The Coffee Book

The Coffee Book

More than 40 Delicious and Refreshing Recipes for Drinks and Desserts

Rosemary Moon

Courage
BOOKS

AN IMPRINT OF RUNNING PRESS
PHILADELPHIA · LONDON

This book was designed and produced by
Quintet Publishing Limited
6 Blundell Street
London N7 9BH

Creative Director: Richard Dewing
Art Director: Silke Braun
Designer: The Design Revolution, Brighton
Project Editor: Diana Steedman
Photographer: Philip Wilkins
Food Stylist: Jennie Berresford

Typeset in Great Britain by
Central Southern Typesetters, Eastbourne
Manufactured in Singapore by Bright Arts Graphics Pte Ltd

Published by Courage Books, an imprint of
Running Press Book Publishers
125 South Twenty-Second Street
Philadelphia, Pennsylvania 19103-4399

Contents

Introduction	6
The History of Coffee Drinking	8
Coffee Houses	12
What Is Coffee?	14
Great Coffee-growing Areas	16
Picking and Processing	26
Roasting	29
Grinding	31
Making Coffee	32
Electric Coffee Makers	33
Espresso and Specialty Coffees	35
Instant Coffee	37
Basic Rules for Enjoying Coffee	38
Coffee Recipes	41
Drinks	42
Cakes and Bakes	51
Ice Creams	60
Desserts	67
Index	80

Introduction

Coffee has been a popular drink for more than a thousand years and now, at the start of a new millenium, it is more popular than ever. The reason lies in its unique qualities: the delicious aroma and taste has made coffee drinking an attractive social pastime in all cultures, and has ensured its lasting appeal.

The coffee bean was first discovered in the Middle East, and in the course of its long history coffee has had many guises, from being a drink treated with almost holy reverence to a reviving brew enjoyed in the early meeting houses of New York and London. From a tradition richly embellished with social customs and rituals, coffee drinking by the twentieth century had become a more informal affair, especially after the development of instant coffee.

Today there is renewed interest in the different varieties and blends, and coffee bars and coffee shops are springing up everywhere, as relaxed, elegant meeting places. Whether your preference is for traditional espresso, cappuccino, cafe latte, or even iced mocha, you will find a coffee shop to meet your needs. Just as the coffee houses of the eighteenth century were the gossip shops and information centers of their time, so cyber-cafés and others offering internet connection over a cup of your favorite brew are very much the information centers of today.

Coffee is the world's most valuable agricultural commodity, of more importance financially than wheat or corn. It is thus one of the most valuable primary products in world trade, second only to oil. What makes it so is a fascinating blend of folklore, historical fact, trade and farming skills, a balance between agri-business and sustainability, mixed with a deep-seated place in the tradition of hospitality around the world from the sixteenth century onward.

Above: A modern espresso machine at the International Club, Washington DC. Espresso, with its many variations, has become one of the most popular drinks on offer today.

For the coffee connoisseur there is a great interest in the skills required to roast beans to perfection, and to blend coffee for the discerning palate. For those who want to try it for themselves, there is a fascinating range of home roasters, grinders and coffee machines to turn a delicious drink into an all-absorbing hobby. There are great coffee houses around the world to provide an endless list of holiday destinations, coffee pots to collect and rare bean varieties to taste.

Coffee is also much more than just a straightforward drink - it is an important flavoring in a whole range of foods. There are coffee liqueurs for the end of a perfect meal, and coffee milk shakes and iced drinks for long summer days. You can make coffee-flavored cakes and cookies for family snacks and elegant entertaining, ice creams, gelatos and granitas, light mousses, trifles and other sophisticated desserts.

The whole subject of coffee is stimulating – the more you discover, the more you will want to find out, to taste and to savor.

The History of Coffee Drinking

How did coffee first come to be brewed? We can't prove anything, but it is almost certain that coffee drinking first originated in Ethiopia – it is known that the arabica strain of coffee plants was cultivated on a small scale from around 575 AD.

The most popular story is that a goatherder noticed one day that his goats were much more frisky than usual. They had been grazing on some bushes which bore round red cherries, and so he decided to try them for himself. Soon he too was affected, becoming alert, awake and full of energy. He took the berries to the local monastery where the abbot made an infusion to test the properties of the berries for himself. Soon the whole community was given the new drink to keep them awake through late night prayers.

Sheikh Omar's name is inseparable from coffee legend, and he is also credited with the discovery of the beans as a result of a miracle performed by Allah. He was a disciple of a great holy man, whom he accompanied on a journey to Mecca, Saudi Arabia, around 1250. Sheikh Omar's guru became ill on the journey, but not before warning him that he would be called upon by Allah's messenger to perform certain holy tasks. A stranger appeared and told Sheikh Omar to dig in the dry dust of the desert, where he willed a spring to appear in the ground. Omar was told that the holy man's spirit was in the water, which was to be carried to Mecca. He did as instructed, passing on the way near the town of Mocha, in the Yemen. When Sheikh Omar set his bowl of water on the ground to rest, another spring appeared just as it had done at the spot where his friend had died.

The Sheikh settled by the spring, building a shelter for himself among the bushes which appeared miraculously in the desert around the water. In due course the bushes produced berries. First he tried eating them, then he boiled them and drunk the liquid. When illness struck the inhabitants of Mocha, it was thought that the Sheikh had cast some sort of wicked spell over them, but he confronted the angry mob with the gift of dried berries from the bushes that surrounded his home. He sent them away with instructions that they should prepare an infusion of the beans for those that were sick. The beans were first regarded as medicine, as they had cured the sick, and then became the favorite drink of the people of Mocha, while Sheikh Omar was revered as a holy man. The name of Mocha is still prominent in coffee language today.

Left: A seventeenth-century copper-plated coffee kettle, known as a "Baghdad boiler."

Above: Lloyd's Coffee House, 1688. In contrast to inns and taverns, coffee houses provided congenial meeting places for the transaction of business, an informal affair in the seventeenth century.

THE HABIT SPREADS

Coffee does not feature again in history until the fifteenth century, when there are records of it being cultivated on quite a large scale in southern Arabia. There are, however, records of the Mufti of Aden, the ruler, visiting Ethiopia just across the Red Sea in 1454 and seeing his own countrymen drinking coffee there. He asked for coffee to be sent to him when he returned home and developed a taste for it. Coffee quickly became popular throughout Aden, the dervishes becoming great coffee drinkers. The popularity of the drink doubtless encouraged the establishment of coffee growing in southern Arabia.

Despite some concern over the fast growing near-addiction of the Islamic peoples of Arabia to coffee, it continued to grow in popularity and became their most valuable trading commodity. The trade in coffee spread east, reaching first Cairo, Egypt, then Constantinople, Turkey in 1517 and Damascus, Syria, by 1530. It did not reach the West until the seventeenth century.

Two Englishmen employed by the East India Company discovered a brisk trade in coffee in Yemen in 1609, although it did not reach England for another forty years. The East India Company began to use coffee to trade for spices and other more saleable items – as yet there was no demand for it in the West.

COFFEE REACHES THE WEST

Coffee was first brought to Europe by Venetian traders at the beginning of the seventeenth century. Cocoa had already been brought from the New World by the Spanish

in 1528, and tea had been introduced from the East. Coming from the Middle East, the land of infidels, coffee was quickly labeled the drink of the devil. However, Pope Clement VIII requested that a cup of coffee be brought to him, so that he could taste the devilish brew, and instantly declared that coffee must be made a drink of the Christian faith. The way into Europe was now open. Coffee drinking spread rapidly throughout the continent, with cafés and coffee houses springing up in all major cities, notably Venice, Italy, and London, England. At first, it was regarded as a medicine, and so commanded a high price.

From Europe it was only a few short years before coffee found its way to the Americas, reaching the north by 1668. Beer, the traditional breakfast-time drink in New York, was quickly replaced by coffee, although tea remained the principal drink until its popularity dwindled as a result of the Boston Tea Party. Such establishments continued to be at the forefront of American social and business life for several decades. The headquarters of the New York Stock Exchange was originally in The Tontine, a coffee house to rival Merchants, on the corner of Wall Street and Water Street.

South America is now one of the major coffee-producing areas of the world but it was not until the early eighteenth century that the plant was first introduced there,

Left: A handful of ripe coffee cherries.

Left: An elegant Chinese porcelain coffee pot.

arriving in Martinique in the French West Indies. This is one of the most romantic tales in the history of coffee. A significant coffee growing industry was established from the safe arrival of just one plant. This was achieved by a French naval officer, Gabriel Mathieu de Clieu, who acquired a coffee plant while on leave in France in the early 1700s, and decided to take it back to Martinique. He managed to keep it alive on the long voyage, in spite of storms, pirates, and a shortage of water. That one plant was grown on successfully and cultivation soon spread to several other islands of the West Indies.

Meanwhile, the Dutch had introduced plants to Surinam on the north-east coast of South America. These plants survived, and plantations quickly spread to Brazil. Indian coffees were introduced to the area around Rio de Janeiro and the British planted coffee on Jamaica in 1730. By 1760 coffee was being grown successfully in Guatemala and by 1780 it had been introduced to Costa Rica from Cuba.

If we accept that coffee was grown in 575 AD in north Africa, it seems quite amazing that it took 1300 years and a journey almost right around the world before the plant was introduced to Kenya. British settlers introduced coffee there in 1878 and Kenya is still the hub of the African coffee industry producing, in the eyes of many, the finest coffees in the world today.

Coffee Houses

The Kaveh Kanes at Mecca were the first coffee houses. Originally established as Islamic prayer houses, they quickly became more general meeting places associated with singing and music, games and gossip. This is a tradition of coffee houses that has continued through the centuries and throughout the world, but in the beginning the spread of coffee houses was inland to Medina, Saudi Arabia, and to the ports of Aden and Cairo, Egypt.

From there, they became established throughout the eastern Mediterranean in the sixteenth century. There are records of cafés, as they were already called, in Damascus, Syria, in 1530, one of the most popular being the Café at the Gate of Salvation. They were popular, not just because of the coffee, but because there had never been such pleasant, exciting, stimulating and inexpensive meeting places offering refreshment before.

Below: One of the new-style American coffee shops.

The first Italian coffee house opened in Venice in 1683, but the most famous one is the Café Florian. Opened in the Piazza San Marco in 1720, it is now the oldest surviving coffee house in Europe. The café was a great success and fitted well with the privileged and elegant lifestyle of many Venetians. Italian coffee is often very finely ground, only a little coarser than pulverized, and it is easy to see the influence of Turkish and Arabic coffees on this première European market. Venetian coffee was considered the best – at least in Italy – and Florian's served a blend that was said to surpass all others. Thus the Café Florian was able to make a commanding charge for its refreshment and it remains, to this day, one of the best-known and most expensive coffee houses in the world.

Coffee houses in London, England, flourished after the first was established in St. Michael's Alley, Cornhill in 1652. However, such cafés quickly fell into disrepute as the government began to suspect the cafés of being hotbeds of discontent and common uprising. There was quite a war of pamphlets about the coffee houses, with leaflets being written both against them and in their support. Coffee houses gained their reputation for rowdiness through the heated debates that they generated – they were, after all, the ideas exchanges and research areas of their times. Lloyds of London was originally a coffee shop, first established in 1688 in Tower Street in the City of London, and later in Lombard Street.

THE CAFÉ PROCOPE
How much we owe to this one Florentine, who introduced both coffee and ice cream to Paris, France. Procope made his mark with the introduction of ices in 1670. He aimed to popularize the drinking of coffee much more in the style

il Caffè

Ristretto	115
Espresso	115
Tallat	130
Cafè amb llet	150
Cappuccino italià	235
Cappuccino amb nata	300
Suis xocolata i nata	300
Triestino cafè amb llet condensada	185
Xocolata	225
Cigaló Anis o Brandy	225
Cigaló Ballers o Whisky	295
Corretto cafè amb grappa	290
Bicherin cafè xocolata i nata	475
Pippo cafè, whisky i llet condensada	300
Mokaccino cafè, Xe condensada i nata	295

set by the Turkish Ambassador in Paris, and became famed for his soirées, at which the coffee was served in elegant porcelain cups by Turkish slaves on their knees! The Café Procope was elegant and sophisticated and soon became the favorite haunt of literary society and intellectuals. The café still flourishes today and is to be found just off the Boulevard Saint Germain.

COFFEE AND THE AMERICAN REVOLUTION

Coffee houses soon opened in New York, Philadelphia, and Boston. American coffee houses were more like taverns, also serving wines, beers and meals. They did, however, follow in the tradition of encouraging free-thinking and conversation, and many even incorporated assembly halls and courtrooms. Coffee houses were the meeting places of the masses and soon became centers of local political activity. Unpopular laws were discussed there and protests mounted. Boycotts on British goods were planned in Merchants' Coffee House in New York, and it was in the Green Dragon Coffee House in Boston that the Boston Tea Party was planned in 1773.

MODERN COFFEE HOUSES

Today, coffee houses are staging a comeback, a movement that began in Seattle, America. The city became known as a center for coffee roasting, and was instrumental in the spread of coffee shops all over the country, although it was not until 1986 that an espresso bar was added to one of the stores.

Chains of coffee bars (the new coffee houses) are now spreading across America, and the trend has crossed the Atlantic to Europe.

What Is Coffee?

There are three species of coffee plant – *Coffea liberica*, *Coffea arabica* and *Coffea canephora*, all of which can range in size from small shrubs to tall trees more than 32 feet high.

Coffea liberica is of the least quality, and the beans require a sympathetic roasting before blending to give a palatable brew. It is grown in Malaysia and West Africa, but demand is low because of its poor flavor.

Coffea arabica produces the best quality, arabica coffee, and was the species first found growing wild in Ethiopia. The plant has luxuriously glossy leaves and very attractive white flowers, followed by red berries which contain the raw green beans. *Coffea arabica* is now cultivated in all the major coffee-producing countries where coffee is grown at altitudes upward of 1800 feet. Arabica beans have the lowest caffeine content and, once extracted, keep well unblended. It represents around 70 percent of the world's production, though arabica trees are more prone to disease than canephora.

Coffea canephora, the species which produces the

Below: Aerial view of a coffee plantation in Colombia.

Right: The flower and the ripe and unripe coffee cherries growing in Brazil.

robusta beans, is better suited to cultivation at lower altitudes and was originally found in the Congo. It is now cultivated in West Africa, Madagascar and other areas of the world that produce arabica beans at high altitude, but still have low-lying land suitable for cultivating coffee. The plant has larger leaves than the arabica and is heavier cropping. The beans have a higher caffeine content and, despite the name, a more neutral flavor which dictates that they are usually mixed to produce commercially prepared coffee blends, often for bulk packaging.

CULTIVATION

It takes between three and five years for coffee trees to come to maturity. Liberica trees will grow to between 20 to 40 feet, but those producing arabica and robusta beans are usually kept pruned to around 6 feet, to direct the energy of the plant into producing a heavy crop and to make it easier to harvest the cherries when ripe. The fruit of the coffee plant, called cherries, contains two flattish seeds – coffee beans. When only one bean develops it is known as a peaberry. The cherries develop as green clusters along the branches of the trees, then turn red when ripe.

It takes six to eight months for arabica cherries to ripen, and nine to eleven for robusta. Harvest times vary: north of the equator, in Ethiopia and Central America, for example, the harvest takes place between September and December. South of the equator, in Brazil and Zimbabwe, the harvest is in April or May, although it may last until August. Equatorial countries such as Colombia and Uganda can harvest fruit all year round, so it is possible to have freshly harvested beans for much of the year.

Propagation is usually from seed, although cuttings are growing in popularity as they can be easily controlled and produce quicker results once planted out. Cuttings must be taken from trees which are known to be healthy, or there is a risk of perpetuating diseased stock.

Coffee trees will last between twenty and thirty years, if conditions are right, with enough sun and rain. Arabica trees prefer a climate of around 59° to 75°F, while robusta prefers warm equatorial conditions with temperatures between 75° and 85°F. Both species die when the temperature falls below freezing. All young coffee plants benefit from a certain amount of shade – indeed, the best mature trees are those which achieve at least two hours shade a day and protective trees are often planted in and around coffee plantations if no natural shade is available. Shade trees not only protect from the sun – they also minimize the difference in temperature between night and day.

Coffee can be grown on large coffee plantations, or on small farms and smallholdings. In Brazil and Guatemala, for example, there are many large estates devoted just to growing coffee. Mechanical harvesters are increasingly used, as well as modern cultivation methods such as fertilizers and irrigation. Weeding is a major issue for coffee growers. The conditions that suit coffee also suit weeds and the traditional method of dealing with them is with scythes, although chemical weedkillers have been introduced on many of the more affluent estates.

Great Coffee-growing Areas of the World

Africa

ETHIOPIA

Ethiopia, the home of coffee, remains one of the major producers in Africa today. Ethiopian coffees for export are arabica beans of top quality, with a slightly unusual winey or gamy flavor that makes them worth seeking out. The best coffees are grown at altitudes of over 5000 feet.

Harrar is the most famous of all the Ethiopian coffee-producing areas and the Harrar Longberry coffee has the typical gamy flavor. Little of the coffee from Yirga Ch'efe, in the south of Ethiopia, reaches the international market as it is bought up for consumption in Japan and parts of Europe. Typical Ethiopian coffees have a full body with a medium to high acidity.

There is still a great deal of wild coffee grown in Ethiopia, much of which is used for the local market. Coffee consumption is the highest in Africa, and in the country the beans are often roasted over an open fire and mixed with a wild herb before being brewed.

KENYA

Kenyan coffees are among the best and the most popular in the world. The beans to look out for are the AA grade and peaberry, the latter distinguished by their unusual round shape and the fact that there is only one bean in each cherry, rather than two. Peaberry is the best type of bean to roast at home as it is the easiest to roast evenly.

Kenyan is one of the most consistently reliable, quality coffees in the world, mainly due to the way it is marketed by the Coffee Board of Kenya. The Board buys all the coffee from the growers, tastes and grades the beans and then auctions them on the international market. Consequently, there are no single estate coffees available from Kenya, but the reliability of the coffee makes up for the lack of individualism.

Kenyan coffees have a medium-full flavor with a high acidity, and are fruity and very well balanced. Striving to maintain their place in the world market, the Coffee Board of Kenya is paying farmers more to produce better-tasting coffees, thus continuing to promote quality rather than quantity.

YEMEN

Although not strictly African, Yemeni coffee is usually classified as such. The most famous of all Yemen beans is the Mocha, almost as round as a peaberry. Yemen Mocha is

Right: Coffee beans drying in the sun on racks, Kenya.

Above: Coffee estate in the highland region of Kenya.

full-bodied with a moderate acidity which gives a roundness of taste comparable to the best Kenyan coffees, but with that indescribable extra gamy, almost chocolate flavor.

The one drawback to this superb coffee is that the beans are sometimes damaged by rough processing. For the very best quality, look for Yemen Mocha from Mattari. Because there is usually only one cropping a year, this coffee is much sought after and demand can easily outstrip supply – the beans are usually only available for export between December and April.

TANZANIA

Tanzania has a potentially vibrant coffee industry which can boast AA grade and peaberry coffees to rival those of Kenya, if only quality can be maintained. The coffees are full-bodied and softly flavored, with less acidity than those from Kenya. Most of the production is from small cooperatives. Tanzania is, however, typical of an African country where production problems can wreck a potentially profitable business through inconsistent quality control. These problems are being addressed, which is good news as coffees such as Kibo Chagga have a superb fragrance, much appreciated by connoisseurs.

MADAGASCAR
Madagascan coffees are the strongest from the east coast of Africa, demanding a dark roast which makes them a good bean for espresso blends. Most coffee produced in Madagascar is of the robusta variety, although the amount of arabica beans is steadily being increased and the island has the potential to develop into a major world producer of quality coffees. Much of the robusta production, which is of high quality, is exported to France. Less full-flavored than some African coffees, it does have a good balance and the high roasting does not over-emphasize the medium acidity of the beans.

CAMEROON
The arabica beans grown in this central African country are from Blue Mountain plants imported from Jamaica, although plenty of robusta coffee is also cultivated. There is a small production of elephant beans, or Maragagype, which are up to a third bigger than other types of bean, and have a very smooth, soft flavor with a low acidity. Cameroon coffee is generally darkly roasted and is often used in Italian-style espresso blends.

BURUNDI
Political unrest is the most likely cause of disruption to the young coffee industry in this developing country. Almost all the coffee production is of rich, full-bodied, high acidity arabica beans, and coffees from the Ngozi area are grown at an altitude over 4000 feet. Both Japan and America are ready markets for the coffee from Burundi.

Left: Quality control check on a production line.

Right: Picking coffee cherries in Brazil.

Other African states that produce coffee include Zimbabwe, Zambia, Uganda, Sudan, Mozambique, and Rwanda. Unfortunately, civil war and political unrest have greatly hampered the development of the industry in these countries, and their coffees therefore rarely appear on the market.

South America

South America produces vast quantities of coffee annually, but it is not all of the best quality. The major producers are Brazil and Colombia, with Venezuela, Peru, Bolivia, and Ecuador also providing valuable quantities of beans. The relatively unknown coffee of the Galapagos Islands is a jewel in the organic coffee crown.

BRAZIL

Brazil, the giant of the coffee producing countries of the world, has at least twice as many producers as the next largest market in Colombia. The peak in the international popularity of coffee is clearly reflected in the importance of the crop to Brazil's economy. In the 1950s, when coffee drinking was at its height, Brazil produced over half the coffee in the world and the beans were therefore a major earner for the Brazilian people. Today, coffee is only responsible for 8 to 10 percent of the gross domestic product, although it still accounts for 30 percent of coffee production world-wide.

Most of the coffee in Brazil is grown along the eastern coast, with Parana, in the far south, responsible for 50 percent of the nationwide production. The quality of Brazilian coffees varies enormously, as do the characteristics of the varieties grown. For years, Bourbon Santos was the best, and there is now a movement to encourage specialty growers to revive these beans. Others to watch for are washed Bahia, which is very popular in America as well as on the domestic market; Capin Branco and Vista Allegre. These are all arabica beans, but Brazil also produces robusta beans, marketed under the name Conillon.

Above: Picking coffee in Colombia, the largest producer of quality coffee in the world.

Brazil has the second largest consumption of coffee in the world, exceeded only by America. Brazilian growers are keenly aware of American market trends and have organized themselves into an effective marketing group, the Specialty Coffee Association of Brazil, to promote individual coffees. All Brazilian coffees are best drunk young as they have a tendency toward acidity.

COLOMBIA
Colombia is the second largest producer in South America after Brazil, but has the distinction of being the largest producer of quality coffees in the world. The importance of the crop is enormous, and all vehicles entering Colombia are sprayed to prevent diseases being introduced into the country which would damage the coffee plants.

The highest grade of Colombian coffee is Armenia Supremo, which is famous in the trade, and therefore with the coffee-drinking public, for its consistent quality. It is medium-bodied with a tangy acidity, and has a sweet and fragrant aroma. All Colombian coffees are marketed as such, as the country is so highly regarded in the coffee world. Coffee from Medellin, which is richly full-bodied and of medium acidity, is also much sought-after. Excelso coffee is the second grade after Supremo.

Colombian coffee is available all year round as it is grown in ranges of mountains in the foothills of the Andes, having many differing micro-climates which encourage the coffee to ripen at varying times. The Federacion Nacional de Cafeteros (FNC), a private company which works with the government to maintain the quality of the coffee, looks after the coffee growers and their produce and is responsible for the highly organized and efficient way in which the Colombian coffee industry is run.

VENEZUELA

The coffee plantations of Venezuela are beginning to enjoy a renaissance as they start to export their own produce in the hope of finding a niche in the growing market for specialty and single-estate coffees. Venezuelan coffees have always been lighter and more delicate than others produced in South America, and their low acidity makes them useful for blending as well as having a good balance for single varieties. Many of the best coffees come from Tachira state in the south-west of Venezuela, bordering Colombia.

THE GALAPAGOS ISLANDS

The coffee plantation on San Cristóbal in the Galapagos Islands was established in 1875 and flourished for many years, producing specialty coffee, until it was forced out of business. However, the plantation was bought by the Gonzalez family in 1990 and, although no chemicals are allowed to be used on the islands and no extra land can be taken into agricultural use (the islands are a national park), the Gonzalez family are increasing production. The coffee is organic and the quality is constantly improving. It is full-bodied and rich with a sweet acidity and is definitely one of the coffees to watch for in the future.

Central America and the Caribbean

All the countries of Central America and most of the Caribbean Islands grow coffee to a greater or lesser extent. They all produce arabica beans, some of better quality than others, and these include the much sought-after coffees of Guatemala, Costa Rica, and the renowned, if somewhat hyped, Blue Mountain coffee of Jamaica.

COSTA RICA

Sandwiched between Panama and Nicaragua and bordered by the Atlantic and Pacific Oceans, Costa Rica has plenty of the well-drained volcanic soil required by coffee and grows arabica beans of excellent quality. It is actually illegal to grow robusta or any of the inferior types of coffee anywhere in the country. Coffee is one

Below: Picking arabica coffee cherries in Costa Rica.

of the major exports from Costa Rica, along with bananas. There are more coffee trees in the country than there are people.

Many coffee experts regard the coffee from Tarrazu, in the center of the country, as among the best in the world, being characterized by a full, mellow body and a high acidity in perfect balance.

All coffee exports from Costa Rica are strictly controlled to maintain the quality, and any inferior beans are dyed blue and released onto the home market. Although Costa Rica is small, its consumption per capita is twice that of America and accounts for around 10 percent of its total production.

GUATEMALA

Guatemalan coffee is quickly regaining its reputation as one of the great coffees of the world. The best beans are SHB (strictly hard bean), grown in the premier growing region around Antigua. They are characterized by a medium body and full acidity and are best described as lively.

Guatemala was one of the premier growers of elephant beans, but the popularity of these larger-than-life beans has declined over the years, and is of little interest now as the coffee connoisseur looks for a stronger roast and flavor – the elephant bean has always produced an easy-drinking, unchallenging cup of coffee.

The Guatemalan coffee industry has been especially troubled by problems with wages for the plantation workers, which led to the decline of the industry from its position among the best in the world. However, American funding is encouraging re-investment in small plantations producing specialist coffees for the increasingly demanding world market, by planting new trees with a better yield of quality beans.

JAMAICA

Jamaican Blue Mountain coffee is probably the most famous in the world, demanding vast premiums as the Japanese would readily snap up the complete crop if they could – they already buy 90 percent of the beans. It is a relatively mild coffee, and to achieve a good flavor you actually have to use almost 20 percent more beans. For many years, the freshness of flavor was compromised by the Jamaican government insisting that all beans should be roasted in Jamaica, but green beans can now be exported for roasting elsewhere.

The Jamaican beans have been through their ups and downs, reaching an all-time low in 1948 when some buyers refused to purchase any more Blue Mountain coffee. The Coffee Industry Board was established to improve the quality and, by 1969, things were on the up again. The actual area of plantations in the Blue Mountains is comparatively small, so not all the coffee labeled with the famous name can possibly come from the mountains, where the coffee plantations are the highest in the world at almost 7000 feet.

MEXICO

Mexico seems an unlikely producer of fine coffees, yet the Tapachula Superior, grown in the mountains of Chiapas state in south-eastern Mexico, is a light to medium-bodied coffee with a crisp dry finish – a good, light dry coffee of similar characteristics to an easy-drinking summer white wine.

Mexico is, surprisingly, the fourth largest producer of coffee in the world. The beans come mainly from

Right: Newly planted coffee on small hillside farm in Jamaica's Blue Mountains.

Above: Coffee growing in Coorg, India, under hardwoods, among cardamoms, with pepper vines growing on the trees.

independent smallholders and the whole production has changed radically from the great estates which once controlled Mexican coffee production. Some elephant beans are still produced, but the coffee growers – those that can afford to make changes to their plantations – are moving away from this mild crop to the more sophisticated and individual coffees being sought in today's market. Most Mexican coffees benefit from a high roasting.

PUERTO RICO

Coffee was once the leading crop on the island of Puerto Rico, but was temporarily replaced in importance by sugar and pharmaceuticals. However, the gourmet coffees produced on the island are of exceptional quality and have a very definite appeal in a discerning market. Yauco Selecto is one of the finest Puerto Rican coffees, grown on only three farms and labeled "high grown." Very few coffee houses stock the beans, which are usually marketed selectively. These beans are full-bodied and very aromatic, the balance between body and flavor being nearly perfect.

Asia and the Indian Ocean

INDIA

The best-known Indian coffees are Mysore and Monsooned Malabar, both of which are produced in the south of the country. Mysore has a spicy, nutty flavor which blends well with both cinnamon and chocolate. It is a medium to full-bodied coffee with a low-to-medium acidity. It is produced toward the south-west of the country, whereas Monsooned Malabar is produced in the south-east.

Monsooning is a process unique to Malabar coffees. Beans are exposed to moisture-laden air during the monsoon season for several days, which causes their color and flavor to change. The beans were originally affected by sea air on their long voyages to the markets of Europe, and the Europeans continued to demand coffee of the same characteristics, even when steam ships shortened the journey and the coffee had less chance to be affected by the weather en route. The moisture-laden beans are then packed in sacks and air-dried, being repacked once a week until they are ready for sale.

Monsooned Malabar is a very full-bodied coffee with

a low acidity, making it an excellent choice for cooking, especially to blend with fruits. Some coffee is also grown at Tellicherry, on the coast to the south-west of Mysore.

INDONESIA

Java and Sumatra are the best known coffee-growing areas of Indonesia, each producing distinctive coffees that are becoming more popular, although they are mainly from robusta beans.

Java coffee is richly and creamily full-bodied, and has quite an explosive flavor. The acidity is medium to low and the coffee is usually medium roasted, although it will happily take a darker roast in the Californian style. Mocha Java is a very popular blend, mixing Indonesian coffee with beans from the Yemen. The best Sumatran coffee is from Lintong and has a low acidity – really just enough to keep it interesting and vibrant in the cup. The small amount of arabica beans grown in Indonesia is mainly in Lintong, which is why many connoisseurs prefer the coffee of this area to that of Java, and also why it is much admired among Indonesian coffees.

Australia and the Pacific Rim

AUSTRALIA

Coffee is grown along the east coast of Australia, from Sydney north to Cairns. The beans are arabica bourbon and are of very high quality. Unfortunately, very little Australian coffee is exported; production costs make it unviable as the beans have to be harvested by hand. The beans are quite light, with a good acidity, and are usually medium roasted.

HAWAII

Hawaiian coffee is of top quality but few coffee drinkers outside America ever get to taste it – being the only coffee actually grown in America, and of such quality, there is a ready home market for it.

The coffee is grown in the west of the island in the region of Kona, where the trees enjoy ideal growing conditions on the volcanic slopes of Mount Loa. Hawaii actually has the highest yield of arabica beans anywhere in the world, but production is limited. The best grades of coffee are Extra Fancy, Fancy and Number One, with Hawaii Kai Farms as an alternative. Hawaiian coffees offer an alternative to California-style roasting, as they are best roasted light or medium.

PAPUA NEW GUINEA

Papua New Guinea is a mountainous country and most of the coffee grown there is at high altitude – between 4265 and 5905 feet, which accounts for its consistently high quality. The only robusta beans are grown in the limited lowlands.

Small grower cooperatives are now re-established to concentrate on producing quality coffees, of which AA, A and AB are the best. AA is rare, but the others are quite widely available. Almost all the coffee from Papua New Guinea used to be sold as Y grade, but quality slipped on these beans, and the image of the country's coffees has been revitalized with the new grading system.

The Arona Valley produces good coffees grown on the root stock imported from the Blue Mountains of Jamaica. The coffee from here is typically medium-bodied with a medium low acidity and a good balance – it is almost sweet and fruity. Other coffees are gamy and richly full-bodied. Coffees from New Guinea are widely used for blending.

Picking ...

Coffee beans are harvested when the berries (called cherries) are bright red and ripe. Coffee picking is a social event as it is mainly done by hand, and requires quite a band of pickers working together in the fields. It is a slow business, and it may take one picker up to five days to pick sufficient cherries to produce enough beans to fill just one hundred pound bag. Ripe cherries shrink very rapidly, so picking has to be completed as quickly as possible, once the crop is ready.

There are two methods of picking: *strip picking* involves only one pass through a plantation, picking the entire crop, so cherries are picked at differing stages of ripeness. This is employed for standard crops. The other method is *selective picking*, taking only red, fully ripe cherries, with several sweeps being made at intervals of eight to ten days, to ensure that the cherries are picked in the best possible condition. Selective picking is obviously more expensive, and is only used for high quality arabica beans.

Hand picking represents about half the total annual production costs of the average coffee plantation. Attempts have been made to introduce mechanical picking, to keep down costs, but it has its limitations. Mechanical picking is initially quick, but the crop that has been shaken into the collecting hoppers then has to be sorted to remove twigs, leaves and other "extras." The equipment is mainly used on low-lying plantations where the trees have been planted in straight lines, allowing the harvester to move easily among them. It is really only one stage on from the traditional technique employed to pick olives — shake the tree and then collect the fruit from netting slung beneath the branches.

Right: Sorting coffee beans in East Java.

and *Processing*

PROCESSING THE BEANS

The first job that has to be done after picking is to separate the beans from the cherries. This is done by one of two methods, either wet or dry processing.

The dry method can only be employed in countries where around three weeks of dry weather can be guaranteed after picking, and is usually only used on lower-grade beans. The cherries are spread out on a flat surface in thin layers in the sun to dry, and are raked and stirred frequently for the first few days to ensure that the process gets under way evenly. Once dried, the cherries are pounded or hulled in mortars until the beans have been separated from the dry covering, a process which can damage the beans and therefore mar the quality of the coffee. Dry processing mutes the acidity in coffee but increases the earthier, fruitier tones in the flavor.

Wet processing is the most widely used method and has to be started as soon as possible after harvesting, ideally within twelve hours, to produce the best quality beans. Wet processing produces crisper and brighter flavors with more impact in the coffee. In this process, the washed, ripe cherries are pulped to extract the beans, which are then washed again. A shiny layer of saccharin mucilage remains on the beans, and this is removed by a brief fermentation.

The beans at this stage are still in a parchment casing and have to be carefully dried so that they can be stored in a stable condition – the parchment is only removed just before export. The parchment is dried by spreading out the beans on drying tables or on concrete floors. They are dried either in the sun, or by mechanical dryers where rain could spoil them. The beans are turned regularly to ensure they dry evenly, the whole process taking twelve to fifteen days. At this stage they are known as "parchment coffee."

Above: Raking the drying coffee beans on an estate in Brazil.

A purely natural coloring will now be assumed by the beans, which is a good indicator of the quality of the crop. The best beans will have a bluish tinge, and a green coloring denotes the next best quality of bean. Any beans which dry slowly in a damp atmosphere will deteriorate quickly and take on a dull, gray-green appearance.

The dried beans must be stored in absolutely stable conditions. The best arabica high-grown coffees are always stored as parchment coffee on the farms that produced them; this maintains the humidity that the beans require. The name parchment comes from the fact that the beans are still covered in a delicate silvery skin, which is removed by milling just before the coffee is exported. Various milling machines are used, as wet and dry treated beans require differing processes. The milling is very critical – several of the machines employ knives which could potentially damage the beans. Beans may be polished after milling to remove any remaining parchment, but this is not always necessary.

GRADING AND SORTING

These are time-consuming, laborious processes but are still best carried out by hand – or by eye – although the mechanical eye may eventually replace the human one. Size is the first indication of quality, as the better coffee is usually from bigger beans. Any rogue beans that have slipped through the previous processes must be removed now, or a whole sack of beans may be ruined. The green coffee beans are then ready for export. There are six export grades, the top grade being SHB (strictly hard bean) which indicates that the beans were produced at a minimum altitude of 4000 feet.

All coffee is tasted before it is bought. Tasting includes green and roasted beans, a ground sample, and then a brewed sample. It is not usually roasted before export as the shelf-life of roasted coffee is very short. Most importers buy and roast the beans themselves, as retailers usually prefer to buy from a local roaster so that they have greater control over the quality.

Roasting

Coffee beans have to be roasted to release their aroma and flavor. Not only do they change color during this process, they also expand considerably, often almost doubling in size. While roasting may produce a light or a dark brown bean, a good roast always remains brown. Black beans are over-roasted or literally burnt, and would produce a very bitter and unpleasant drink if brewed. The lighter the roast, the milder the coffee, and an insufficiently roasted bean will produce a weak and flavorless drink.

Of all the processes associated with the production of a perfect cup of coffee, it is roasting that is probably the most critical. Each coffee has its own individual characteristics which must be enhanced and not masked during the roasting process.

Roasting should encourage the natural sugars and oils in the coffees to develop. However, roasting also begins a rapid staling of coffee – the green beans will store well for up to a year if conditions are right, but once they have been roasted, the beans will start to lose their natural flavor and will only remain at their best for up to two weeks. It is therefore essential to buy small quantities of freshly roasted coffee on a regular basis.

Roasts are generally described as low, medium, or high, and sometimes light, medium, and dark, but these can mean different things to different people. In general, however, the darker the roast the lower the eventual quality, as darker roasts mean that less of the character of the bean will come through.

The time and temperature required for each variety of bean must be very carefully controlled. If the coffee is not packed as soon as possible after roasting, the aromatic oils which have been brought to the surface can oxidize, producing a sooty and rancid flavor.

Roasting is done at extremely high temperatures. Coffee beans are roasted to an internal temperature of between 400°F and 450°F, depending on the roast required. At these temperatures, the beans will have turned brown, going through a gradual transition to yellow at 200°F, and then starting to color and swell at about 300°F. At 400°F the oils start to emerge.

The beans must be kept moving in the roaster to prevent them from burning and to ensure an even roast – this may be done by turning the roaster as a drum or, for larger quantities, by forcing the beans through the machine from one end to the other, with a screw.

Roasted beans must be cooled quickly to allow them to be packed, and also to halt the roasting or cooking process. The cooling may be done in water but a better result is achieved if the beans are air-cooled.

ROASTING BEANS AT HOME

Stove-top roasters are available for home use, or beans can be roasted in the oven. The chances of creating as good a roast as any specialist roaster is minimal, but a delicious aroma will waft around as you try.

It is possible to roast your own beans in a frying pan, and it is most successful if you use peaberry coffee. This has just one bean per berry and, as the name suggests, they are round and pea-like in appearance, roasting more evenly than the more usual split beans. A large, heavy skillet is essential and the peaberries should be roasted slowly in a single layer over a medium heat until they are a good color. While home roasting produces wonderful aromas, I am certain that some of the volatile gases must be lost by this open processing. It is fun, but coffee roasting is really best left to the experts.

Above: An American coffee-roasting plant. The machine keeps the beans moving constantly, to ensure an even roast.

Grinding

Coffee beans have to be ground before they can be brewed to make coffee. Green beans can last for years, but once the beans are roasted there is only a week or two of full flavor. And after grinding, the coffee will only last a few days.

If you buy beans in a good coffee shop, where they grind the coffee for you, they will ask what grind you want. This will depend on how you are planning to brew the coffee. The basic categories are coarse, medium, and fine. The fine grinds do not need to be brewed for as long as the coarse grinds. Coarse grinds are used in the classic jug method, where you spoon in the coffee and pour on hot, not boiling water. Medium grinds are used in cafetières with a plunger, and medium-fine in filter methods. Espresso machines need a fine grind, and for Turkish coffee the beans are pulverized.

cafetières or filter machines. Some hand-cranked grinders collect the coffee in a little drawer under the mechanism, while the screw types may be locked onto a work surface or bolted to a wall. Elaborately crafted and decorated grinders were popular at the turn of the twentieth century for use at the table when entertaining.

Electric grinders may be large or small. The large ones have the disadvantage of taking up a great deal of work surface but produce grinds suitable for all styles of coffee, including espresso and sometimes even Turkish coffee. The Gaggia electric grinder is one of the best available, with 36 different grind settings. It uses burr plates, which give a much more even grind, resulting in a better quality of flavor.

Small, blade-operated electric grinders are much cheaper, though they do not produce such an even grind. They are similar to a spice grinder, but do not use the same machine for spices and coffees as the flavors will mingle and taint each other. Although the coffee produced in these grinders is really finely chopped rather than ground, it does not harm the beans.

HOME GRINDERS

The best flavor is obtained if you grind the beans at home just before brewing the coffee. Home grinders may be manual or electric. They should produce an even grind, but only the more sophisticated manual machines have a variable setting making the resulting coffee suitable for

Making Coffee

The simplest way of making coffee is in a jug. Just measure in the coffee grounds, add hot (not boiling) water then stir, cover the pot and leave to stand for five minutes. Add a few spoonfuls of cold water to the pot to encourage the grounds to sink to the bottom of the jug, then gently pour the coffee into cups or mugs. You should use a coarsely ground coffee in a jug, and the coffee may be strained if you wish.

Cafetière

The French press or cafetière is one stage on from the jug, incorporating a plunge filter to hold the grounds at the bottom of the pot after brewing. Always choose a pot of this type with a stainless steel mesh rather than one made of nylon – the metal mesh will last much longer. It is very simple to use: just warm the pot, spoon in medium ground coffee, pour in hot water, stir and allow to steep for four to five minutes. The plunger is then pushed down to separate the grounds before pouring.

The Napolenta

Many people swear by their Napolentas – neat little metal coffee pots with two chambers and a simple but stylish design. These Italian stove-top pots attract a devoted following and make excellent espresso coffee, although they are more of a fiddle than the cafetière. The ground coffee is put into a holder screwed into place between the two chambers, the water being poured into the lower chamber. The pot is then placed on the heat and the hot water is forced up into the top chamber through the coffee.

Turkish Coffee Pots

These are small saucepan-like pots with a narrow top and a long handle. They are often made of copper with a tinned lining and the long handle is to protect your hand during the repeated boiling of the coffee. Use 2 teaspoons of pulverized coffee for each cup and 2 teaspoons of sugar. Pour in the water and put on the heat. When it comes to a boil, take it off the heat. Do this three times before serving. The fine grounds sink to the bottom of the cup and are not filtered off in any way.

Cona Vacuum

This was once a popular way of making coffee, but the machines are rarely seen nowadays. A goblet is placed over a jug of water with a simple glass rod between the two to filter the ground coffee which is placed in the goblet. The vacuum is placed on the heat and the water boils up into the upper chamber. Once removed from the heat, the coffee will drain back down through into the jug, leaving the used grounds in the top.

Filter Machines

This is now one of the most popular methods. The machine heats the water then passes it through the coffee, which is held in a paper filter in the upper section. The coffee drips down through the filter into the jug below. Some machines are fitted with a permanent filter, rather than using disposable paper ones.

Electric Coffee Makers

Electric coffee makers range from filter machines to the most amazing, state-of-the-art, espresso machines complete with milk frothers. Some of the latter are real coffee centers and even incorporate a grinder.

Basic Filter Machines

These heat water which is then forced through an arm into a conical filter containing finely ground coffee. The resulting brewed coffee then drips into a jug and is kept warm over a heated plate. The machines originally used paper filters, but they are gradually being replaced by permanent plastic filters, although many people feel that the papers are actually more efficient. There is some evidence that filtered coffee actually contains a higher concentration of caffeine than that made by other methods.

Espresso and Cappuccino Machines

Really serious coffee drinkers may purchase an espresso machine for home use that looks more as if it should be in a restaurant than a domestic kitchen! Gaggia, the company that led the modern coffee bar revolution by supplying commercial espresso machines in the 1950s, have since turned their attentions to domestic machines and now supply a range of coffee makers

to suit the pockets of most serious coffee drinkers.

Non-electric espresso machines are admired for their looks, with their polished copper and brass or stainless steel finish, long handles, pressure gauges and nozzles. These piston-operated machines look wonderful, but are quite difficult to operate, and most stores now sell more electric espresso makers than manual machines.

Perfect Espresso

Most home espresso fails because the concentration of coffee is not correct. It is very easy to think that a larger helping of espresso can be achieved simply by forcing more water through the coffee, but all that happens is that the brew becomes too weak to be a drink of note – home espresso is very often even more diluted than the espresso-based Cafe Americano (see page 36).

Making espresso is a passion, like surfing the Net or following a favorite football or baseball team. You mustn't be disappointed if the coffee isn't perfect – just keep trying and enjoy all the paraphernalia that goes with the process.

The coffee used must be very finely ground – this is best done commercially as few home grinders will produce the required grade. You will need 1½ to 2 tablespoons to a cup. The coffee must then be packed into the filter basket with a tamper.

One: A tamper is used to pack down the finely ground coffee in an espresso machine.

Two: The best coffee from the espresso machine comes first followed by the *crema*.

Three: For cappuccino place the steam jet under the surface of the milk.

This is not as easy as it sounds, for coffee that is not packed tightly enough will produce a weak and watery cup, but if the coffee is packed too tightly the water will drip through very slowly, resulting in a very bitter cup of coffee. It's all trial and error.

It is essential to remember that the first coffee through the espresso machine is the best. Just a few spoonfuls of almost black coffee, followed by the nutty brown froth or *crema*, and that is all you want. Carry on for too long and the coffee will be bitter. Remember to warm the cups while the machine is heating the water; this will help to keep the coffee hot as it is often quite tepid before it is ready for drinking.

Crema is the mark of a good espresso. It is caused by the essential volatile oils from the coffee mixing with water and air as the coffee is made. A good *crema* is evenly colored and covers the whole surface of the coffee in the cup.

CAPPUCCINO

Most espresso machines incorporate a nozzle for frothing milk for cappuccino. When buying an espresso machine that you will also use for cappuccino, you should check that the frothing nozzle or pipe for the milk is easy to use and can be completely removed from the machine for washing. If this is not possible, sour milk will collect in the frother and taint all future cups of frothy coffee. Use semi-skimmed milk, as whole cream milk will mask the flavor of the coffee. It also helps to use cold milk, though it takes longer, as cold milk foams better and tastes fresher.

One development in the search for the perfect home espresso is pellets of coffee for use in specific machines. The German manufacturer Krups has led the way in this field, but most other manufacturers are bound to follow. At the time of writing, I have yet to see the coffee capsules available in any major supermarkets, which may dictate the success or otherwise of the coffee makers.

Espresso and Specialty Coffees

The interest in specialty coffees is being led by a taste for stronger, more distinctive brews made from darker roasted, and therefore fuller flavored beans.

This movement started on the West Coast of the US and is based in Seattle and San Francisco. Just as Americans have taken pizza and made it their own, so they have taken espresso one stage further than its Italian creators dared. Traditional espresso, once found only in Italian restaurants, was effectively introduced to the mass market. Seattle became creative with coffee, offering it frothed, foamed, flavored, or even iced.

Coffee bars have become popular once more, to cater for this gourmet coffee culture, offering high quality coffee in hotels, airports, bookstores, shopping malls and offices. The craze has spread to Europe, where chains of coffee bars have opened. Those establishments that do not roast and grind their own coffee often air-freight it in to maintain the maximum possible freshness.

Espresso bars are becoming very big business and many are now offering stylish snacks and light meals. New York has led the way in offering sophisticated snacks in stylish espresso bar surroundings. In the UK, convenience food chains specialize in quality sandwiches and snacks for office workers, and also offer espresso-based coffees in large take-away beakers. Designer snacking is here for food and coffee.

Enthusiasts for the Italian espresso have criticized the American desire for a higher roast for this style of coffee, but consumer demand is certainly indicating that Americans today like their coffee this way. In Italy, a mixture of around 80 percent arabica beans to 20 percent robusta is used to achieve the espresso blend, whereas American roasters prefer to use pure arabica and some critics say that this dictates a need for a higher roast to achieve the required concentration of flavor.

The Espresso Vocabulary

Espresso The standard espresso is a very short drink, about 1¹/₂ fl oz – and is served in tiny coffee cups. It is little more than a mouthful, so many people order a double espresso.

Ristretto is a double strength, standard espresso, made by switching off the machine sooner, so that the coffee is denser.

Above: A range of coffee beans offered by an American supplier includes organic coffee.

Above: The modern, upscale coffee shop was first introduced in America, and the craze has now crossed the Atlantic to Europe.

Cappuccino is espresso topped with foamed milk – this is usually achieved by an injection of steam under the surface of the milk. This popular drink is named after the creamy colored robes worn by Capuchin monks. Purists argue as to whether a cappuccino should be topped with a seasoning of nutmeg, cinnamon, cocoa, or chocolate, or left completely plain. Some plunger coffee pots are now being adapted to froth milk for cappuccino.

Cafe Latte is a long milky espresso drink. The standard Italian blend for the brew is equal parts of espresso, milk, and foam, which works well in a cup of not more than 6 fl oz, but in a larger mug or beaker that mixture will not hold. So, for a standard 12 fl oz measure, it is usual to use about half and half espresso and steamed milk, and then to top the coffee off with just a thin layer of froth.

Cafe Americano is espresso diluted with enough hot water to make a regular cup of coffee.

Cafe Mocha is the hot fudge sundae of espresso drinks – coffee with chocolate syrup and steamed milk, topped with whipped cream and then decorated with grated or flaked chocolate.

Instant Coffee

It seems amazing to me that the spread of real coffee throughout the world took around a millennium, and yet international dependence on instant coffee came about in just forty to fifty years.

Although coffee purists would hardly acknowledge instant coffee in the same breath as the carefully nurtured product of beans, it cannot be ignored. The first convenience coffee was developed by an English chemist living in Guatemala. He was inspired after noticing powdery deposits on the spout of his silver coffee pot. Experimentation led to a way of producing the powder in marketable quantities, and he launched his new product (called Red E Coffee) in America in 1909. Its success inspired the launch of a similar product for the European market four years later.

Instant coffee was a boon during the years of the Second World War, providing an instant, fashionable drink. Far from disappearing when peace came, instant coffee remained.

In order to satisfy demand, and also to preserve its surplus coffee, the Brazilian government worked with other South American coffee producing countries to find a way to produce larger quantities of better quality instant coffee. Spray drying came first, whereby freshly brewed coffee was sprayed into a drying chamber in which all liquid evaporated, leaving only a powder of instant coffee. This was the normal method of production until the 1960s, when freeze drying became more popular.

FREEZE DRYING

This process was perfected in 1966 in an attempt to maintain the flavor and aroma of the coffee, both of which were completely lost in the spray drying process. It involves a slush of coffee being frozen and then broken or smashed into granules. The water content is then extracted in a high-pressure vacuum chamber, leaving just the freeze-dried granules. These even look better than the spray-dried product as the resulting dried coffee is left in distinctive granules or chips.

I do use spray-dried instant coffee in recipes, especially for baking, as I find that the texture and flavor are both good and that the coffee can be incorporated pretty much as it is, without having to be made into a liquid which tends to alter the consistency of a baking mix.

DRINKING INSTANT COFFEE

One of the problems with instant coffee is that, believe it or not, it is often badly made! Yes, it is possible to mess up adding hot water to coffee granules! The problem lies in the amount of coffee put into the cup. Most freeze-dried instants are developed to be made with 1 teaspoon of coffee in a 6 fl oz cup, but many people just ladle the coffee in, following the old adage that a cup of strong coffee is a cup of good coffee.

The chemists and food scientists who work in the instant coffee industry will argue vociferously that a good cup of freeze-dried instant coffee, properly made to the right strength, is often better than a poorly brewed cup of fresh coffee, especially if the beans are past their best. I am certain that you get what you pay for with instant coffee, just as you do with beans, and that the more expensive brands are definitely worth the extra cost. You should also consider that instant coffee loses its volatile gases when exposed to air in exactly the same way as freshly ground coffee and coffee beans do. I would always suggest buying small jars of good quality freeze-dried instant coffee, and drinking it quickly. A catering size tin for one or two people is a very false economy.

Basic Rules for Enjoying Coffee

Most of the "rules" about making coffee concern storing the beans and keeping the coffee well, rather than dictating what coffees should be drunk when, or what sort of cup the drink should be served in. Although coffee drinking is still, in some countries, a very formal event, for most of us it is an opportunity to relax, or to revive our failing concentration through a coffee break.

STORING COFFEE
There are just a few tips to follow:
• Buy coffee regularly in small amounts.
• Buy directly from the roaster if possible. This will ensure that the coffee is as fresh as possible.
• Store coffee, either as beans or ground, in a cool place. If your house is very warm you might store it in the fridge, but keep it well wrapped so that moisture does not get to it.
• Coffee should be kept in the dark, so don't transfer it from a bag to a glass jar.
• Remember that coffee is only at its best for about ten days to two weeks in beans. Ground coffee starts to loose its flavor after just a couple of days.
• If you buy in bulk you should store your coffee, well wrapped, in the freezer. Even so, it will only be in peak condition for about four weeks.

WHAT TO DRINK WHEN
There are no hard and fast rules as to which style of coffee should be drunk at certain times of the day. Your mood and the task in hand are most likely to dictate the coffee that you drink, but here are a few suggestions.
• Many people like a strong coffee to start the day. For a regular coffee choose a French or Continental blend which are very darkly roasted. For a single variety you might choose Java, which is rich and full in flavor, or a Costa Rican coffee which is full and mellow, but has a great depth of flavor.
• Cappuccino is one of the most popular morning coffees. Although many people drink it throughout the day, traditionalists would only serve it at breakfast or for a mid-morning drink.
• Mysore is a favorite after-lunch coffee. Its spiciness helps to prevent the onslaught of an afternoon nap!
• Espresso and ristretto are good after a heavy meal – they almost work as a digestive.

MATCHING TASTES TO MOODS
The full flavor of coffee will only really be appreciated if you grind your own beans, and enjoy the aroma of the drink in the nose as well as the flavor in the cup.

Volatile oils are essential to the full enjoyment of coffee – this is why freshly ground is so much more satisfying than the average instant. You are unlikely to enjoy your coffee as much as usual if you have a cold.

Body, acidity and balance are more difficult to explain. Body could be described as the strength or depth of flavor; acidity is roughly translatable as brightness, and the balance is really the overall roundness of the flavor. Beyond these characteristics you should be able to find individual taste sensations or flavors in the coffee – chocolate, spice, nuttiness, smoke. Don't linger too long over the tasting or the coffee will be cold by the time you stop tasting and actually drink it!

A FEW RULES FOR COFFEE MAKING
• Coffee should be as hot as possible when served, so do warm the pot, or the cups that you will use if serving espresso or an espresso-based drink.

• With the exception of Arabic coffee, no coffee is made with boiling water as it scorches very easily, producing a bitter flavor. Either boil a kettle and let it stand for 30 to 60 seconds to go off the boil, or try to catch it just before it bubbles. Electric coffee makers will heat the water to the optimum temperature for you.

• Purists will suggest using filtered or bottled water if your tap water is heavily chlorinated or very chalky.

• Coffee should not be reheated. Of course it is drinkable, but the flavor changes dramatically. Coffee will keep hot in a better condition if poured into a warmed vacuum flask, rather than keeping it on a hot plate. However, it should not be left standing for longer than 30 minutes.

• The most important part of brewing is to use the correct amount of coffee. A good rule of thumb is 2 level teaspoons of ground coffee for each 6 fl oz (¾ cup). Of course, it is all a matter of taste.

COFFEE IN COOKING

The recipes use a variety of coffees. For ice creams, make a very strong brew using about 4 tablespoons of ground coffee to 5 fl oz (⅔ cup) water, which works very well. However, for baking and desserts you can use a freeze-dried instant coffee, or coffee extract, as they do not cause such a change in the texture of the mixture. Coffee extract is thick and syrupy, and is often a blend of coffee and chicory, the latter being an old-fashioned filler or bulker for cheaper coffees. Coffee extract is an essential store-cupboard ingredient; just a teaspoonful can add an edge to mixtures that would otherwise be far too sweet. In some ways it is the salt and pepper of the coffee world, a flavoring in its own right, or a seasoning for sweet dishes.

Coffee Recipes

Drinks

WARMING PUNCHES ENLIVENED WITH BRANDY OR RUM, REFRESHING ICED COFFEES, SPICY AFTER-DINNER TREATS, AND SOOTHING MILK SHAKES — THERE'S SOMETHING HERE FOR EVERYONE.

Cakes and Bakes

COFFEE IS THE MAGIC INGREDIENT IN THESE DELICIOUS BAKES, FROM SATISFYING COOKIES AND MUFFINS TO RICH GATEAUX, PETIT FOURS, TRUFFLES, AND SHORTBREAD.

Ice Creams

INDULGE IN LUSCIOUS TREATS, RICH WITH EGGS AND CREAM; IMPRESS WITH A SUCCULENT VIENNESE CLASSIC; REFRESH YOUR TASTE BUDS WITH A TANGY GRANITA OR YOGURT ICE.

Desserts

COFFEE GIVES A DELICIOUS NEW TWIST TO SOME OLD FAVORITES — SOUFFLE, CREME CARAMEL, CHOCOLATE MOUSSE — AND HIGHLIGHTS A SURPRISE REFRIGERATOR CAKE AND TINY PECAN PIES.

Drinks

Coffee makes an excellent base for many hot or cold drinks. It is a natural partner for whiskey, brandy, rum, and numerous liqueurs, and also marries well with carbonated drinks, milk, and some fruit juices to make cold punches and cups.

Coffee should ideally be freshly brewed for drinks, but, if you are in a rush, you could use cold left-overs providing they are well diluted. There are one or two suggestions about the variety of coffee to use, but as a general rule a full-flavored, high-roasted coffee will be fine.

Coffee Punch à la Russe

An interesting hot coffee punch with plenty of fresh fruit; leave the skins on for extra color. Choose a coffee such as Mocha, which is best drunk black.

Serves 4

**1 red eating apple,
   cored and diced**
**1 ripe but firm dessert pear,
   cored and diced**
Juice of 1 lemon
3 cups strong hot coffee
Sugar to taste
½ cup brandy or vodka

1 Toss the diced fruits in the lemon juice, then place in a warmed glass jug. Add the coffee and sweeten to taste, without losing the tang from the lemon juice.

2 Heat the brandy or vodka in a metal ladle over a low heat, until it ignites, then pour over the coffee. Leave until the flames subside, then stir and serve in warmed cups or glasses.

Cardamom Topper

Café Brûlot

Café Brûlot is a classic hot spiced brew from the South, traditionally made in a large silver or copper bowl.

Serves 4 to 6

Pared rind of 2 oranges
Pared rind of 2 lemons
2 cups strong hot coffee
1 cinnamon stick
2 tsp cloves
2 Tbsp granulated sugar
¼ cup curaçao
1 cup brandy

1 Cut the orange and lemon rinds into slivers with a small, sharp knife. Place in a warmed jug with the coffee, spices, sugar and curaçao and stir until the sugar has dissolved.

2 Warm the brandy in a large metal ladle or a small pan over a low flame then carefully ignite it. Pour the brandy into the jug and wait for the flames to subside. Stir briefly, then strain into warmed cups or glasses.

Cardamom Topper

An excellent coffee to round off a spicy meal. You can sweeten the cream a little more, but don't overpower the cardamom flavor.

Serves 1 to 2

2 green cardamom pods, crushed
  and seeds removed
1 tsp superfine sugar
1 or 2 Tbsp heavy cream,
  lightly whipped
1 cup strong hot coffee,
  such as Mysore

1 Crush the cardamom seeds in a pestle and mortar or with the end of a rolling pin. Mix the spice and sugar into the cream.

2 Pour the coffee into a warmed glass, then spoon the spiced, sweetened cream over. Sip the coffee slowly through the cream.

Coffee Egg Nog

The ultimate reviver or pick-me-up; more appealing than a bowl of onion soup after a night on the tiles!

Serves 2

1 tsp light brown sugar
1 egg yolk
1 cup whole milk
1 cup strong hot coffee
2 cinnamon sticks

1 Beat the sugar and egg yolk with a small whisk until creamy. Heat the milk until almost at a boil, then add to the egg with the hot coffee, whisking all the time.

2 Pour into mugs, and stir the coffee with cinnamon sticks, adding a little extra sugar if necessary.

Coffee Rum Punch

Coffee and rum are natural partners, sharing a South American pedigree. Add liquidized banana as a natural sweetener with cream and nutmeg. Use white or dark rum, whichever you prefer.

Serves 2

1 large ripe banana
⅔ cup heavy cream
⅓ cup rum
2 cups strong hot coffee
Freshly grated nutmeg
Sugar to taste

1 Chop the banana, then put in a blender with the cream and rum. Blend until smooth, then add the coffee and blend again.

2 Pour the coffee into 2 mugs, and grate a little nutmeg into each. Add sugar to taste.

Mocha Liqueur Cocktail

There are so many recipes for coffee and chocolate liqueurs, but this is my favorite. Add whipped cream as a topping if you feel self-indulgent.

Serves 2

2 Tbsp cocoa powder or flaked drinking chocolate
1 or 2 tsp light brown sugar
1 cup whole milk
1 cup strong hot coffee
4 Tbsp brandy
1 Tbsp finely grated chocolate

1 Blend the cocoa with the sugar and a little milk. Put the remaining milk in a small pan and bring almost to a boil. Pour the hot milk onto the paste and stir until smooth and blended. Return the cocoa to the pan with the hot coffee and heat gently until very hot but not boiling.

2 Pour into large mugs and add 2 tablespoons of brandy to each. Top with finely grated chocolate and serve immediately.

Irish Coffee

Serves 1 or 2

¼ cup Irish whiskey
1 tsp light brown sugar
1 cup strong hot coffee
¼ cup heavy cream

1 Warm 1 large or 2 small glasses. Pour in the whiskey, add the sugar, then add the coffee and stir until the sugar has dissolved.

2 While the coffee is still revolving slowly in the glass, pour in the cream over the back of a spoon so that it floats on the top of the coffee. Don't stir again, or you will lose the layers in the glass.

This classic liqueur is sometimes called Dublin Coffee James Joyce. I have never been brave enough to ask an Irishman whether it's true that this drink was actually invented in San Francisco!

Coffee and Whiskey Hooligan's Soup

Hooligan's Soup is a popular dessert in many South African restaurants after a filling main course. It's really an alcoholic milk shake!

Serves 2

3 generous scoops vanilla ice cream
1 cup cold coffee
1 Tbsp coffee extract
Whiskey, as much as you dare
1 cup crushed ice

1 Place all the ingredients in a food processor or blender and process to a thick, smooth shake. Add a little extra coffee, milk (or whiskey) if necessary. Pour into tall glasses, and drink through a thick straw.

Orange-flavored Turkish-style Coffee

Many people find Turkish coffee too sweet, but the addition of a little orange rind and juice lifts the flavor.

Serves 2 to 4

2 cups water
3 Tbsp granulated sugar
3 Tbsp very finely ground coffee
Finely grated rind and juice
  of 1 orange
½ cup Cointreau
4 Tbsp heavy cream, whipped
  until thick enough to hold
  its shape

1 Bring the water to a boil with the sugar in a small pan. Stir in the coffee then return the pan to the heat. Bring to a boil so that the coffee froths up, then remove from heat for about 2 minutes until the grounds have settled. Repeat this process twice more, allowing the grounds to settle each time.

2 Add the orange juice and Cointreau to the coffee, then pour into 2 glasses or 4 cups. Mix the grated orange rind into the cream, then spoon it over the coffee. Serve immediately. Do not strain the coffee; the grounds will settle to the bottom of the cups.

Creamy Iced Coffee

Serves 2

1 cup whole milk
**1½ cups double strength hot
 coffee**
Sugar to taste
Crushed ice
**3 Tbsp heavy cream, lightly
 whipped until thick and soft**
Coffee sugar crystals to decorate

1 Heat the milk until almost boiling, then add to the coffee and stir in sugar to taste. Leave to cool, then chill for 30 minutes.

2 Place 2 or 3 tablespoons of crushed ice in 2 tall glasses, then pour the chilled coffee over. Top with the lightly whipped cream and a few sugar crystals for decoration. Serve immediately, with a long swizzle stick in each glass to stir up the coffee and ice.

This is one of the few iced coffees made with a strong brew as the coffee really is the main ingredient. The milk is essential to take the edge off the cold drink, which might otherwise be slightly bitter.

Iced Coffee Punch

The fruit must be in even-sized small dice if you are to drink them from the glass, otherwise you will have to supply spoons with the punch. For a slightly more gingery flavor, grate a small piece of fresh gingerroot, then squeeze the juice into the coffee.

Serves 4

1 ripe peach, stoned, peeled and diced
1 ripe dessert pear, cored and diced
1 Tbsp lemon juice
2 cups cold coffee
1 cup dry ginger ale
2 scoops vanilla or ginger ice cream
⅔ cup light cream
1 cup crushed ice

1 Toss the diced fruit in the lemon juice. Place all the remaining ingredients in a blender or food processor and blend to a thick, shake-like consistency. Divide the fruit between 4 chilled glasses and pour in the coffee. Serve immediately, adding a little sugar to taste if necessary.

Mocha Milk Shake

A traditional milk shake on a creamy coffee base. I like to add chocolate ice cream and a banana for extra thickness. This works extremely well with left-over cold coffee.

Serves 2

1 cup cold black coffee
1 Tbsp coffee extract
1 cup whole milk
2 scoops chocolate ice cream
1 banana, chopped
1 cup crushed ice
Crushed flaked chocolate or finely grated chocolate, for decoration

1 Process all the ingredients together in a blender until thick and smooth, then pour into tall glasses. Alternatively, pour the milk shake into 2 glasses filled with the crushed ice.

2 Top with flaked or grated chocolate and serve immediately.

Spanish-style Iced Coffee

Serves 2

4 cloves
2 tsp light brown sugar,
**   or to taste**
1 cup strong hot coffee
1 cup orange juice
5 Tbsp brandy
1 orange
Crushed ice

1 Add the cloves and sugar to the coffee and stir until the sugar has dissolved. Leave to cool for 10 minutes, then stir in the orange juice. Strain the coffee into a jug, then leave to cool completely. Add the brandy, then chill for 30 minutes.

2 Cut away the top and bottom of the orange, then cut the fruit into thin slices. Chop into segments, then mix with crushed ice in 2 tall glasses. Pour the chilled coffee into the glasses and serve immediately.

Most iced coffees include milk or cream, but this one is definitely to be drunk black. It is a sweet coffee, fortified with brandy and mixed with orange juice and sliced oranges; a long, luxurious iced coffee which is deliciously different.

Cakes and Bakes

In baking, the addition of coffee can transform what might otherwise be a straightforward recipe into something very special.

A rich fruit cake is enhanced with coffee, a Madeira mix takes on a completely new character and muffins become the ultimate breakfast food when made with coffee and banana – a complete breakfast in a cake.

Instant coffee is often used in baking recipes because it is better for the consistency of the mixture. Be sure to use a good quality, freeze-dried instant, which comes in the form of granules, rather than powdered instant coffee. Coffee extract is also used in a number of the bakes. This is a strong mixture of coffee and chicory which can completely lift the flavor of a cake or frosting.

Banana and Raisin Muffins

Makes 12

1 Tbsp butter
2¼ cups flour
1½ tsp baking powder
½ tsp bicarbonate of soda
2 Tbsp freeze-dried instant coffee granules
⅓ cup raisins
⅓ cup superfine sugar
3 large bananas, mashed
1 cup buttermilk
2 eggs, beaten
Granulated sugar for sprinkling

These are ideal for breakfast, quick to mix and quick to bake. Muffins are best eaten on the day that they are made.

1 Preheat the oven to 400°F and line 12 deep muffin tins with double paper cases. Melt the butter, then leave it to cool.

2 Mix together all the dry ingredients in a bowl and make a well in the center. Add the bananas, butter, buttermilk and eggs, then quickly combine the ingredients together with a palette knife until just mixed; the mixture will seem quite wet.

3 Divide the mixture between the paper cases; speed is the secret of successful muffins. Bake in the preheated oven for 20 to 25 minutes, until set and lightly browned. Sprinkle a little granulated sugar over the muffins as soon as they are cooked. Cool slightly on a wire rack before serving.

A classic cake for all those with a sweet tooth! The walnuts help to take away a little of the richness. Based on a French recipe from the town of Mocha in Brittany, the town's name bearing witness to the importance of the coffee trade to its citizens.

Mocha Gateau aux Noix

Serves 8 to 10

1 cup all-purpose flour
Pinch of salt
3 Tbsp unsalted butter
3 eggs
½ cup superfine sugar
2 Tbsp strong cold coffee

1 Preheat the oven to 350°F and line a 8-inch round springform pan with baking parchment. Sieve the flour and salt together. Melt the butter and allow it to cool.

2 Whisk the eggs and sugar with an electric beater until they are pale and very thick. The mixture should leave a long thick ribbon trail when the beater is lifted.

3 Sieve the flour again, then add it to the mixture one-third of a cup at a time, folding it in lightly with a wire whisk. Add the cooled butter and the coffee with the last lot of flour. Scrape the mixture into the prepared pan and bake for 30 to 40 minutes, until lightly golden. The cake will shrink slightly from the sides when ready, and should spring back when lightly touched. Remove the cake from the pan, peel off the paper and allow to cool on a wire rack.

Frosting
8 oz (2 sticks) unsalted butter, softened
4 Tbsp strong cold coffee or 2 Tbsp coffee extract
2 cups confectioners' sugar, sieved
½ cup walnut halves

4 Beat the butter for the frosting until creamy, then add the coffee. Gradually beat in the confectioners' sugar. If you prefer a very buttery, French-style frosting use only about two-thirds of the sugar.

5 Slice the cake horizontally into two, and spread the bottom half with frosting. Sandwich the layers together, then frost the top, reserving sufficient frosting to pipe around the edge in swirls or rosettes. Decorate with walnut halves and serve cut into small slices.

Makes about 25

1⅔ cups all-purpose flour
2 tsp baking powder
1 tsp bicarbonate of soda
2 tsp ground ginger
1 tsp mixed spice or pumpkin
   pie spice
1 Tbsp superfine sugar
7 Tbsp butter or margarine, plus
   extra for greasing
⅔ cup light corn syrup

Frosting
2 oz (½ stick) butter, softened
¼ cup superfine sugar
1 tsp coffee extract
½ cup confectioners' sugar,
   sieved

Ginger and Coffee Creams

Crisp ginger nut cookies sandwiched together with a coffee cream: perfect with a large mug of steaming coffee, and very good for dunking!

1 Preheat the oven to 375°F and butter 2 or 3 cookie sheets.

2 Sieve all the dry ingredients together into a bowl, stir in the sugar and make a well in the center. Melt the butter slowly, then stir in the syrup and pour the mixture into the well. Mix thoroughly to give a soft but not sticky dough.

3 Scoop up half teaspoons of the mixture and roll into balls. Place on the prepared cookie sheets, leaving some space between the cookies as they will spread during cooking, and flatten them slightly. Bake in the preheated oven for 15 to 20 minutes until set. Leave to cool for a few minutes on the cookie sheets, then remove to a wire rack to cool completely.

4 To prepare the frosting, beat the butter and superfine sugar together with the coffee extract until well blended. Gradually beat in the confectioners' sugar, sieving it into the bowl, and mix to a stiff paste. Sandwich the cookies together with a little frosting; don't be too generous or it will ooze out when you bite into the cookies.

5 Store the cookies for 2 to 3 days in an air-tight tin. The frosting will make them go a little soft, but they are very crisp cookies and will not spoil.

Swedish-style Coffee and Cardamom Buns

Makes 12

**1 heaped Tbsp green cardamom
pods, crushed and seeds
removed**

**½ oz fresh yeast or 1 tsp dried
fast-acting yeast**

½ cup warm water

3½ cups white bread flour

½ tsp salt

**1 Tbsp freeze-dried instant
coffee granules**

1 egg, beaten

**1 cup warm milk, plus extra
to glaze**

¼ cup superfine sugar

**7 Tbsp unsalted butter, softened,
plus extra for greasing**

**Coffee sugar crystals or light
brown sugar, to decorate**

*Cardamom is used extensively in Scandinavian baking, and it is also a very
good spice to use with coffee. These yeasted buns are delicious for breakfast,
spread with butter and jelly, and are also a welcome snack with a
mid-morning cup of coffee.*

1 Crush the cardamom seeds in a
pestle and mortar or with the end of
a rolling pin. Crumble the fresh
yeast into the water in a large bowl
or the bowl of a food processor,
leave for 3 to 4 minutes, then stir
until completely dissolved. If using
dried yeast, add to the flour.

2 Mix the flour, salt and coffee
together. Add the egg, milk, sugar,
and butter to the fresh yeast liquid
and whisk until blended. Change to
the dough hook if using a food
processor, then gradually add the
flour to make a soft and very sticky
dough. Knead thoroughly until the
dough is smooth and shiny, and
ready to leave the sides of the bowl.
This kneading is easiest to do with a
food processor. Add a little extra
flour if necessary, but the dough
should be too soft to knead by hand
on a work surface. Cover and leave
in a warm place for 1 hour, or until

doubled in size.

3 Knock back the dough on a
floured surface and divide into
12 pieces. Shape into buns and
place on a buttered or floured
cookie sheet, then cover and leave
in a warm place for 20 minutes.
Meanwhile, preheat the oven to
400°F.

4 Brush the buns carefully with
milk, then scatter them with the
sugar and bake in the preheated
oven for 20 to 25 minutes until
lightly golden. Cool on a wire rack.
Serve the buns still slightly warm.

Florentines

These rich and sophisticated cookies have always been a favorite. I like to put a little coffee extract in the chocolate as it adds a bite to the cookies, preventing them from being too sweet.

Makes about 16

**1 cup roughly chopped
   mixed nuts**
**6 glacé cherries, rinsed
   and chopped**
⅓ cup mixed chopped peel
1 Tbsp all-purpose flour
3 Tbsp butter
¼ cup superfine sugar
¼ cup light cream
**⅓ cup bittersweet chocolate,
   broken into squares**
1 tsp coffee extract

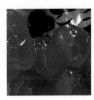

Florentines and Chocolate Chip Shortbreads

1 Preheat the oven to 350°F. Line 2 heavy cookie sheets with baking parchment.

2 Mix the fruit and nuts together and chop them finely, then toss them in the flour. Heat the butter, sugar and cream together until the butter has melted, then bring just to a boil. Add the prepared fruits, and stir well.

3 Place spoonfuls of mixture on the prepared cookie sheets, allowing plenty of room for the Florentines to spread. Bake for 15 to 20 minutes, until golden brown, then carefully neaten the edges of the Florentines while still warm, to make circular cookies. Cool slightly, then transfer to a wire rack to cool completely.

4 Melt the chocolate in a bowl over a pan of hot water, or heat it in the microwave. Stir in the coffee extract. Spread a little of the chocolate thinly over the back of each Florentine, then leave them face down on the wire rack for the chocolate to set. Store the cookies in an air-tight tin if you can resist the temptation to eat them immediately.

Cranberry and Blueberry Coffee Madeira

Serves 10

2 cups flour
1 tsp baking powder
6 oz (1½ sticks) butter, slightly softened, plus extra for greasing
1 cup superfine sugar
3 eggs, beaten
1 Tbsp coffee extract, or 1 Tbsp instant coffee dissolved in 1 Tbsp hot water
⅓ cup dried cranberries
⅓ cup dried blueberries
Milk to mix

The flavor of coffee with the slightly tart taste of the dried berries makes a much more interesting Madeira cake than the traditional variety.

1 Preheat the oven to 350°F and lightly grease and line an 8 x 4 inch loaf pan. Sieve together the flour and baking powder.

2 Cream the butter and sugar in a bowl until pale and creamy, then gradually beat in the eggs and coffee. Fold in the flour, then add the dried berries and mix to a fairly stiff dropping consistency with about 2 tablespoons of milk.

3 Spoon the mixture into the prepared pan, smooth the top and bake in the preheated oven for about 1 hour, until a skewer inserted into the middle of the cake comes out cleanly.

4 Carefully remove the cake from the pan and allow it to cool completely on a wire rack. Serve sliced with morning coffee.

Coffee and Chocolate Chip Shortbreads

Always make shortbread with butter for the best flavor.

Makes about 20

6 oz (1½ sticks) butter, plus extra for greasing
1¼ cups all-purpose flour
2 tsp freeze-dried instant coffee granules
½ cup confectioners' sugar, sieved
Few drops of vanilla extract
⅓ cup fine chocolate chips

1 Cream the butter in a bowl until soft, then gradually work in all the remaining ingredients except the chocolate. Continue working the dough until it begins to come together, then add the chocolate and knead into a firm dough. Shape into a roll about 15 inches long, then cover in plastic wrap and chill in the refrigerator for about 1 hour.

2 Preheat the oven to 350°F and lightly grease 2 cookie sheets. Slice the dough into 24 pieces, then place on the cookie sheets and flatten slightly with a fork. Bake the shortbreads in the preheated oven for 20 to 25 minutes, until lightly golden.

3 Allow the shortbreads to cool for 1 to 2 minutes on the cookie sheets, then transfer them carefully with a palette knife to a wire rack until completely cold. Store in an airtight tin.

Coffee Truffles

The success of the truffles depends on the quality of the chocolate.

Makes 30 to 35

1⅓ cups bittersweet chocolate, broken into squares
7 Tbsp butter
1¼ cups confectioners' sugar, sieved
1 Tbsp coffee extract
Confectioners' sugar for decoration (optional)

1 Melt the chocolate in a bowl over a pan of hot water, or in a microwave oven. Beat thoroughly, then allow to cool for about 5 minutes; the chocolate must still be liquid but not so hot that it will melt the butter when added to it.

2 Beat the butter and sieved sugar into a paste, but don't cream them as you would when making a cake. Stir in the coffee extract, then gradually add the cooled chocolate.

The mixture will start to harden as you beat it into a thick paste.

3 Fit a large star tube into a piping bag and spoon the truffle mixture into the bag. Pipe bite-sized rosettes onto a cookie sheet lined with baking parchment, or into small truffle or petit-fours cases. Chill for 1 to 2 hours and leave them in the refrigerator until required. Dust lightly with confectioners' sugar just before serving.

Coffee and Cinnamon Puff Pinwheels

Crisp and flaky, these cookies may be served with morning coffee or as an accompaniment to any number of fruit fools, mousses and soufflés.

Makes 32

½ lb prepared puff pastry, defrosted if frozen
2 Tbsp butter, melted, plus extra for greasing
½ cup finely chopped raisins
3 Tbsp light brown sugar
1 Tbsp freeze-dried instant coffee granules
Superfine sugar
Confectioners' sugar for dusting

1 Preheat the oven to 400°F and lightly grease 2 cookie sheets.

2 Roll the pastry out to a large rectangle on a lightly floured surface. It should measure about 9 x 14 inches. Trim the edges, then brush the pastry liberally with melted butter. Mix the raisins, sugar and coffee together, then scatter the mixture evenly over the pastry.

3 Roll the pastry up tightly from the long edge, then brush the roll with any remaining butter and sprinkle it with superfine sugar. Cut into about 32 thin slices, then arrange the pinwheels on the cookie sheets.

4 Bake in the preheated oven for 12 to 15 minutes until golden brown. Carefully transfer the pinwheels to a wire rack using a palette knife, then dust the best side with sieved confectioners' sugar. Leave to cool completely before serving.

Coffee and Almond Petit Fours

Makes about 12

Just the thing for using up the odd egg white when entertaining. These are quick to make and I prefer to make them a few at a time when needed as I think they are much better when fresh. A hand mixer is probably the best way of whisking up just one egg white.

Pinch of cream of tartar
1 tsp coffee extract
1 Tbsp finely chopped blanched almonds
1 egg white
⅓ cup superfine sugar

1 Preheat the oven to 275°F and line a cookie sheet with baking parchment.

2 Mix the cream of tartar, coffee extract and chopped almonds together. Whisk the egg white until stiff, then gradually whisk in most of sugar until the meringue is smooth and glossy. Fold in the almond mix; I like the effect if the coffee stays slightly streaky in the mix.

3 Place 12 little piles of the mixture on the prepared cookie sheet and sprinkle any remaining sugar over the top of the meringues. Bake in the cool oven for 40 minutes, until the meringues are set and crisp. Cool completely before serving.

Truffles, Pinwheels and Petit Fours

Ice Creams

Coffee is my all-time favorite flavoring for ice creams. Rich ice creams take at least four hours to prepare because of cooling and chilling times, so you must leave yourself plenty of time to make them.

Instant espresso is very good for the Italian ices. But be careful if you use a commercially ground coffee in a cafetière. It will be too finely ground for the mesh of the plunger to remove all traces of the coffee, and the result will be a rather grainy texture. If in doubt, strain the coffee through a paper filter. Make fresh coffee as it definitely has the best flavor.

Note: Some of these recipes contain uncooked egg white.
It is recommended that expectant mothers and those with weak immune systems should not eat raw eggs.

Creamy Coffee Ice Milk

Ice milks are best eaten as soon as they are made, or they may become crystalline during storage.

Serves 4

½ **cup instant espresso**
½ **cup light brown sugar**
2 **cups whole milk**
⅔ **cup light cream**
1 **egg white**

1 Put the coffee and sugar in a bowl. Heat the milk until almost boiling, then pour it onto the coffee. Stir until the sugar has dissolved, then leave to cool completely. Stir the cream into the cold coffee mixture.

2 Whisk the egg white until frothy, then gradually add the coffee and cream and continue whisking until thoroughly combined. Turn the ice milk into an ice cream machine and freeze-churn until ready to serve. Ice milks are best served immediately as there is little fat in the mixture to prevent ice crystals from forming during freezer storage. However, the mixture may be hardened for 30 minutes or so in the freezer if you wish to serve it in scoops.

Coffee Ice Cream with Chocolate Ripple

Serves 6 to 8

⅔ cup hot water

4 Tbsp coarsely ground high
   roast coffee

4 egg yolks

⅔ cup light brown sugar

½ tsp ground mixed spice

1¼ cups light cream

1¼ cups heavy cream

Chocolate fudge sauce

⅔ cup bittersweet chocolate,
   broken into small pieces

⅓ cup light corn syrup

2 Tbsp hot water

1 tsp coffee extract (optional)

A luxuriously rich ice cream sweetened with a chocolate fudge sauce ripple.

1 Pour the hot water over the coffee and leave to stand for 10 minutes. Whisk the egg yolks and sugar in a bowl with the mixed spice until pale and thick.

2 Strain the coffee through a fine sieve into a pan with the light cream and heat gently until almost boiling. Pour the mixture onto the egg yolks, stirring all the time. Rinse the pan in cold water, return the custard to the pan and cook slowly until thickened just enough to coat the back of a wooden spoon. Transfer the custard to a bowl. Leave to cool completely, then chill for 1 hour.

3 Meanwhile, make the sauce. Place all the ingredients in a small, heavy-bottomed pan and heat very gently until melted and blended together. Pour into a small bowl, allow to cool, then chill until required.

4 Fold the heavy cream into the chilled custard, then turn the mixture into an ice cream machine and freeze-churn until ready to serve, or freeze in a suitable plastic container for about 4 hours, stirring once or twice.

5 Pack scoops of the ice cream into a clean freezer box, then spoon the chocolate sauce over, pressing the ice cream down so that there are no gaps. Harden for at least 30 minutes in the freezer before scooping and serving.

Coffee and Coconut Sherbet

Sherbets are light ices made with whipped egg whites and comparatively little fat.
Of all the home-made ices, they are really the most like commercial ice creams in texture.

Serves 6 to 8

⅔ cup water
1 cup superfine sugar
Pared rind and juice of ½ lemon
3 Tbsp filter ground, high roast
   coffee
1¾ cups coconut milk
1 Tbsp lemon juice
3 egg whites
½ cup heavy cream

1 Bring the water, sugar and lemon rind slowly to a boil, stirring until the sugar is dissolved, then simmer for 15 minutes. Remove the pan from the heat, discard the lemon rind and allow the syrup to cool briefly, then stir in the coffee. Leave to stand for 10 minutes, then strain through a fine sieve into a bowl and leave until completely cold. Chill for at least 30 minutes.

2 Stir the coconut milk and lemon juice into the chilled coffee mixture. Whisk the egg whites until frothy, then gradually whisk in the coffee. Stir in the cream, then pour into an ice cream maker and freeze-churn until ready to serve. Alternatively, freeze in a suitable plastic container for 4 hours or until firm, stirring once or twice during freezing.

Coffee and Cardamom Frozen Yogurt

Serves 4

½ cup hot, not boiling, water
3 Tbsp coarsely ground high
   roast coffee
1 Tbsp green cardamom
   pods, crushed
1½ cups plain yogurt
¾ cup heavy cream
½ cup superfine sugar

A spicy, creamy frozen yogurt with a tang! Once the coffee has cooled, this ice just needs mixing and freezing. It is much quicker to make than ice cream. I find that this recipe increases in bulk quite considerably during churning if using an ice cream machine, so do not be tempted to add more ingredients than the recipe states.

1 Pour the water over the coffee and cardamom pods, then leave to stand for 10 minutes. Strain the coffee through a fine sieve into a large bowl, then leave until completely cool. Add all the remaining ingredients and beat until smooth.

2 Turn into an ice cream machine and freeze churn until ready to serve, or freeze in a suitable plastic container for 3 to 4 hours until hard, stirring once or twice. Serve immediately, or store in the freezer.

Viennese Ice Cream

Serves 8

1¼ cups hot, not boiling, water
8 Tbsp coarsely ground coffee
1⅓ cups roughly chopped,
   ready-to-eat dried figs
5 Tbsp Tia Maria
⅔ cup hot, not boiling, water
1¼ cups light cream
4 egg yolks
⅔ cup light brown sugar
1¼ cups heavy cream,
   lightly whipped

1 Pour the water over the coffee and leave to stand for 10 minutes, then strain through a fine sieve. Place the figs in a bowl. Pour half the coffee over the figs and stir in the Tia Maria, then leave to soak.

2 Gently heat the remaining coffee in a pan with the light cream until almost boiling. Beat the egg yolks and sugar in a bowl until pale and thick, then pour the hot cream onto the eggs, whisking continuously.

3 Rinse the pan in cold water then return the custard to the pan and heat slowly, stirring all the time,

Figs are the secret flavoring ingredient in the classic Viennese coffee blend. With that combination in mind I have made a rich and delicious coffee ice cream, enriched with a thick and succulent fig purée. Resist it if you can!

until just thick enough to coat the back of a wooden spoon. Pour into a clean bowl and leave until completely cold. Chill the custard for at least 1 hour.

4 Fold the heavy cream into the custard and freeze churn in an ice cream machine until almost ready to serve. Meanwhile, place the figs in a food processor or blender and blend to a smooth purée. Turn the thickened ice cream into a large bowl and fold in the figs, then pack

into an ice cream container and freeze for at least 1 hour. Alternatively, blend the chilled custard and fig purée together in a food processor, then turn into a large freezer box and freeze for 4 to 5 hours, stirring once or twice.

Coffee and Pistachio Kulfi

Serves 10 to 12

3 Tbsp coarsely ground Mysore, or other medium flavored coffee
½ cup hot, not boiling, water
About ⅔ cup whole milk
1⅓ cups light brown sugar
1 cup evaporated milk, well chilled
1¼ cups heavy cream
½ cup finely chopped pistachio nuts

Kulfi is traditionally frozen in tall conical molds, but you can use ice lolly shapers or individual dessert molds, or freeze it in a plastic box. If you do use a mold, try serving the kulfi in the traditional way by scoring the tip to make four leaves.

1 Pour the hot water over the coffee, then leave it to stand for about 10 minutes. Strain through a fine sieve into a jug and leave until cold. Add sufficient cold milk to make 1 cup.

2 Pour the coffee into a bowl, add the sugar, then stir until it has dissolved. Stir in the chilled evaporated milk and the cream. Pour into molds or a freezer box, and freeze until solid, 4 to 6 hours.

3 To serve, dip the molds into hot water for a few seconds, then turn out the kulfi onto serving dishes. Leave to stand in a cool kitchen or in the refrigerator for 10 to 15 minutes before serving sprinkled with the finely chopped pistachios.

Mocha Ice Cream

The best way to chop the chocolate is in a food processor.

Serves 6 to 8

⅔ cup hot water
4 Tbsp coarsely ground high roast coffee
1¼ cups light cream
4 egg yolks
½ cup light brown sugar
⅔ cup finely chopped chocolate chips
1¼ cups heavy cream

1 Pour the hot water over the coffee, leave to stand for 10 minutes, then strain the coffee into the cream in a saucepan.

2 Whisk the egg yolks in a bowl with the sugar until pale and thick. Heat the coffee-flavored cream until almost boiling, then add the chocolate. Stir until the chocolate is dissolved, then pour the mixture onto the egg yolks, whisking all the time.

3 Place the bowl over a pan of hot water until the mixture has thickened just enough to coat the back of a wooden spoon. Remove the bowl from the pan and leave it to cool completely. Chill for at least 1 hour.

4 Whip the heavy cream until thick and floppy, then fold it into the mocha custard. Turn into an ice cream machine and freeze-churn until ready to serve, or freeze in a plastic container for 4 to 5 hours, stirring once or twice. Store in the freezer.

Cafe au Lait Gelato

An intensely flavored Italian-style coffee ice cream. Serve in scoops in sugared cornet wafers, with whipped cream or with a dollop of mascarpone.

Serves 6

2½ cups whole milk
⅓ cup instant espresso
½ cup superfine sugar, or more
 according to taste
6 egg yolks, beaten

1 Heat the milk in a pan with the instant espresso and sugar, stirring until the sugar has dissolved.

2 Beat the egg yolks in a bowl until pale, then pour on the hot milk, stirring constantly. Rinse the pan, return the custard to the pan and heat gently, stirring all the time, until the mixture has thickened just enough to coat the back of a wooden spoon. Pour the custard into a clean bowl and allow it to cool completely. Chill for 1 hour.

3 Scrape the custard into an ice cream machine and freeze-churn until ready to serve. Alternatively, freeze the gelato in a suitable plastic box for 3 or 4 hours, stirring several times during freezing. Serve immediately, or store in the freezer.

Spiced Coffee Granita

Serves 8

1 cup water
Pared rind of 1 lemon
1 piece star anise
3 cloves
1 cinnamon stick
1 cup light brown sugar
2¼ cups cold strong coffee
2 or 3 Tbsp coffee liqueur, such
**   as Kahlua or Tia Maria**

1 Bring the water slowly to a boil with the lemon rind, spices and sugar, stirring constantly to dissolve the sugar. Remove the pan from the heat and add the coffee, then leave to cool for 10 minutes. Strain into a bowl and leave until completely cold. For a more spicy flavor, leave the spices to infuse until the coffee is cold.

2 Stir in the liqueur, then chill the cold coffee for at least 1 hour. Pour into a large flat freezer container and freeze, stirring with a fork after 1 hour, and then every 30 minutes until full of small ice crystals, which should be evenly sized. Serve immediately.

A granita is stirred with a fork during the freezing process, which gives a very granular ice. If the granita is too crystalline you could whizz it in a food processor before serving, but that would give it more of the texture of a sorbet.

Desserts

Coffee makes an excellent flavoring for desserts, especially when fruits are scarce but you wish to create an elegant, stylish conclusion to your meal.

Most of the recipes use fresh coffee, often very strong to achieve the required flavor. Use a good quality freeze-dried instant coffee if you prefer, but make it up to double strength.

Cut chocolate chips from good quality plain chocolate, rather than using ready-made. The best chocolate contains at least 70 percent cocoa solids.

Gelatin is used to set the mousses and soufflés, but use the vegetarian equivalent or agar-agar if you prefer.

Una's Coffee Sponge Pudding

If you love Lemon Surprise Pudding, where a tangy lemon sauce oozes out from under a baked lemon sponge, then you will love this variation on the theme – a coffee sponge with a difference.

Serves 4

6 Tbsp butter, plus extra for greasing
1 cup superfine sugar
⅓ cup strong cold coffee
2 Tbsp Tia Maria
2 large eggs, separated
1 cup all-purpose flour
1½ tsp baking powder
¾ cup milk

1 Preheat the oven to 350°F. Butter 4 large ramekin dishes.

2 Beat the sugar and butter together until pale and fluffy, then add the coffee, liqueur and egg yolks. Sieve the flour and baking powder into the mixture, then fold lightly together. Whisk the egg whites until stiff, then fold them into sponge mix.

3 Divide the pudding between the 4 ramekins in a deep roasting pan. Half fill the pan with hot water, then bake the puddings in the preheated oven for 20 to 25 minutes, until the sponge has set over a runny coffee sauce. Serve immediately with custard, chocolate sauce or ice cream.

Coffee and Almond Pavlova

Serves 8 to 10

1⅓ cups superfine sugar, plus
    extra for sprinkling

⅓ cup ground almonds

1 tsp cream of tartar

1 Tbsp cornstarch

4 egg whites

Pinch of salt

½ tsp almond extract

1 tsp white wine vinegar

2 Tbsps coarsely ground high
    roast coffee

⅓ cup hot water

¼ cup blanched almonds

1¼ cups heavy cream

⅓ cup roughly chopped
    bittersweet chocolate

My Mom's favorite dessert, a marshmallowy meringue topped with coffee and toasted almond cream, then drizzled with chocolate. The best pavlovas are crisp on the outside and sticky in the middle. I don't add sugar to the cream as the meringue base is very sweet, but you may sweeten it slightly if you wish.

1 Preheat the oven to 300°F. Cover a cookie sheet with baking parchment and mark out a 10-inch circle. Scatter a little superfine sugar over the parchment to prevent the pavlova from sticking to the paper.

2 Toast the ground almonds under a medium broiler until golden, stirring them once or twice, then allow to cool. Mix together the sugar, cream of tartar and cornstarch in a small bowl.

3 Whisk the egg whites with the salt until stiff. The mixture should remain firm in the bowl when tipped upside down. Add the almond extract and whisk again. Gradually add the sugar mixture, and stop whisking as soon as it is combined. Quickly fold in the vinegar and the cold toasted almonds using a wire whisk. (Do not attempt to add the almonds with an electric whisk as the fat from them will oil the mixture and the meringue will collapse.)

4 Pile the meringue onto the cookie sheet, spreading it lightly over the marked circle, then fork up the edges into soft peaks. Bake the meringue in the preheated oven for 2 hours, until crisp on the outside and a pale golden color.

5 Prepare the coffee while the meringue is cooking. Pour the hot water over the grounds then leave for 15 minutes. Strain through a fine sieve, then leave until completely cold. Toast the blanched almonds for 3 to 4 minutes under a medium broiler until browned, stirring and turning them once or twice, then leave them to cool. Chop the almonds roughly.

6 Turn off the oven and leave the cooked meringue to stand for about 10 minutes, then lift it carefully onto a wire rack and leave until completely cold.

7 Whip the cream until thick and soft, then add the cold coffee – you should have 3 to 4 tablespoons.

Continue whipping until soft peaks form, then fold in the chopped toasted almonds. Carefully peel away the paper from the meringue base, then gently place it on a large serving plate. Spoon the coffee and almond cream onto the meringue. Spread it over the center and fork it up gently into tiny peaks.

8 Melt the chocolate pieces in a bowl over a pan of hot water, or in a microwave. Spoon the melted chocolate into a waxed paper piping bag, snip off the end, then drizzle the chocolate over the pavlova. Leave for a few minutes before serving, to allow the chocolate to set.

Tiramisu

This classic Italian coffee trifle now comes in many variations. I do hope my version pleases – the secret is in the rich, custard-like topping. Make the tiramisu either in one large dish or layered in large wine glasses.

Serves 4 to 6

½ **cup hot water**

4 **Tbsp coarsely ground Italian-roast coffee**

3 **egg yolks**

1 **cup mascarpone or 2 Tbsp superfine sugar beaten into 1 cup cream cheese**

3 **Tbsp orange liqueur**

12 **Italian ladyfinger cookies**

⅓ **cup finely chopped or grated bittersweet chocolate**

1 Pour the hot water over the coffee then leave to stand for 10 minutes. Strain the coffee through a fine sieve, then leave until completely cold.

2 Beat the eggs yolks in a bowl, then add the mascarpone (or sugar and cream cheese) and beat until smooth. Add 1 tablespoon of the orange liqueur and beat again. Add the remaining liqueur to the cold coffee.

3 Dip the cookies into the coffee as you use them. Either arrange all the cookies in the bottom of a trifle dish and top them with the custard, or arrange cookie pieces in layers with the custard in wine glasses. Sprinkle with the chocolate just before serving.

Coffee and Raisin Pecan Pies

Coffee is used as a seasoning in these pies, to add a touch of spice to the filling without too much sweetness. The result is delicious!

Serves 6

**4 Tbsp coarsely ground high
roast coffee**
⅔ cup hot water
1 cup seedless raisins
7 Tbsp salted butter
½ cup honey
1 Tbsp coffee extract
2 cups pecans

Pastry
1¾ cups all-purpose flour
7 Tbsp butter or margarine
Cold water to mix
**Sieved confectioners' sugar
for decoration**

1 Pour the hot water onto the coffee and leave to stand for 10 to 15 minutes. Strain through a fine sieve into a small bowl, add the raisins and leave them to soak for 10 minutes. Preheat the oven to 400°F.

2 Prepare the pastry. Rub the butter into the flour until the mixture resembles fine breadcrumbs, then bind to a firm, manageable dough with cold water. Divide the dough into 6 pieces and roll them out to line six 4-inch tart pans. Chill the pastry cases.

3 Drain the raisins. Beat the butter until soft, then add the honey and coffee extract and beat until well mixed. Roughly chop half the pecans and add them to the butter with the raisins, 2 tablespoons of the cold coffee, and the coffee extract – don't worry if the mixture appears curdled. Divide the mixture between the chilled pastry cases and smooth it down, then decorate with the remaining pecans.

4 Bake for 10 minutes, then reduce the heat to 375°F and cook for a further 15 minutes. Allow the tarts to cool slightly, remove from their pans, then sprinkle with a little sieved confectioners' sugar before serving.

Coffee Soufflé

A wonderfully light soufflé, ideal to serve after a heavy main course or on a summer's evening in the garden with a glass of chilled dessert wine.

Serves 8

⅔ **cup hot water**
4 **Tbsp coarsely ground high roast coffee**
4 **eggs, separated**
½ **cup superfine sugar**
1 **Tbsp powdered gelatin**
3 **Tbsp boiling water**
1¼ **cups heavy cream, whisked until thick and soft**
⅔ **cup heavy cream**

Decoration
⅔ **cup heavy cream**
10 **to 12 coffee beans, or chocolate-coated coffee beans**

1 Pour the hot water over the ground coffee then leave to infuse for 10 to 15 minutes. Meanwhile, place a 1½ pint soufflé dish on a cookie sheet (which makes it easier to handle) and tie a double thickness collar of waxed paper or baking parchment around the dish, to stand about 1½ inches above the top.

2 Strain the coffee through a fine sieve into a large bowl, then add the egg yolks and sugar. Whisk in a food processor for about 10 minutes, until very thick, and the beaters leave a ribbon trail when lifted. If whisking by hand, place the bowl over a pan of hot water as the heat will help to thicken the mixture.

3 Sprinkle the gelatin over the boiling water in a small bowl and stir, then leave to stand for 2 to 3 minutes. Stir again to make certain that the gelatin has dissolved. If necessary, heat the bowl for 30 to 60 seconds in a shallow pan of hot water or in the microwave, until the gelatin has completely dissolved.

4 Stir a spoonful of the coffee mixture into the gelatin, then whisk it all into the mixture, and fold in the whipped cream. Chill in the refrigerator for 20 minutes, or until starting to set and thicken around the edges of the bowl.

5 Whisk the egg whites until stiff, then fold them into the soufflé mixture using a wire whisk. Turn into the prepared soufflé dish, then chill in the refrigerator for 2 to 3 hours.

6 To decorate the soufflé, carefully loosen the paper from the top with a sharp, thin-bladed knife and peel away from around the dish. Whip the cream until stiff, then pipe it into rosettes either around the top of the soufflé or around the base of the dish on a serving plate. Top each rosette with a coffee bean.

Coffee and Chocolate Cheesecake

A smooth, sophisticated cheesecake for all those with a not-too-sweet tooth. You can decorate the cheesecake with grated chocolate, a rich chocolate fudge sauce, or whipped cream.

Serves 10 to 12

⅔ **cup hot, not boiling, water**
**4 Tbsp coarsely ground high
  roast coffee**
**4 oz (1 stick) unsalted butter,
  plus extra for greasing**
**2 cups crushed chocolate-coated
  cookies**
¼ **cup superfine sugar, plus 1 tsp**
1 Tbsp gelatin
3 Tbsp boiling water
1 cup cream cheese
2 egg yolks
1¼ **cups sour cream**

1 Pour the hot water onto the coffee and leave for 10 minutes. Lightly butter a deep 8-inch springform pan.

2 Melt the butter in a pan, then stir in the crushed cookies and 1 teaspoon of sugar. Press the mixture evenly over the base and about halfway up the sides of the pan, then chill until required.

3 Sprinkle the gelatin over the boiling water, stir well then leave for 3 to 4 minutes to dissolve. Beat the cream cheese in a bowl until smooth, then beat in the egg yolks and remaining sugar. Strain the coffee into the mixture through a fine sieve, whisk thoroughly, then whisk in the sour cream.

4 Stir the gelatin to ensure that it has dissolved completely, then stir in a little of the coffee mixture. Whisk the gelatin into the coffee mixture. Pour into the pan and chill for 2 to 3 hours until set. Serve sliced.

Pear and Coffee Charlotte Russe

A very light dessert, a perfect end to a late summer meal. I like to serve this with a really ripe dessert pear, or perhaps a fig, and a spoonful of mascarpone cheese.

Serves 6 to 8

⅔ **cup cold coffee**
3 **Tbsp Tia Maria**
16 **Italian ladyfinger cookies**
⅔ **cup cold water**
¼ **cup superfine sugar**
Pared rind and juice of 1 lemon
1 **vanilla pod**
3 **pears, peeled, cored and chopped**
1 **Tbsp gelatin**
3 **Tbsp boiling water**
⅔ **cup heavy cream, lightly whipped**
Whipped cream and fruit in season to serve

1 Mix together the coffee and 1 tablespoon Tia Maria, then pour into a shallow bowl. Dip the cookies in the coffee, then stand them up around the sides of a 1 pint soufflé dish.

2 Heat the water, sugar, lemon rind and vanilla in a frying pan until the sugar is dissolved, then simmer for 5 minutes. Add the pears and poach for 5 minutes, or until just soft.

3 Sprinkle the gelatin over the boiling water and stir. Leave for 2 to 3 minutes. Allow the pears to cool slightly, then remove the vanilla and purée the fruits and their liquor in a blender with the lemon juice. Stir in the remaining Tia Maria.

4 Stir the gelatin to make certain that it is completely dissolved, then add it to the pear purée. Whip the cream until thick and soft, then fold it into the pears. Spoon the mixture carefully into the soufflé dish, then weight the cookies down with a small upturned plate.

5 Chill the charlotte for 2 to 3 hours until firmly set. Just before serving, run a thin-bladed knife around the edges of the dish, then invert the charlotte onto a serving plate. Tie or pin a ribbon around it, then decorate with whipped cream and berry fruits in season.

Rich Mocha Refrigerator Cake

This delicious dessert cake is based on an Italian recipe. It is very rich and should be served with just a small dollop of sweetened yogurt. Leave out the eggs if you prefer, for a slightly heavier cake, which is still utterly delicious.

Serves 8

1⅓ cups bittersweet chocolate, broken into small pieces
2 Tbsp instant espresso
⅓ cup hot water
3 Tbsp Tia Maria or other coffee liqueur
½ lb (2 sticks) unsalted butter
2 Tbsp superfine sugar
2 eggs, separated
1 cup roughly chopped blanched almonds
12 petit beurre cookies, cut cleanly into halves
Confectioners' sugar

1 Line a 2-pound loaf pan with non-stick baking parchment. Melt the chocolate in a large bowl over a pan of hot water, or in a microwave. Dissolve the instant espresso in the hot water, then add it to the melted chocolate with the liqueur and stir until thoroughly blended together. Leave to cool slightly.

2 Beat the butter in a bowl until soft, then add the sugar and egg yolks, one at a time. Stir in the almonds and the cooled chocolate.

3 Whisk the egg whites until stiff, then fold them into the mixture. Carefully add the cookie halves one at a time, tossing them gently until they are coated with the chocolate. Make sure they remain separate and do not stick together.

4 Carefully spoon the mixture into the prepared pan, pressing down lightly to ensure there are no gaps, but avoid breaking the cookies. Try to ensure that the cookies are evenly distributed throughout the loaf. Chill for at least 2 hours.

5 Carefully turn the loaf out onto a serving plate and remove the paper. Sprinkle with sieved confectioners' sugar, if you wish, and serve in slices. Keep the cake chilled until you are ready to serve.

Mocha Mousse

Everyone loves chocolate mousse, but it can be overly rich. This coffee-flavored mousse is lighter, and makes a very welcome alternative.

Serves 8

1⅓ cups chocolate, broken
   into small squares
1 Tbsp freeze-dried instant
   coffee granules
1 Tbsp brandy
1 Tbsp warm water
4 eggs, separated
½ cup superfine sugar
1¼ cups heavy cream
Toasted flaked almonds
   for decoration

1 Melt the chocolate in a bowl over hot water or in a microwave, then allow it to cool slightly. Stir the coffee into the brandy and add the warm water. Stir until dissolved.

2 Whisk the egg yolks with the sugar until the mixture is thick and very pale, and leaves a trail when the beaters are lifted. Add the coffee and brandy, and the chocolate, and beat until combined.

3 Whisk the cream until thick and soft, then fold into the mixture. Whisk the egg whites in a clean bowl with clean beaters until stiff, then fold them into the mousse.

4 Divide the mixture between 8 ramekins and scatter the mousses with some toasted almonds. Chill for 1 to 2 hours before serving.

Coffee Crème Caramel   *Serves 6 to 8*

Butter for greasing
⅔ cup hot, not boiling, water
4 Tbsp coarsely ground high
**   roast coffee**
1¼ cups superfine sugar
Pinch of mixed spice
3 eggs
1¼ cups whole milk
⅔ cup heavy cream

1 Lightly butter a 1½ pint soufflé dish. Pour the hot water over the coffee and leave to infuse. Preheat the oven to 300°F.

2 Heat 1 cup of sugar in a heavy-bottomed pan, tipping it backward and forward without stirring until dissolved. Bring to a boil and cook until a pale golden brown without stirring. Pour into the prepared dish and tip it gently so that the caramel coats the bottom and the sides of the dish. Set the caramel pan on one side.

3 Beat the eggs in a bowl with the remaining sugar until thick and pale. Strain the coffee through a fine sieve into the caramel pan, add the milk and cream, then heat gently until almost at a boil. Pour the hot milk onto the eggs and sugar, stirring all the time, then strain the custard into the dish.

4 Place the dish in a small roasting pan and fill the pan with boiling water to come halfway up the sides of the soufflé dish. Bake slowly in the preheated oven for 1¾ to 2 hours, until just set. Leave the custard to cool, then chill for at least 4 hours.

5 Loosen the custard from the edges of the soufflé dish with a sharp, thin-bladed knife, then invert the dish into a deep serving dish – this is important as you need to catch the caramel that will run out. Do not unmold. Chill for a further 2 hours, then remove the soufflé dish before serving.

Cappuccino Mousse   *Serves 8*

2¼ cups double strength cold
**   coffee (add 2 Tbsp instant**
**   espresso to regular cold**
**   coffee to get the right flavor)**
1 Tbsp gelatin
3 Tbsp boiling water
3 eggs, separated
⅓ cup superfine sugar
1¼ cups heavy cream
Grated bittersweet or semisweet
**   chocolate to decorate**

1 Mix the instant espresso into the cold coffee. Sprinkle the gelatin over the boiling water, stir well, then leave for 3 to 4 minutes to dissolve completely.

2 Whisk together the egg yolks and sugar until thick and pale, then gradually whisk in the cold coffee. Stir the gelatin to check that it is completely dissolved, then blend 1 or 2 spoonfuls of the coffee mixture into the gelatin – this helps it to blend into the mousse more easily. Fold the gelatin into the coffee mixture.

3 Lightly whip the cream until thick and soft, then fold it into the coffee mixture. Pour the mousse into a glass bowl, then chill for 2 to hours until set. Sprinkle with grated chocolate before serving.

Index

AA grade   16, 17, 25
acidity   38
Aden   9
African coffees   16–19
Armenian Supremo beans   20
Asian coffees   24–5
Australian coffees   25

Bahia beans   19
balance   38
Banana & Raisin Muffins   51
Blue Mountain beans   18, 21, 22
body   38
Bourbon Santos beans   19
Brazil   19–20
Burundi   18

Café Brûlot   43
Café at the Gate of Salvation,
    Damascus   12
Café au Lait Gelato   65
Cafe Americano   36
Café Florian, Venice   12
Café Latte   36
Café Mocha   36
Café Procope, Paris   12–13
cafetiere method   32
Cameroon   18
Capin Branco beans   19
cappuccino   34, 36, 38
Cappuccino Mousse   78
Cardamom Topper   43
Central American coffees   11, 21–4
Charlotte Russe, Pear & Coffee   75
Cheesecake, Coffee & Chocolate   74
Coffea arabica   14, 15
Coffea canephora   14, 15
Coffea liberica   14, 15
Coffee & Almond Pavlova   68–9
Coffee & Cardamom Buns,
    Swedish Style   55
Coffee & Cardamom Frozen
    Yogurt   64
Coffee & Chocolate Cheesecake   74
Coffee & Cinnamon Puff
    Pinwheels   58
Coffee & Coconut Sherbet   64
Coffee Crème Caramel   78

Coffee Egg Nog   44
coffee extract   39
coffee houses   11, 12–13, 35
Coffee Ice Cream with
    Chocolate Ripple   61
coffee making   38–9
Coffee & Pistachio Kulfi   62
Coffee Punch à la Russe   42
Coffee & Raisin Pecan Pies   71
Coffee Rum Punch   45
Coffee Soufflé   72
coffee trade, spread of   9–11
Coffee Truffles   58
Coffee & Whiskey Hooligan's
    Soup   46
Colombia   20–1
cona method   32
Conillon beans   19
Costa Rica   21–2, 38
Creamy Coffee Ice Milk   60
crema   34
cultivation   15

de Clieu, Gabriel Mathieu   11

Egg Nog, Coffee   44
electric coffee makers   33–4
elephant beans   18, 22
espresso bars   35
espresso machines   33–4
Ethiopia   8, 16
Europe, introduction of coffee to   11

filter method   32
Florentines   56
freeze drying   37
Frozen Yogurt, Coffee &
    Cardamom   64

Galapagos Islands   21
Granita, Spiced Coffee   66
Green Dragon Coffee House,
    Boston   13
grinding   31
Guatamala   22

Harrar beans   16
Hawaii   25

Hooligan's Soup, Coffee &
    Whiskey   46
ice creams   60–6
Iced Coffee, Creamy   48
Iced Coffee, Spanish Style   50
Iced Coffee Punch   49
India   24–5
Indonesia   25
instant coffee   37
Irish Coffee   46

Jamaica   22
Java   25, 38
jug method   32

Kaveh Kanes   12
Kenya   11, 16
Kibo Chagga beans   17
Kulfi, Coffee & Pistachio   62

Lintong beans   25
Lloyds of London   9, 12

Madagascar   18
Merchant's Coffee House,
    New York   13
Mexico   22–4
Milk Shake, Mocha   49
Mocha (town)   8
Mocha Gâteau aux Noix   52
Mocha Ice Cream   62
Mocha Java   25
Mocha Liqueur Cocktail   45
Mocha Milk Shake   49
Mocha Mousse   77
Mocha Yemen   16–17
Monsooned Malabar beans   24
Muffins, Banana & Raisin   51
Mysore beans   24, 38

napolenta method   32

Omar, Sheikh   8
Orange-flavored Turkish-style
    Coffee   47

Papua New Guinea   25
'parchment coffee'   27

Pavlova, Coffee & Almond   68–9
peaberry beans   15, 16, 17
roasting   29
Pear & Coffee Charlotte Russe   75
Pecan Pies, Coffee & Raisin   71
picking   26
processing   27–8
Puerto Rico   24

Rich Mocha Refrigerator Cake   76
ristretto   35, 38
roasting   29
robusta beans   15
Rum Punch, Coffee   45

SHB grade   22, 28
Seattle   13, 38
Sherbet, Coffee & Coconut   64
South America, coffee
    production in   11, 19–21
Spiced Coffee Granita   66
storing coffee   38
Sumatra   25
Swedish Style Coffee &
    Cardamom Buns   55

Tanzania   17
Tapachula Superior   22
Tiramisu   70
Truffles, Coffee   58
Turkish coffee   32
    Orange-flavored   47

Una's Coffee Sponge Pudding   67
USA, coffee houses in   11, 13

Venezuela   21
Venice   11, 12
Viennese Ice Cream   63
Vista Allegre beans   19

wild coffee   16

Yauco Selecto beans   24
Yemen   8, 16–17
Yirga Ch'efe beans   16

Picture Credits

The Publishers have made every effort to identify and obtain copyright permission but apologize for any omissions, and would like to thank the following for their help and contribution to this book:

Bramah Tea and Coffee Museum; Gregory K. Clark Photographics, photograph on page 7; International Coffee Organization, photographs on pages 6, 10, 14–21, 26, 28, 30; Anita Leroy of Monmouth Coffee Company, London, photograph on page 24; Lloyd's, London, photography on page 9; Phyllis Luntta, photograph on page 23; Platingum Homewares of Halifax for the provision of the Gaggia Espresso Machine; Robot Coupe (UK) Limited of Middlesex for the provision of the Robot Coupe ice cream maker; Seattle Coffee Company, Seattle, photograph on page 36; Starbucks Coffee Company, photograph on page 12; Diana Steedman, photograph on page 13; Tea & Coffee Trade Journal for information and guidance.

THE
BORDER
BOOK

THE
BORDER
BOOK

ANNA PAVORD

DORLING KINDERSLEY
LONDON • NEW YORK • STUTTGART

A Dorling Kindersley Book

To Oenone and her future garden

Project Editor Claire Calman
Project Art Editor Gillian Andrews
Editorial Assistant Melanie Tham
Designer Bob Gordon

Managing Editor Jane Aspden
Managing Art Editor Ina Stradins

Principal Illustrators Sharon Beeden, Martine Collings

FRONT COVER: *A Low-maintenance Scheme pp.82–85*
BACK COVER: *A Tropical Summer Border pp.32–35*

FACING TITLE PAGE:
*A shady spring planting with strong foliage interest, the deep purple leaves
of* Viola labradorica *contrasting with the green-gold ribbons of Bowles' golden
grass,* Milium effusum 'Aureum'. *The soft pink flowers of* Anemone nemorosa
form a foil for the sharper colours of the other plants.

First published in Great Britain 1994
by Dorling Kindersley Publishers Limited,
9 Henrietta Street, London WC2 8PS

Reprinted 1994

Copyright © 1994 Dorling Kindersley Limited, London
Text copyright © 1994 Anna Pavord

A CIP catalogue record for this book is available from the British Library.

ISBN 0 7513 0084 5

Reproduced by Bright Arts (HK) Ltd, Hong Kong

Printed and bound by Butler & Tanner, Frome, Great Britain

PREFACE

———— ❧ ————

WHY DO WE GARDEN? Fortunately, this is a question that psychologists have never tackled. Their findings might put us off for life. Central to the activity is the fact that when you garden you abandon a timetable constructed around dentist appointments, car services, and the possible arrival of trains, to be subsumed into a different one, an immense and inexorable one that is entirely outside your control. This calendar controls the growth of plants, their living, seeding, and dying. In order to garden successfully, we have to respect and become part of that cycle.

But a garden is an artificial construct. It is not usually the same as the natural landscape that may lie over the boundary wall. We garden to provide a setting for ourselves in which we feel comfortable. We garden because we like looking after things. We garden because we want to create but cannot paint or sculpt.

Apprentice gardeners often want a neat set of rules: now is the time to plant the daffodils, this is the way to prune your clematis, here is how to sow your seeds. As with bringing up babies, this information was once absorbed by example rather than swotted up from books. But rules tend to be of limited use in gardening. They act as a kind of lifebelt when you first start off, but they can be deceptive. In the end, a gardener is better served by his own powers of observation. The vagaries of climate and season and soil constantly force the gardener to rewrite the rule book. In gardening, the learning never stops. The more you know, the more you realise how much there is still to learn.

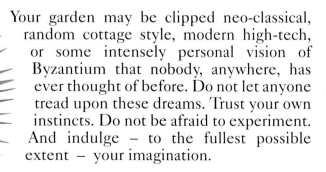

Your garden may be clipped neo-classical, random cottage style, modern high-tech, or some intensely personal vision of Byzantium that nobody, anywhere, has ever thought of before. Do not let anyone tread upon these dreams. Trust your own instincts. Do not be afraid to experiment. And indulge – to the fullest possible extent – your imagination.

ANNA PAVORD

CONTENTS

❧

HOW TO USE THIS BOOK 8

CREATIVE PLANTING 10

MIXED BORDERS 22

COOL COLOURS *for* DAMP SHADE 24
PRETTY PASTELS 28
A TROPICAL SUMMER BORDER 32
A LUSH POOLSIDE 36
BRIGHT BERRIES *for* AUTUMN 40
COTTAGE-GARDEN BORDER 44
AN AUTUMN–WINTER DISPLAY 48
BORDER *of* MINIATURES 52

❧

ISLAND AND OTHER BEDS 56

A BED *of* ROSES 58
A BOLD DESERT BED 62
INSTANT FLOWERS 66
A YEAR-ROUND DISPLAY 70
A FORMAL HERB DESIGN 74
FLOWERS *and* FRUITS 78
A LOW-MAINTENANCE SCHEME 82

CORNER SITES 86

WATERSIDE TEXTURES 88
COLOURED FOLIAGE 92
A SCHEME *for* SCENT 96
PLANTING *by the* SEA 100
SUNNY YELLOWS *and* BLUES 104

VERTICAL SPACES 108

PLANTS *for a* PERGOLA 110
COLOUR *for* AUTUMN–WINTER 114
SCREENING *the* GARDEN 116
A PLACE *in the* SUN 120
A RETAINING WALL 122
CLIMBING FRAMES 124
WALLS *without* SUN 126

———— ✿ ————

FORGOTTEN PLACES 128

A POTTED DISGUISE 130
PATIO PLANTING 132
A NARROW STRIP 134
BETWEEN *the* STEPS 136
A STONY PATCH 138
OCCASIONAL POTS 140
SPLENDOUR *in the* GRASS 142

PLANTER'S GUIDE 144

CARE AND CULTIVATION 146

PREPARING *the* SOIL *and* PLANTING 146
CARING *for* PLANTS 148
PRUNING *and* TRAINING 150
PROPAGATING PLANTS 152

INDEX 154

ACKNOWLEDGMENTS 160

HOW TO USE THIS BOOK

THERE ARE MANY THOUSANDS OF PLANTS available and countless ways of combining them. *The Border Book* demystifies the art of creating effective plant associations and provides a diversity of planting plans for all sorts of sites – from a large, formal border for a hot, sunny garden to a small, informal design for a stony patch of ground. You can use the planting schemes like recipes in a cookery book – follow them precisely or play around with the combination of ingredients to produce your own unique creation. For each scheme, a glorious full-colour illustration shows what the design will look like if you reproduce it to the letter. Supplementary plans offer suggestions on ways of introducing alternative plants to suit different growing conditions or different tastes.

THE INTRODUCTION – CREATIVE PLANTING
At the beginning of the book, an introductory chapter on creative planting outlines basic principles of sound design, exploring ways of combining plants to establish pleasing echoes and exciting contrasts of colour and form. This chapter also looks at style, foliage interest, texture, and scent, and how to select appropriate plants for the conditions in your garden.

THE PLANTING SCHEMES
The book is divided into five chapters, each comprising a particular type of scheme. *Mixed Borders* includes plans designed to be seen mainly from one side, while *Island and Other Beds* shows schemes that are effective from more than one viewpoint. *Corner Sites* provides designs for awkward corners, and *Vertical Spaces* includes plans for planting up walls, pergolas, and frames. *Forgotten Places* is a collection of schemes for difficult areas – for example, patios and steps. Each scheme is self-contained and includes a complete plant list, clear planting plan, and illustration of the established planting.

PLANTING PLAN KEY
The key below shows the symbols used to denote each type of plant included in the schemes – whether a tree, shrub, perennial, or bulb, for example.

 Tree

 Shrub

 Conifer

 Perennial

 Annual

 Bulb

Succulent

Evergreen

PLANT LIST
Each scheme includes a complete list of all the plants used and the number of plants required. Full botanical names are given, with common names where appropriate. The quantities should be taken only as a rough guide, depending on the area you have available; you can use fewer plants but it will take longer for them to fill the allotted space.

PLANTING PLAN
A clear planting plan shows the type, number, and position of each plant. Numbers around the plan correspond with those on the plant list. The dimensions of the bed as shown are given as a rough guide, but you can easily adapt a scheme for a smaller or larger area, or a site of a different shape, by using the same combination of plants.

DESIGN POINTS
Important design features or characteristics of a scheme, such as distinctive colour combinations or strong interest from handsome foliage or architectural plants, are picked out to help you decide whether a scheme will suit you and your garden.

PLANTING SCHEME
A large, full-colour artwork, specially commissioned to bring each plan vividly to life, illustrates clearly what a design will look like once it is established. Each planting scheme is shown in the season when it will be at its peak overall, but in order to maintain a long period of interest, some of the plants included will be at their best earlier or later in the year.

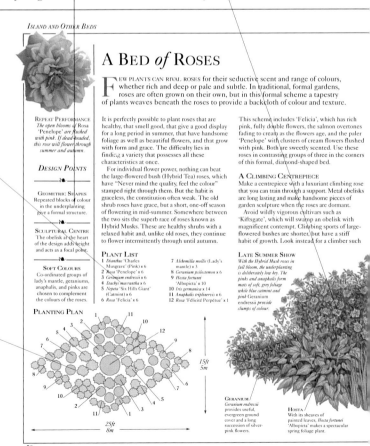

ISLAND AND OTHER BEDS

A BED *of* ROSES

FEW PLANTS CAN RIVAL ROSES for their seductive scent and range of colours, whether rich and deep or pale and subtle. In traditional, formal gardens, roses are often grown on their own, but in this formal scheme a tapestry of plants weaves beneath the roses to provide a backcloth of colour and texture.

REPEAT PERFORMANCE
The open blooms of Rosa 'Penelope' are flushed with pink. If dead-headed, this rose will flower through summer and autumn.

DESIGN POINTS

GEOMETRIC SHAPES
Repeated blocks of colour in the underplanting give a formal structure.

SCULPTURAL CENTRE
The obelisk at the heart of the design adds height and acts as a focal point.

SOFT COLOURS
Co-ordinated groups of lady's mantle, geraniums, anaphalis, and pinks are chosen to complement the colours of the roses.

It is perfectly possible to plant roses that are healthy, that smell good, that give a good display for a long period in summer, that have handsome foliage as well as beautiful flowers, and that grow with form and grace. The difficulty lies in finding a variety that possesses all these characteristics at once.

For individual flower power, nothing can beat the large-flowered bush (Hybrid Tea) roses, which have "Never mind the quality, feel the colour" stamped right through them. But the habit is graceless, the constitution often weak. The old shrub roses have grace, but a short, one-off season of flowering in mid-summer. Somewhere between the two sits the superb race of roses known as Hybrid Musks. These are healthy shrubs with a relaxed habit and, unlike old roses, they continue to flower intermittently through until autumn.

This scheme includes 'Felicia', which has rich pink, fully double flowers, the salmon overtones fading to cream as the flowers age, and the paler 'Penelope' with clusters of cream flowers flushed with pink. Both are sweetly scented. Use these roses in contrasting groups of three in the corners of this formal, diamond-shaped bed.

A CLIMBING CENTREPIECE
Make a centrepiece with a luxuriant climbing rose that you can train through a support. Metal obelisks are long lasting and make handsome pieces of garden sculpture when the roses are dormant.

Avoid wildly vigorous cultivars such as 'Kiftsgate', which will swamp an obelisk with magnificent contempt. Climbing sports of large-flowered bushes are shorter, but have a stiff habit of growth. Look instead for a climber such

PLANT LIST
1 *Dianthus* 'Charles Musgrave' (Pink) x 6
2 *Rosa* 'Penelope' x 6
3 *Geranium endressii* x 6
4 *Stachys macrantha* x 6
5 *Nepeta* 'Six Hills Giant' (Catmint) x 6
6 *Rosa* 'Felicia' x 6
7 *Alchemilla mollis* (Lady's mantle) x 3
8 *Geranium psilostemon* x 3
9 *Hosta fortunei* 'Albopicta' x 10
10 *Iris germanica* x 14
11 *Anaphalis triplinervis* x 6
12 *Rosa* 'Félicité Perpétue' x 1

PLANTING PLAN

15ft
5m

25ft
8m

LATE SUMMER SHOW
With the Hybrid Musk roses in full bloom, the underplanting is deliberately low key. The pinks and anaphalis form mats of soft, grey foliage while blue catmint and pink Geranium endressii provide clumps of colour.

GERANIUM
Geranium endressii provides useful, evergreen ground cover and a long succession of silver-pink flowers.

HOSTA
With its sheaves of painted leaves, Hosta fortunei 'Albopicta' makes a spectacular spring foliage plant.

58

PLANT GALLERY AND SUPPLEMENTARY SCHEMES

Each scheme includes photographs of all the plants used, while practical tasks needed to maintain the plants are outlined under the Care and Cultivation reminders. Plans that extend to four pages include one or two supplementary artworks that give ideas on substituting alternative plants or adding extra ones. These help you adapt a scheme, either for a different site or to create a different visual effect – by changing the colour scheme, for example.

SUPPLEMENTARY SCHEME TEXT
This text suggests ways of altering the main plan to suit different growing conditions, change the colour balance, or alter the principal season of interest.

SUPPLEMENTARY SCHEME ARTWORKS
Unique artworks graphically show the effect of using the substitute or additional plants. The original scheme is shown in a pale tint, while the new plants are portrayed in full colour so that they stand out clearly.

CARE AND CULTIVATION
Brief reminders on the basic care needed for each scheme are given in the left-hand column. The tasks are divided so you can see at a glance what needs to be done in each season.

PLANT PORTRAITS
For every scheme, there is a photographic gallery of all the plants included. Each colour photograph is accompanied by a caption that describes the plant and gives its expected height and spread.

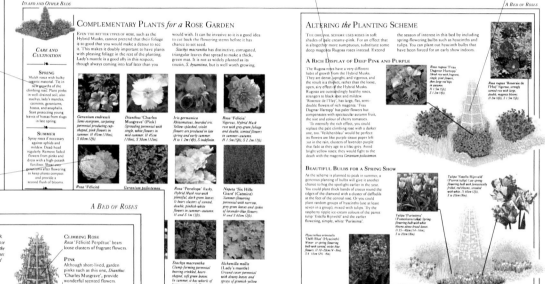

SECOND SEASON DISPLAY
Schemes that are particularly attractive in another season are illustrated by a second artwork, showing what the design will look like then – in spring, for example, when bulbs that would not show in summer, would be in full flower.

PLANT CHARACTERISTICS
Every plant that is included in a scheme is clearly annotated to point up a particular feature or characteristic.

PRACTICAL ADVICE

All the information you need to recreate and maintain the schemes in this book is included in *Care and Cultivation* (pp.146–153). This section covers basic routine tasks such as planting, staking, mulching, pruning and training, and propagation.

To help adapt a scheme for a particular site, use the *Planter's Guide*; this groups plants according to their tolerance of various growing conditions.

If you want to look up a specific plant, turn to the index, which lists all the plants under both botanical and common names.

CREATIVE PLANTING

Matching plants to positions is the key to good gardening, but in deciding what to put where, you have to consider the plants' needs as well as your own desires. It is no use being determined to have a plant unless you can give it the kind of conditions it would choose for itself, if it had that luxury. Not everything that you fall in love with will necessarily love you in return. Rhododendrons, for instance, demand acid soil, as do a whole group of other woodland shrubs,

such as pieris. It is pig-headed to try and grow them in alkaline soil. If you feel you must have them, but do not have the right soil, grow them in pots in a special ericaceous compost.

Space is also an important consideration. A shrub with a ten-foot soul is never going to look happy if it has constantly to be butchered to fit into a four-foot strait-jacket. Think ahead when you are planting and, in your schemes, allow some plants the guarantee of living happily ever

▲ EXPLOITING YOUR SPACE

An out-of-the-way corner in this gravelled yard is transformed by a mass of plants, many of them half hardy, all grown in pots. This suits the spiky agaves, plain and variegated, the waxy aeoniums by the door, the leafy ginger, and the yellow gazanias in the foreground.

► PLANTING TO SUIT THE SITE

Rich, damp ground, such as you might find beside a pool, is what you need to make Rodgersia podophylla *happy. Its handsomely veined, hand-shaped leaves make a superb foil for the tall, candelabra flowers of* Primula pulverulenta *and the blue-flowered* Iris sibirica.

after in the positions you have chosen for them. A garden that consists only of ephemeral planting will never be truly satisfying.

In the wild, plants are opportunists, adapting themselves to a wide range of growing conditions. You can exploit this, finding plants that will colonize the least desirable areas of the garden. A gravel path can stand in for an alpine scree; a dark corner by the dustbins can be brought to life with plants that do not need sun to blossom.

ADAPTING SCHEMES

The dimensions given in this book, both for plants and for schemes, are approximate. Rate of growth depends on climate, soil, and – it must be said – the skill of the gardener. You may need to adjust schemes as they mature, transplanting a shrub to allow its neighbour to spread its wings.

The schemes have been arranged into sections such as beds, borders, and corners, but there is no reason why you should not adapt a bed plan for a corner or a corner planting as part of a border. Do not, however, expect plants such as the rodgersia included in a scheme for a damp poolside to be happy in a dry, hot slope in full sunshine. Remember, too, that vagaries of climate and season will sometimes wreck the most carefully laid plans – or bring you results more magical than in your wildest dreams.

▲ PLANTS FOR A DRY, SUNNY BED
Architectural plants dominate this scheme suitable for a dry, sunny site. The European fan palm, Chamaerops humilis, *is the main focus with* Aeonium arboreum 'Atropurpureum' *in front of it. To the right is spiky* Yucca filamentosa 'Variegata', *its form echoing the leaves of the palm.*

► SPRING COLOUR
The Lenten rose, Helleborus
orientalis, *is at its best in
early spring with flowers
ranging from deep plum-
purple to purest white. The
insides of the petals are often
freckled with darker colour.
The leaves are as handsome
as the flowers.*

►► EXTENDED
INTEREST
*Ferns are confident enough
to dispense with flowers
altogether. Form is all and,
undistracted by colour, you
can settle to the engrossing
business of finding them
suitable partners. They
have a long period of
interest, at their most
dramatic unfurling, as
here, in late spring.*

SEASONAL IMPACT AND CONTINUITY

In spring it is impossible to resist the call of the
nursery and garden centre. There is a beguiling
sensation of making a fresh start. Blinded by
an optimism of the most irrational kind,
mesmerised by the ranks of plants all bursting
into life, you ricochet from magnolia to
rhododendron, from ceanothus to chaenomeles,
each plant the centre of a new dream.

The danger of this spring euphoria is that you
may end up with a garden crammed with plants
that give their all in spring and early summer
and have nothing to show for the rest of the year.
Not all areas of the garden will be equally
attractive in all seasons – nor do they need to be.
You may plan it so that one bed stars in autumn
and winter, for example, while another is at its
best in spring and summer. Your garden must
have an underpinning of structural planting,
however, shrubs that are the equivalent of the
most important pieces of furniture in a room.

In choosing these structural plants, look for
ones with a long season of interest; they may be
architectural in form or have handsome foliage.
Some should be evergreen, so that in winter the
garden does not entirely dissolve into a mess of
rotting leaves and skeletal branches. The spurge,
Euphorbia characias subsp. *wulfenii,* is a fine
example of a plant that has presence all year
round, not just when it is flowering.

◄ SEASONAL DISPLAY
*Dark-leaved annual dahlias
and tumbling nasturtiums
are added to more permanent
planting for hot summer
colour. Seasonal displays
such as this are a good way of
changing a garden's emphasis.*

▲ AUTUMN
DELIGHTS
*Bead-like berries and the
changing colours of leaves
are a particular pleasure of
autumn. Sorbus 'Joseph
Rock' bears pale, creamy
berries that deepen to yellow
as they age. The leaves turn
from green to warm orange,
red, and purple.*

With these key plants in place, you can start filling in the gaps in between. Foils are as important as features when you are combining plants in the garden. Not everything should be screaming "Look at me!" You need bright pools of summer annuals, but you also need plants that are no more than quietly supportive. After a while, these are the plants that you actually might come to prefer.

It often helps to think of planting as a three-tier affair. Three separate groups of plants can occupy the same piece of ground, though not all will necessarily peak at the same time. High up you have trees and large shrubs, in the middle tier herbaceous perennials, and scrabbling around underneath, low-growing ground-cover plants and bulbs. By using the space carefully, you can arrange it so that a spring-flowering tree has summer-flowering perennials under it, interspersed with bulbs, perhaps colchicums, that come spearing through the soil in autumn. That patch of ground will be earning its keep over a long period in the garden.

▲ FOLIAGE INTEREST
For long-lasting impact, choose plants with good foliage rather than a brief flush of flowers. The combination of Crocosmia 'Lucifer' *and* Dahlia 'Bishop of Llandaff' *used here provides late summer colour but both plants earn their space twice over with their fine leaves – the upright swords of the crocosmia and the dark bronze foliage of the dahlias make a contribution long before the flowers start to appear.*

◄ SCULPTURAL SEEDHEADS
The flowers of this poppy, Papaver somniferum, *are coming to an end, but the sculptural seedheads will continue to look good until the end of the summer. They also dry well for use later in indoor flower arrangements. Poppies such as this self-seed liberally, making handsome clumps of glaucous foliage among earlier spring flowers.*

13

PLANTING STYLES

Gardeners are usually told that the first step when laying out a garden is to make a plan, but before you can even begin on this task, you have to decide on the mood of the garden: formal, exotic, wild, cottagey. In a large garden, you can combine several of these styles in different areas, with screens, hedges, and walls dividing one stage set from the next. In a small garden, this is more difficult to arrange. You need more restraint if the design is to cohere well.

The mood of a garden is dictated by its general design and layout, but the right plants are important, too. Particular plants reinforce particular styles. In a formal garden you expect clipped box and yew, fruit trees trained into espaliers and fans. Single colour borders would be at home here and borders with bold plants such as red hot pokers or acanthus used at regular intervals to break up the planting. Although the formal style of gardening grew in the grand manner out of the Italian Renaissance with its balustrades, elaborate stone seats, urns,

▶ INFORMAL ABUNDANCE
Bold clumps of Euphorbia characias *subsp.* wulfenii *dominate this informal planting, which relies as much on foliage as flowers for its impact. The central terracotta pot gives a focus to the group, but does not draw too much attention to itself. Grey foliage, used here in quantity, acts as a buffer between plants, softening the effect of colour contrasts.*

▼ FORMAL PATTERNING
Regularly repeated blocks of plants – alchemilla and mats of acaena in the foreground, bold clumps of rudbeckia behind – emphasize the formal nature of this scheme. The symmetrically placed urns accentuate the formality.

and terraces, it adapts more easily than any other genre to a small town garden. For this sort of style you need symmetry, evergreens, stone, and – if you can run to it – water.

In a wild garden, you use glorified versions of wild flowers: papery poppies with petals like coloured tissue left in the rain, small-flowered narcissus, foxgloves extravagantly marked at the throat, all planted under apple blossom. Wild gardening can take many forms: lush planting by a stream, a meadow swaying with long grasses and colourful flowers, an overgrown orchard, or a woodland idyll where azaleas flame lazily over banks of bluebells. The trick always is not to try too hard – sweet disorder is the key. You can't be tidy and wild at the same time.

Many of the most exciting gardens fit into no category at all. These are the ones fired by a personal vision. They may be eccentric, but their creators show unfailing sympathy for plants and the way that they grow. You too could free yourself from the yoke of conformity.

▲ ON THE WILD SIDE
*Borage and dill, both fast-growing culinary herbs, combine
here to make an effective informal planting, which will be
at its peak in mid-summer. Self-seeding plants such as the
opium poppy with pink flowers are natural allies in areas
where you want a casual, spontaneous effect.*

ADAPTABLE PLANTS

Some plants, like the best sort of aunts, get
along in any company and can adapt themselves
to all styles of planting. Euphorbias immediately
come to mind in this context. The flowers,
though an extraordinary, wild lime green, tone
well with any colour you put with them. They
are elegant with white, cool with blue, stunning
with pink, sophisticated with yellow. Structure
is important, too; the plants hold themselves
well and have excellent foliage. You soon learn
to recognize your best friends when you are
planning planting schemes. Whatever the style,
include a high proportion of plants that offer
more than the colour of their flower.

► MIXING STYLES
*The frame is formal, the iron bower visually anchored to the
ground by two beautifully clipped box balls, but the planting in
this large pot is wonderfully exuberant, peaking in late summer
with melianthus, skirts of helichrysum, and a long succession of
daisy flowers from the argyranthemum 'Chelsea Girl'.*

PLAYING WITH COLOUR

Colour has dominated theories of garden design for most of this century, ever since the famous plantswoman Gertrude Jekyll laid out her carefully graded borders, working through pale, recessive tones to a crescendo of fiery oranges and reds. But there are no unbreakable rules about using colour. In the end a gardener is best served by his own powers of observation.

Single-colour borders are vogueish, but deceptively difficult to do well. And in restricting yourself this way, you deny yourself the pleasures of a wider palette. Use foliage plants as buffers between colours that make you anxious and make a resolution never, ever, ever to plant a white garden. You will not regret it.

Yellow is the colour that gardeners appear to be most cautious about, but a certain shade of sugar pink is the only colour that it quarrels with noisily. Combined with blue, yellow will give you the authentic Monet effect. Yellow with white and the kind of sharp lime green provided by alchemilla makes an extremely fresh colour scheme. Create quieter combinations using pastel shades interspersed with grey foliage plants. They should not be so quiet that you fall asleep while looking at them.

► BENDING THE RULES

The star plant in this group is the yellow crocosmia which tones beautifully, against all the so-called rules, with the pink Japanese anemones behind it and the richer pink mats of phuopsis in front. Some yellows are easier to work with than others, but it is criminal to ban them altogether from the garden as some highly strung gardeners feel they must. If you are nervous, use them with blue as with the agapanthus here.

► COOL COLOURS

Blue and white flowers, as with these mixed annual echiums and nemophilas, have an appealing crisp freshness. This cool combination can be achieved within a single season from spring-sown seed.

◄ FOLIAGE BUFFER

The dark foliage of a purple cotinus is used as a buffer between the fiery tones of a red hot poker and the pink of the foreground phlox. Purple foliage, which absorbs and deadens light, is not always easy to place in the garden but is used well here.

► **LIMITED PALETTE**
The chalky whiteness of the foreground flowers in this delicately controlled colour scheme is subtly underpinned by the pale pink Alba rose behind and the hints of cream and blue to the right. All benefit by being displayed against the strong shapes of the foliage behind them.

▼ **FRAGRANT ARCHWAY**
Roses scrambling over this simple metal arch bring flower smells just where you need them – right under your nose. Summer gardens are bursting with scents: plant climbing roses, honeysuckle, and sweet peas.

THE PLEASURES OF SCENT

Scent is one of the most dangerously evocative of the senses. In the garden it creates a fourth dimension – a separate, unseen landscape hanging in the air, changing shape with the seasons. Many heavily scented flowers are white – mock orange, summer jasmine, madonna lilies, lily-of-the-valley – and look their best planted against dark backgrounds. Some, such as evening primrose, save their scent for evening, which is thoughtful, since that is when we most often have time to notice them.

Too often plant breeders sacrifice scent in pursuit of other objectives: bigger flowers, a wider range of colours. The loss of natural scent in flowers too highly bred for our own good is ironically paralleled by the rise in aromatherapy. We always knew that smells were good for us, only now we are being asked to pay through the nose for the privilege. Ignore those expensive bottles. Plant some real smells instead.

► **PERFUMED LEAVES**
Plants that have scented foliage, such as many herbs and this pelargonium 'Sweet Mimosa', are a delight – reach out and crush the leaves as you pass by to release their perfume.

SHAPE AND FORM

Shape and form are just as important as colour when you are looking for plants to set each other off in the garden. The clever juxtaposition of contrasting shapes may make a less immediate impact than a daring mêlée of magenta and orange but it is the subtle interplay of height, scale, and substance in a garden that will provide a more sustaining diet. The orange-pink shock will only work once. The contrast of rodgersia, say, with a filmy fern such as *Adiantum pedatum*, pierced by the tall stems of a group of white lilies, will draw you back again and again.

Form of one sort or another is vital in a garden and if it is lacking in the overall design, you can reinforce it by patterning the planting. This does not mean restricting the planting to a formula – one of this, two of those and then one of this again – but it does often mean using more of less. In a small garden this requires superhuman restraint, for the urge to cram in as many different plants as possible is strong.

Reinforcing the lines of paths can have a marked effect on the look of a garden. Those that are straight and wide will probably not need this help, but the lines of narrower, curving paths easily become swamped and can look muddled. Think of edging the path with the same plant for the whole of its length. This immediately makes the path more important. The edging also has a unifying effect on the planting behind it. It all begins to look less random, more cohesive. Of course, you need to use the right

▲ CONTRASTING FORMS
The huge umbrella leaves of gunnera are stunning in their own right but also make a fine backdrop for the different leaf forms in the foreground. The heart-shaped, metallic blue leaves of the hosta form a neat mound, while a pointed contrast is made by the strong verticals of a white Iris sibirica *and tall stems of airy seedheads.*

◄ SCULPTURAL PLANT
Eryngium giganteum *is a biennial sea holly, rising in the second year to make a statuesque plant, the flowers poised like candles in a candelabra.*

kind of plant for the job. Avoid anything that will flop all over the path or anything so tall that it will obscure the plants behind it.

STRUCTURAL PLANTING

Gardens also need landmarks. A landmark plant is the opposite of one that you would use for edging. It must be a bold one-off, strongly architectural, an extrovert, a shark among minnows. Its leaves and general habit of growth will probably be more important than its flower. The variegated aralia is a classic landmark plant, but unfortunately it is not evergreen. Mahonia has all the necessary attributes – and scent, too. How you site landmark plants will influence the way that your eye moves over the garden – and the way *you* move round the garden, too. Use tall crambe as a promontory where you want to create a visual obstacle, masking what lies round the corner, making it more intriguing.

HEIGHT AND SCALE

The scale of a plant in relation to the space that it is sitting in provides endless opportunities to experiment. The tallest plants do not always have to be at the back of a border. A clump of a willowy, tall perennial such as *Verbena bonariensis* makes a dramatic feature in the foreground of a planting. Nor should you feel that because you have a small garden, you have to fill it with small plants; a plethora of miniature plants can look fussy and lacking in emphasis. A fig tree growing in a small enclosed courtyard has immense drama. So does a yucca. Try it and see.

▶ FOUNTAIN OF FOLIAGE
The ostrich-feather fern, Matteuccia struthiopteris, *has no need of flowers to impress – its arching fronds spread out like spokes, creating a strong, architectural shape.*

▼ STRENGTHENING INFORMAL PLANTING
The euphorbia here adds substance to this unstructured planting and is as handsome in winter as it is in summer. The controlled colour scheme shifts extra emphasis on variations in plant form.

▲ LIVING LANDMARK
The sculptural skeleton of a towering onopordum dominates this section of an informal mixed border, complemented by the shapely spires of purple delphiniums. Architectural plants such as these are ideal for adding structure and substance to a scheme of airy or mound-forming plants.

FINE FOLIAGE

Many useful border plants, such as asters, penstemons, and members of the daisy family, are sadly deficient in the matter of leaves. When they are out of flower there is little else on offer. Although when you first garden you may think always in terms of flowers, the benefits of foliage soon creep up on you. Leaves bring form, bulk, and texture to mixed plantings. They also bring colour, though in a more subtle way than flowers: as well as variegated leaves, there are purple, gold, blue, grey, silver, and a thousand different shades of green.

All the most satisfying plant groups include plants with strong foliage – fat bergenia leaves, plumes of artemisia, swords of phormium and yucca. Sword leaves are especially useful in punctuating the low, rounded masses of so many herbaceous plants. You do not want too many of them, in the same way that you do not want to keep tripping over commas in a piece of prose, but well used, they are invaluable.

SURFACE TEXTURES

When you are combining plants, think about contrasts and echoes of texture as well as form. Some leaves, such as the glaucous, waxy foliage of *Melianthus major*, provide the pleasures of both. Contrast it with a smooth, shiny, purple *Hebe* 'La Séduisante' or with a spiky phormium. Texture is provided both by the surface of a leaf – like the thick, felted covering on lamb's tongues, *Stachys byzantina* – and by the effect of leaves *en masse*. Soft, hairy leaves such as those of alchemilla and *Meconopsis regia* hold raindrops in a dazzling way, each one a perfect bead shining like mercury. Foliage such as this will be your true ally in the garden.

▲ **BURNING BUSH**
The stag's-horn sumach, Rhus typhina, *is ablaze with colour when its leaves turn shades of fiery orange and red in autumn.*

◄ **PATTERNED LEAVES**
The bright, gold-splashed foliage of euonymus enlivens this planting of pale trilliums. Variegated leaves are as variously patterned as birds' feathers, splashed, striped, spotted in silver, cream, or gold. The trilliums' lush leaves provide a sober background to offset its pagoda blooms.

► **FERN COLLECTION**
Ferns are the ultimate foliage plants, their finely fragmented fronds contrasting here with the smooth bulk of the large stones. The gleaming hart's tongue ferns in front form a foil for the divided foliage of the other ferns behind, Adiantum venustum *creeping over the wall flanked by the shield fern,* Dryopteris affinis, *on the left and the chain fern,* Woodwardia unigemmata, *on the right at the rear. They will thrive wherever the ground is cool and damp and are ideal in shady courtyard gardens.*

◄ TEXTURAL CONTRASTS
A filmy haze of fennel surrounds the newly emerging flowers of Alchemilla mollis, *which, though a rampant and determined self-seeder, is a magnificent plant in foliage as well as flower. The lobed, pleated leaves of the alchemilla have a distinctive shape and downy texture that complements the diaphanous foliage of the fennel.*

▲ GLOSSY COAT
Although the leaves of this holly, Ilex aquifolium 'Argentea Marginata', *are variegated, the cream markings are hardly more of a pleasure than the surface texture – as shiny as a well-waxed car.*

MIXED BORDERS

⁂

Flexibility is the keynote of the modern border, which is created on altogether more relaxed lines than the grand (and difficult to maintain), old-fashioned borders of carefully staked herbaceous perennials. Modern borders contain a more eclectic mix of plants: shrubs to provide structure and extend the display, bulbs to carpet the ground in spring, annuals for a burst of summer colour. And you do not need acres of garden to create the right effect.

COOL COLOURS *for* DAMP SHADE

THERE IS A SENSE of luxuriance and mystery about plants growing in shade that you can never match in full sun. In shade, pale colours float like moths at dusk. In sun, they just look washed out. Despite this, many gardeners treat shade as a problem. Think of it instead as a heaven-sent opportunity: plenty of plants grow far better in shade than anywhere else.

HYDRANGEA HEADS
On this Hydrangea aspera *subsp.* aspera, *compact heads of tiny flowers are circled by showy sterile flowers of palest pink or even white.*

DESIGN POINTS

SERENE SHADE
A tranquil scheme that makes the most of a shady situation. Colours are generally muted apart from the warm glow of Bowles' golden sedge, *Carex elata* 'Aurea'.

LIVING CARPET
Shade-loving epimediums, variegated arums, bugles, and ginger mint provide an attractive, weed-suppressing carpet under the shrubs.

Shade brings a change of mood to a garden. It is contemplative, introverted. It slows you down, giving you time to notice the magnificently extravagant diversity of plants and flowers. From a distance, you may think that the lacecap flowers of the *Hydrangea aspera* subsp. *aspera* that features in this border are rich violet, for example. When you stop and rub noses with them, however, you can see that the outside bracts are actually pink and that the violet effect is created by the brilliant blue stamens of the small, pink, knobby flowers in the centre of the head.

PLANT LIST

1 *Polygonatum* x *hybridum* (Solomon's seal) x 12
2 *Arum italicum* 'Pictum' x 3
3 *Hydrangea quercifolia* (Oak-leaf hydrangea) x 1
4 *Scilla siberica* 'Atrocoerulea' x 75
5 *Cotoneaster horizontalis* 'Variegatus' x 2
6 *Carex elata* 'Aurea' (Bowles' golden sedge) x 3

7 *Viburnum plicatum* 'Mariesii' x 1
8 *Epimedium perralderianum* x 5
9 *Mentha* x *gentilis* 'Variegata' (Ginger mint) x 3
10 *Hydrangea aspera* subsp. *aspera* syn. *H. villosa* x 1
11 *Ajuga reptans* 'Atropurpurea' (Bugle) x 3
12 *Decaisnea fargesii* x 1

TIERED PLANTING

The large shrubs in this scheme form the topmost layer of a three-tiered planting plan. Underneath them, you can fit in a middle tier of herbaceous plants, such as Solomon's seal (*Polygonatum* x *hybridum*), with another colony of low-growing plants at ground level. Some of the smaller shrubs, such as the cotoneasters suggested for the foreground of this scheme, are themselves ground huggers and can only share their space with miniature bulbs, like the scillas, which will not crowd them out.

The two hydrangeas are the stars of this scheme, together with a late spring-flowering viburnum, a cultivar of *Viburnum plicatum* that is built up in tiers like a wedding cake. The peak season of most hydrangeas is late summer when they are in flower, but the species used here also have handsome foliage for more lasting pleasure.

Like the hydrangeas, the viburnum has a long season of interest; this makes these plants particularly welcome in small gardens, where

A SHOW FOR LATE SUMMER
In summer, the hydrangeas are at their finest with their white and misty mauve flowerheads. More dramatic colour comes from the unusual dark pods of the decaisnea and the bright, bead-like berries of the arums.

OAK-LEAF HYDRANGEA
Hydrangea quercifolia is included as much for its handsome foliage as its heads of white flowers.

SOLOMON'S SEAL
Polygonatum x *hybridum* is a graceful plant with arching stems of small bell flowers.

ARUM
Arum italicum 'Pictum' has spear-shaped leaves, marbled in pale cream, which are particularly welcome in winter.

PLANTING PLAN

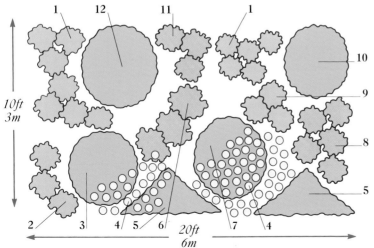

10ft
3m

20ft
6m

every inch of space must be used to the full. The overall form of the viburnum, with its branches held out in ascending horizontal layers, is pleasing even when it is not in flower. It needs plenty of space around it, so that its fine form is not spoiled by other plants lurching into its orbit. The flowers are white, and rather like those of a lacecap hydrangea, with a ring of sterile florets around a central cluster of much smaller flowers.

COOL COLOURS AND FINE FOLIAGE

White predominates in this scheme, with white flowers hanging from the arching stems of Solomon's seal and greenish-white clusters of flowers on *Decaisnea fargesii*, though these are its least important attribute. The real surprise is the fruit: long, navy blue seed pods the size and texture of sausages. The foliage is supremely elegant: each leaf is very long and is made up of pairs of leaflets arranged along a central rib.

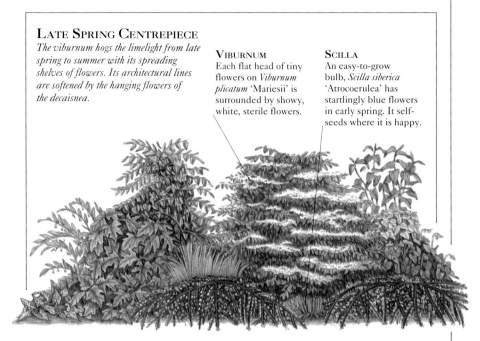

LATE SPRING CENTREPIECE

The viburnum hogs the limelight from late spring to summer with its spreading shelves of flowers. Its architectural lines are softened by the hanging flowers of the decaisnea.

VIBURNUM
Each flat head of tiny flowers on *Viburnum plicatum* 'Mariesii' is surrounded by showy, white, sterile flowers.

SCILLA
An easy-to-grow bulb, *Scilla siberica* 'Atrocoerulea' has startlingly blue flowers in early spring. It self-seeds where it is happy.

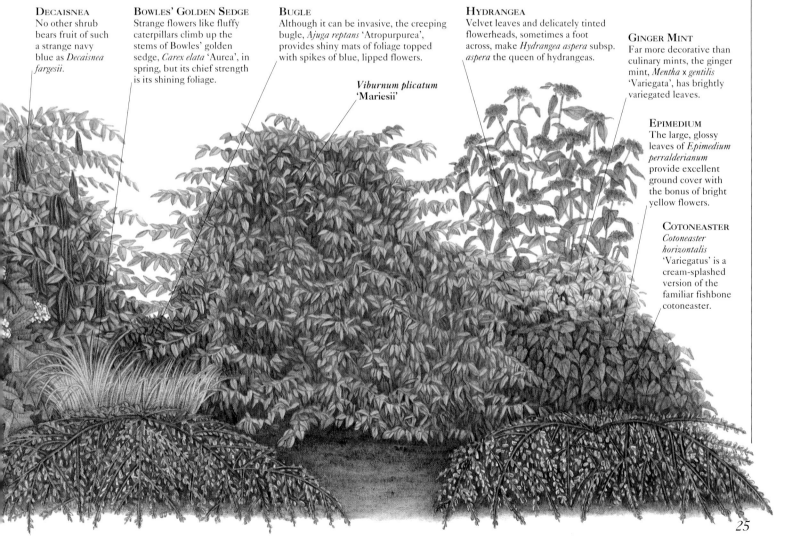

DECAISNEA
No other shrub bears fruit of such a strange navy blue as *Decaisnea fargesii*.

BOWLES' GOLDEN SEDGE
Strange flowers like fluffy caterpillars climb up the stems of Bowles' golden sedge, *Carex elata* 'Aurea', in spring, but its chief strength is its shining foliage.

BUGLE
Although it can be invasive, the creeping bugle, *Ajuga reptans* 'Atropurpurea', provides shiny mats of foliage topped with spikes of blue, lipped flowers.

Viburnum plicatum 'Mariesii'

HYDRANGEA
Velvet leaves and delicately tinted flowerheads, sometimes a foot across, make *Hydrangea aspera* subsp. *aspera* the queen of hydrangeas.

GINGER MINT
Far more decorative than culinary mints, the ginger mint, *Mentha x gentilis* 'Variegata', has brightly variegated leaves.

EPIMEDIUM
The large, glossy leaves of *Epimedium perralderianum* provide excellent ground cover with the bonus of bright yellow flowers.

COTONEASTER
Cotoneaster horizontalis 'Variegatus' is a cream-splashed version of the familiar fishbone cotoneaster.

PLANTS *for a* SHADY SITE

MANY SUN-LOVING PLANTS flower better when they are half-starved. Shade plants need to be nourished, however, and this scheme is planned for a place that is shady but not starved or dry.

Give the viburnum plenty of space and resist the urge to prune it. This shrub is an object lesson in symmetry: if you cut a branch, you may unbalance the entire form. Keep decaisnea in check by cutting out one or two of the oldest stems entirely each year. Both bugle and ginger mint spread quite rapidly by runners and, if not checked, may squeeze out the scillas. Leave the skeletal heads on the hydrangeas until spring; they look particularly good rimed with frost.

CARE AND CULTIVATION

SPRING
Plant carex, mints, and bugles. Mulch Solomon's seal. Plant hydrangeas now or in autumn, and mulch established plants heavily to conserve moisture around the roots. Remove their dead flowerheads. No regular pruning is necessary, but if plants get too big, cut them back now. Shear off old leaves of epimediums and top-dress with fine compost before the flower spikes appear.

SUMMER
If necessary, thin out some of the older stems of the decaisnea after it has finished flowering. Plant arums while dormant.

AUTUMN
Plant the viburnum, Solomon's seal, decaisnea, and cotoneasters. Stop neighbouring plants encroaching on the cotoneasters, as they die back if other plants lie on top of them. Plant epimediums and scilla bulbs, setting the latter 8cm (3in) deep.

WINTER
Clear away old stems of Solomon's seal.

Polygonatum × hybridum (Solomon's seal) *Arching perennial with hanging, greenish-white flowers in spring. H 1.2m (4ft), S 1m (3ft).*

Decaisnea fargesii *Deciduous shrub with drooping tassels of light green flowers, followed by large, navy seed pods. H and S 3m (10ft).*

Ajuga reptans 'Atropurpurea' (Bugle) *Low, evergreen perennial with glossy leaves and blue spring flowers. H 15cm (6in), S 1m (3ft).*

Hydrangea aspera subsp. **aspera** syn. **H. villosa** *Deciduous shrub flowering from late summer to mid-autumn. H 3m (10ft), S 2.5m (9ft).*

Hydrangea quercifolia (Oak-leaf hydrangea) *Deciduous, mound-forming shrub with fine autumn foliage and white flowers from mid-summer. H 2m (6ft), S 2.2m (7ft).*

Carex elata 'Aurea' (Bowles' golden sedge) *Evergreen perennial with golden-yellow, grassy leaves and small brown flower spikes in summer. H to 40cm (16in), S 15cm (6in).*

Viburnum plicatum 'Mariesii' *Deciduous, bushy shrub with tiered branches and large, rounded flowerheads from late spring to early summer. H 3m (10ft), S 4m (15ft).*

Mentha × gentilis 'Variegata' (Ginger mint) *Spreading perennial with aromatic, gold-splashed leaves and mauve flowers. H 45cm (18in), S 60cm (2ft).*

Arum italicum 'Pictum' *Early spring-flowering perennial with variegated autumn foliage followed by spikes of red berries. H to 25cm (10in), S to 30cm (12in).*

Scilla siberica 'Atrocoerulea' *Bulbous perennial with glossy leaves, producing spikes of bell-shaped, blue flowers in early spring. H 15cm (6in), S 5cm (2in).*

Cotoneaster horizontalis 'Variegatus' *Deciduous shrub with herringbone branches covered with cream-variegated leaves, and red berries in autumn. H 60cm (2ft), S to 1.5m (5ft).*

Epimedium perralderianum *Semi-evergreen, carpeting perennial with glossy foliage and yellow spring flowers. H 30cm (12in), S 45cm (18in).*

ALTERING *the* PLANTING SCHEME

THERE ARE SEVERAL WAYS to adjust this planting to suit specific conditions. The hydrangeas are easy-going about soil type, provided that it is moist and enriched with good compost, but if you have an acid soil, you could substitute a pieris for the tall hydrangea and low-growing rhododendrons for the cotoneasters. Another option is to vary the ground-cover plants: here, a combination of white, gold, and blue is used.

COLOURFUL GROUND COVER

Unrelieved carpets of hypericum have given ground cover a bad name, but at its best it can be as rich and intricate as a Turkish rug. Try to combine plants with modest territorial ambitions and complementary characters that provide interest over a long season.

Choose a hosta with warmth in the leaves. For this scheme, the white-flowered variety of lily-of-the-valley, with its startling, malachite purity, is preferable to the pink.

Omphalodes cappadocica
Perennial with bright blue flowers carried in spring–summer above crinkled leaves. H 15–20cm (6–8in), S 25cm (10in) or more.

Hosta 'Gold Standard'
Perennial with pale green leaves that turn to gold from mid-summer and are margined with dark green. H 75cm (2½ft), S 1m (3ft).

Tiarella wherryi (Foamflower) *Perennial with feathery flowers. H 10cm (4in), S 15cm (6in).*

Convallaria majalis (**Lily-of-the-valley**) *Low-growing perennial with matt, dark green leaves and sprays of fragrant, bell-shaped flowers. H to 30cm (12in), S indefinite.*

A BORDER WITH SPRING INTEREST FOR ACID SOIL

Certain shrubs such as rhododendrons, camellias, and pieris thrive only on acid soils. In the wild, these plants are most often found in woodland habitats and, similarly, in the garden they prefer some shade. Choose rhododendrons with pale flowers to blend with the rest of the planting. Offset the beefy effect of the rhododendrons by using ground-cover plants with filigree or divided leaves.

Pieris is a distinguished, evergreen shrub, at its showiest in spring when the young foliage is suffused with a rich coppery-red. The small, scented, cream flowers hang in drooping spikes.

Rhododendron 'Snow' *Low, mound-forming shrub that is covered with pure white flowers in early spring. H and S to 60cm (2ft).*

Pieris 'Forest Flame'
Shrub with glossy leaves that turn from red when young to pink, cream, and then dark green. H 4m (12ft), S 2m (6ft).

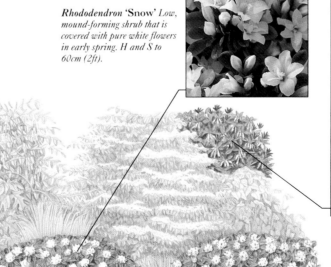

DESIGN POINTS

LONG-LASTING DISPLAY
Creamy broom and pink and white tulips bring interest in spring, while the seedheads of the sea hollies last well into winter.

CALMING COLOURS
Soft coloured pastel flowers and cool foliage combine to create a serene, restful scheme.

CHANGING SPECTRUM
If you include tulips, which are not always great stayers, you can change the balance of the colour scheme slightly each year. Dark purple parrot tulips will provide a contrast with the surrounding pale foliage.

PRETTY PASTELS

MELIANTHUS, THE STAR of this border, is the most sumptuous foliage plant that a gardener could imagine. It has magnificent leaves of a strange, glaucous sea-green. In bud, they are tightly pleated, but they shake themselves open to display neatly crimped edges, each leaf a masterpiece.

The melianthus is a native of South Africa and may need to be nursed through winters of frost and icy winds. Like all stars, it is used to a life of luxury and ease. Treat it right and it will out-perform any other plant in the garden.

COLOUR MIXING WITH HAZY TONES
Pale, misty mauves and blues are the keynotes of this border, drifting around the pools of grey and cool sea-green made by foliage plants such as the melianthus and amiable lamb's tongues, *Stachys byzantina*. Even the yellow broom used here is a muted, creamy shade, rather than the brilliant, custard yellow of many of the family.

Plants of strong, bold form prevent the border from being too sleepy in tone. The spherical seedheads of the alliums last as stiff skeletons long after the flowers have faded. The sea hollies, too, look as though they have been forged by a sculptor working in spun metal.

If you want to expand this scheme, include more plants with soft tones: penstemons, blue Canterbury bells (*Campanula medium*), lavender (*Lavandula*), abutilon, and cranesbills (*Geranium*).

Silver-leaved plants such as lamb's tongues are excellent foils for pale flowers whose own foliage is nothing special. Interplant them with bulbs such as tulips, lilies, and alliums. Do not include too many silver-foliaged plants in the same bed, however, or you will lose contrasts of colour and texture. Either grey or lime-coloured helichrysum could be used in this border; the lime will give the more interesting effect. Both types grow prodigiously, but they will thread attractively through other plants rather than steamroller over them.

PLANT LIST
1 *Eryngium* x *oliverianum* (Sea holly) x 10
2 *Lilium regale* (Regal lily) x 25
3 *Aster* x *frikartii* 'Mönch' (Michaelmas daisy) x 8
4 *Melianthus major* (Honeybush) x 2
5 *Viola cornuta* (Horned violet) x 15
6 *Stachys byzantina* (Lamb's tongue) x 3
7 *Tulipa* 'Angélique' and 'White Triumphator' x 50
8 *Helichrysum petiolare* 'Limelight' x 8
9 *Astrantia major* 'Shaggy' (Masterwort) x 4
10 *Cytisus* x *praecox* (Warminster broom) x 1
11 *Allium giganteum* x 16
12 *Eupatorium ligustrinum* x 1

PLANTING PLAN

11 12 1 11 4

1

2

3

4

5

6 7 8 2 5 7 3 9 10 6 5

20ft
6m

10ft
3m

A SEA OF FOLIAGE AND FLOWERS
By late summer, the melianthus has built up to maximum effect, providing a sea-green background to the skeleton heads of the alliums and the sea hollies' striking, metallic, thistle-like heads.

SEA HOLLY
In a family noted for its good looks, this sea holly, *Eryngium* x *oliverianum*, is one of the most handsome.

MICHAELMAS DAISY
Far less disease-prone than normal Michaelmas daisies, *Aster* x *frikartii* 'Mönch' has shaggy, daisy flowers of rich lavender.

HONEYBUSH
Although tender, the supreme foliage plant *Melianthus major* is worth fussing over for the sake of its glorious leaves.

HORNED VIOLET
The flower power of violas is astonishing, given their miniature size. Here, the pale *Viola cornuta* is used.

SHRUBS FOR SUBSTANCE AND SHOW

The shrubs are there to give bulk and height to the border. The broom, *Cytisus* x *praecox*, will enjoy the same growing conditions as the grey foliage plants. In late spring, the flowers drip down the branches like melting ice cream.

The evergreen eupatorium is an antidote to the greys, which look their worst in winter. To call it a useful shrub is demeaning. It is a low-key shrub certainly, its dark leaves exactly like the privet's from which it takes its name. But in late summer it sheds its sobriety, covering itself with a mass of flattish flowerheads, each made up of hundreds of tiny, white, filament flowers. The effect is charming – a banker surprised at his own frippery.

SPRING SPECTACLE
The broom steals the show in mid-spring, with clumps of tulips filling the gaps between later-flowering perennials.

Tulipa 'Angélique'

WARMINSTER BROOM
A strong, spicy scent is an added bonus with the Warminster broom, *Cytisus* x *praecox*, covered with creamy flowers in spring.

TULIPS
Use tulips to ring colour changes in the border. Here, lily-flowered 'White Triumphator' and pink 'Angélique' (left) continue the pastel theme.

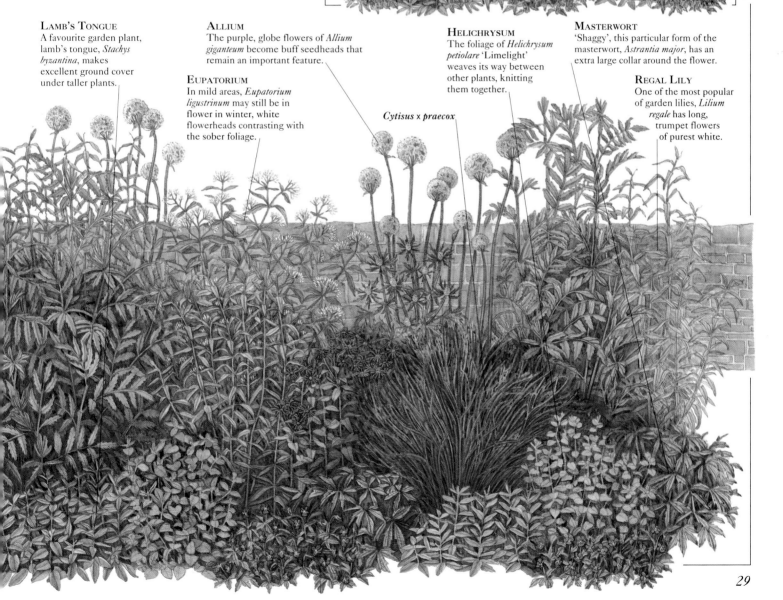

LAMB'S TONGUE
A favourite garden plant, lamb's tongue, *Stachys byzantina*, makes excellent ground cover under taller plants.

ALLIUM
The purple, globe flowers of *Allium giganteum* become buff seedheads that remain an important feature.

EUPATORIUM
In mild areas, *Eupatorium ligustrinum* may still be in flower in winter, white flowerheads contrasting with the sober foliage.

Cytisus x *praecox*

HELICHRYSUM
The foliage of *Helichrysum petiolare* 'Limelight' weaves its way between other plants, knitting them together.

MASTERWORT
'Shaggy', this particular form of the masterwort, *Astrantia major*, has an extra large collar around the flower.

REGAL LILY
One of the most popular of garden lilies, *Lilium regale* has long, trumpet flowers of purest white.

PLANTS *for a* WELL-DRAINED SITE

ALL THE PLANTS IN THIS BORDER need an open, sunny situation. In cold areas, think of the half-hardy melianthus as a pelargonium. Take cuttings in autumn and overwinter them inside ready for the following season. Or buy fresh plants each year. They will not cost much more than a bottle of wine, and the effect will be twice as intoxicating. Once established, melianthus will survive zero temperatures. The problem lies in getting it through its first few winters. It may help if you protect the crowns with straw. Where it is not butchered by frost, it will grow up to 3m (10ft), but if it has to start from scratch each spring, it will not reach half that. Winter damp is as much an enemy of plants such as melianthus as is winter cold. This is true of a whole family of silver-leaved plants such as lamb's tongues; they all grow best in light, well-drained soil.

Allium giganteum
Summer-flowering bulb with a stout stem and dense purple flowerheads 12cm (5in) across. H 1.2m (4ft), S 35cm (14in).

Eupatorium ligustrinum syn. **E. micranthum**
Evergreen, rounded shrub with fragrant flowers. H and S 2m (6ft).

Eryngium x **oliverianum (Sea holly)** *Upright perennial with thistle-like, lavender-blue flowerheads in late summer. H 1m (3ft), S 60cm (2ft).*

Lilium regale (Regal lily) *Summer-flowering bulb with fragrant, outward-facing, funnel-shaped blooms. H to 2m (6ft), S to 30cm (12in).*

Aster x **frikartii 'Mönch' (Michaelmas daisy)** *Bushy perennial bearing daisy-like flowers in autumn. H 75cm (2½ft), S 45cm (18in).*

Melianthus major (Honeybush) *Evergreen shrub with brownish-red flowers from spring to summer. H and S 2–3m (6–10ft).*

Tulipa 'White Triumphator' *Bulb that flowers in late spring, bearing white blooms with reflexed petals. H 65cm (26in), S to 20cm (8in).*

Cytisus x **praecox (Warminster broom)** *Deciduous, densely branched shrub flowering from mid- to late spring. H and S 1.5m (5ft).*

Viola cornuta (Horned violet) *Perennial with toothed leaves and purplish-blue flowers in spring–summer. H 12–20cm (5–8in), S 20cm (8in) or more.*

Stachys byzantina syn. **S. lanata (Lamb's tongue)** *Evergreen perennial with mauve-pink flowers in summer. H 38cm (15in), S 60cm (2ft).*

Helichrysum petiolare syn. **H. petiolatum** *Evergreen, mound-forming shrub with grey, felted leaves. It produces creamy-yellow flowers in summer. H 30cm (12in), S 1.5m (5ft).*

Astrantia major 'Shaggy' (Masterwort) *Clump-forming perennial that bears a mass of small flowers from summer to autumn. H 60cm (2ft), S 45cm (18in).*

ALTERING *the* PLANTING SCHEME

ANY SUBSTITUTE PLANTS must be suited to dry, well-drained soil, although you can heavily mulch areas that you want to make more nourishing. For a dramatic foliage contrast, include a purple-leaved shrub instead of the eupatorium. To complement the melianthus at its opulent best, substitute late summer-flowering plants for some of the bulbs.

COLOUR FOR ALL SEASONS

For richly coloured foliage, choose the smoke tree *Cotinus coggygria*, a purple-leaved hebe such as 'La Séduisante', or a purple berberis (although the flowers can be a particularly savage orange). Use a spring-flowering clematis to twine through the smoke tree, and blowsy pink poppies to contrast with its summer foliage.

For a late summer show, replace some of the tulips and lilies with pink nerines and blue agapanthus.

Cotinus coggygria **'Notcutt's Variety' (Smoke tree)** *Deciduous shrub with rich reddish-purple leaves. To encourage foliage growth rather than flowers, cut the shrub back hard in autumn. H and S to 5m (15ft).*

***Agapanthus* Headbourne Hybrids** *Perennial with arching leaves and large heads of deep purple-blue flowers on erect stems. H 1m (3ft), S 50cm (20in).*

***Clematis alpina* 'Frances Rivis'** *Deciduous climber that produces nodding, mid-blue flowers in spring followed in summer by fluffy, silvery seedheads. H 3m (10ft), S 1.5m (5ft).*

***Papaver orientale* (Oriental poppy)** *Hardy, spreading perennial that forms mounds of coarse, hairy, deeply cut leaves. Large, showy blooms are borne singly on straight stems during early summer. These may be salmon-pink, white, orange, or a rich mahogany-red, usually with an inky blotch at the base of each petal. H 75cm (2½ft), S 30cm (12in).*

Nerine bowdenii *Autumn-flowering bulb with strap-shaped, basal leaves. Each stem carries a head of pretty, glistening, pink flowers that curl back at the tips of the petals. H 45–60cm (18–24in), S 12–15cm (5–6in).*

A TROPICAL SUMMER BORDER

THINK OF THE JUNGLE as your inspiration for this border. The effect should be leafy, luxuriant, strange, exotic. It is not a style that is worth considering in any place where summer comes late and winter frosts early. Nor does it have any pretension to be low-maintenance, but for anyone prepared to put in the extra effort it requires, this sumptuous border is a star attraction.

COLOURFUL CLEOME
Long, leggy stamens protrude from the flowers of Cleome hassleriana *'Colour Fountain', giving it its common name, spider flower. It flowers generously, flourishing especially well in hot summers.*

DESIGN POINTS

A BORDER WITH BRAVADO

This is a border that throws caution to the wind. Strong shapes, lush foliage, and hot colours combine to create a dazzling display.

KALEIDOSCOPE OF COLOUR

The cannas and castor oil plants are particularly effective seen against the light, the bronze of the leaves fractured into a hundred different colours. In late summer, the plants are set alight by flame-coloured flowers.

PRIME POSITION

The border is designed to be viewed head on. It would be ideal, for instance, sited at the end of a sheltered courtyard where you could look on to it from the windows of the house, but it will be bare in winter.

In the grand gardens of Edwardian England where there was never a shortage of labour, borders such as this were commonplace. Landowners competed with each other to produce ever more outrageous effects and head gardeners were as familiar with the needs of a tropical banana palm as they were with the homegrown cabbage. The style lives on in the famous red borders at Hidcote Manor in Gloucestershire, England, where in summer tender cannas and cordylines, rich red lobelias, and luscious dahlias are bedded out among the more hardy inhabitants of the border.

FORMAL PATTERNING

An unashamedly theatrical border such as this looks its best if the artifice is stressed, not squashed. Plant in a formal fashion, with groups of plants repeated at regular intervals like the pattern on a roll of wallpaper. Once the pattern is established, you can extend the border to the length you need. Vary the positions of some of the foreground plants, however, so that the overall effect is not too mechanical.

The heavyweights in this border are the banana palms, the castor oil plants, and the cannas. For the full *fortissimo* effect, you need all three. The bananas give height

A SHOW-STOPPING SCHEME
Plants with bold foliage – bananas, castor oil plants, cannas – set the tone for this tropical-looking border, while cleomes, cosmos, and tobacco plants contribute colour and scent.

ARGYRANTHEMUM
Argyranthemum frutescens 'Jamaica Primrose' provides yellow flowers throughout summer.

AEONIUM
Aeonium arboreum 'Schwarzkopf' has neat, wine-dark, fleshy rosettes.

and importance: few other plants provide their kind of bulk and beefiness. You are growing them for their huge leaves, which unfurl with all the drama of the best conjuring trick. Outside the tropics, bananas will not produce edible fruit and, during winter, they will need a warm berth

CASTOR OIL PLANT
Ricinus communis is included for its lush, deeply lobed leaves.

COSMOS
Cosmos 'Sensation' forms a bushy mound of fine, feathery leaves and hovering pink flowers.

(such as a heated conservatory) where they can dream of the tropics between their summer performances. The castor oil plants and cannas also provide the leafiness and succulence essential in a tropical border, as does the tall tobacco plant, *Nicotiana sylvestris*. Other exotics such as phormium, tetrapanax, yucca, and the Japanese cartwheel tree, *Trochodendron araloides*, would also be at home in this border.

ADDING SCENT AND COLOUR
Cosmos, cleomes, and tobacco plants provide scent as well as colour. All these annuals are available in pink, mauve, and white. Decide whether you prefer single colours or a mixture. Too much white could be counter-productive as it would dilute the boldness of the scheme.

PLANTING PLAN

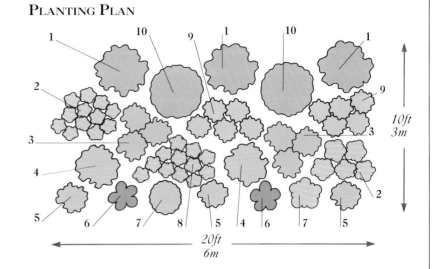

10ft
3m

20ft
6m

BRONZE CASTOR OIL PLANT
Ricinis communis 'Carmencita' is just one of a number of forms of the castor oil plant that has bronze or reddish leaves.

BANANA PALM
The arching, quill-like leaves of banana palms – *Ensete ventricosum* – add height and dramatic sculptural interest.

TOBACCO PLANT
These tall tobacco plants, *Nicotiana sylvestris*, provide scent and cool touches of pure white.

CANNA
Broad, bronze leaves and fiery flowers of *Canna indica* add an exotic look.

CLEOME
Cleome hassleriana 'Colour Fountain' adds tall spires of pink, purple, and white flowerheads.

FELICIA
The blue heads of *Felicia amelloides* 'Santa Anita' add a cool note to offset the scheme's hot colours.

PELARGONIUM
Use *Pelargonium* 'Royal Oak' for its spicy-scented leaves splashed at the centre with deep brown.

PLANT LIST
1 *Ensete ventricosum* (Banana palm) x 3
2 *Cleome hassleriana* 'Colour Fountain' x 17
3 *Canna indica* x 6
4 *Argyranthemum frutescens* 'Jamaica Primrose' x 2
5 *Pelargonium* 'Royal Oak' x 3
6 *Aeonium arboreum* 'Schwarzkopf' x 2
7 *Felicia amelloides* 'Santa Anita' x 2
8 *Cosmos* 'Sensation' x 12
9 *Nicotiana sylvestris* (Tobacco plant) x 10
10 *Ricinus communis* (Castor oil plant) x 1 and *R. c.* 'Carmencita' x 1

CARE AND CULTIVATION

SPRING

In early spring, repot bananas in rich compost and plant cannas in pots under cover. Sow seeds of cleomes and grow on in pots. Harden off cosmos, tobacco plants, and castor oil plants, and plant out with the felicias and pelargoniums after last frosts. Tall castor oil plants may need staking.

SUMMER

Plant out cannas. Plant argyranthemums and dead-head regularly. Plunge pots of aeoniums in the border. Water bananas well and give occasional liquid feeds to all plants. Shear over felicias after flowering. Take cuttings of felicias and pelargoniums for overwintering.

AUTUMN

Bring in bananas and aeoniums before first frosts and keep at a minimum of 10°C (50°F). Take cuttings of argyranthemums for the following season. Lift cannas after first frosts and dry off rhizomes.

WINTER

Sow seeds of cosmos, tobacco plants, and castor oil plants in late winter or early spring. Cut leaves and roots from cannas before storing rhizomes in moist compost.

PLANTS *for a* HOT SPOT

IN COOL OR TEMPERATE REGIONS, tender plants such as the bananas and aeoniums grown here must be overwintered in a heated greenhouse or conservatory. The easiest way to deal with the bananas is to keep them permanently in pots, which you can plunge in the border for the summer display once all danger of frost has passed. As winter approaches, unearth the pots, hose them down, and then bring them in under cover for the cooler months. The other two stars of this exotic border, the castor oil plants and the cannas, are equally tender. In autumn, lift and store the cannas under cover for the winter. The castor oil plant comes from tropical Africa. Although by nature an evergreen shrub, in temperate climates this fast-growing plant is usually treated as a half-hardy annual, raised each year from seed.

Cleome hassleriana 'Colour Fountain' *Bushy annual with divided leaves, flowering in summer. H 1.2m (4ft), S 60cm (2ft).*

Argyranthemum frutescens 'Jamaica Primrose' *Bushy, evergreen perennial with fern-like leaves and yellow flowers throughout summer. H and S to 1m (3ft).*

Ensete ventricosum (Banana palm) *Evergreen, upright, palm-like perennial with huge, veined leaves that have a reddish midrib. H to 6m (20ft), S to 3m (10ft).*

Ricinus communis (Castor oil plant) *Fast-growing, evergreen shrub with heads of green and red flowers in summer. H 1.5m (5ft), S 90cm (3ft).*

Nicotiana sylvestris (Tobacco plant) *Branching perennial with panicles of fragrant, tubular, white flowers in late summer. H 1.5m (5ft), S 75cm (2½ft).*

Canna indica *Perennial with broad, branching leaves, sometimes tinged red-purple, and red or orange flowers in summer. H 1.2m (4ft), S 45cm (18in).*

Pelargonium 'Royal Oak' *Bushy evergreen with compact, scented leaves and small, mauve-pink flowers. H 38cm (15in), S 30cm (12in).*

Aeonium arboreum 'Schwarzkopf' *Perennial succulent with distinctive rosettes of stiff, dark purple leaves. H to 60cm (2ft), S 1m (3ft).*

Cosmos 'Sensation' *Bushy annual with feathery leaves and daisy-like flowers from early summer to early autumn. H 90cm (3ft), S 60cm (2ft).*

Felicia amelloides 'Santa Anita' *Evergreen shrub with daisy-like flowers in late spring–autumn. H and S 30cm (12in).*

Altering *the* Planting Scheme

In areas where summers are short, you could substitute hardier species for some of the more tender plants. This will help to make the scheme less labour-intensive, although the dramatic effect will diminish along with the man hours. The bananas, which need special care in winter, are the most obvious candidates for replacement.

Plumes of Pampas for a Cool Climate

In cool climates, pampas grass will make the border easier to manage as it can stay in the ground all year. Choose an early type that puts on its plumes before the rest of the plants have died back.

Cordylines may be plunged in their pots, then lifted and brought into a frost-free place for winter. Tie the leaves together in a bundle for extra protection. Dahlia tubers should be lifted after the first frosts.

Cordyline australis **'Atropurpurea'** *Slow-growing tree with arching leaves. H 1.2m (4ft), S to 1m (3ft).*

Cortaderia selloana **'Sunningdale Silver' (Pampas grass)** *Grass with feathery plumes from late summer on. H 2.1m (7ft), S 1.2m (4ft).*

Dahlia **'Bishop of Llandaff'** *Tuberous perennial with bronze-green leaves that complement the border's colour scheme. In summer–autumn, it produces large, vivid red flowers. H and S 1m (3ft).*

Rich Colour Combinations

Choose rich purple *Verbena patagonica* and gladioli in magenta, crimson, and purple against a backcloth of variegated aralia and the shining bronze castor oil plants. Use the silver-variegated aralia, rather than the gold: it is a finer foil for the vibrant flowers. The gladioli have splendid flower spikes that enhance the scheme's exotic effect.

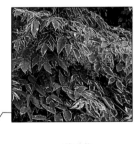

Aralia elata **'Variegata'** *Deciduous tree or shrub with white-edged leaves. In late summer–autumn, it produces large, flat heads of tiny, creamy-white flowers. H and S to 2.5m (8ft).*

Gladiolus **'Robin'** *Corm that produces erect spires of flowers in late summer. The stems need discreet staking. H 1.2m (4ft), S 20cm (8in).*

Verbena patagonica *Tall perennial with upright stems topped by pinkish-purple flowers in summer–autumn. It self-seeds happily, and never needs support. H 1.5m (5ft), S 50cm (20in).*

HANDSOME FOLIAGE
The distinctively veined leaves of Rodgersia podophylla *are washed over with bronze. In summer, they form a good foil for airy sprays of creamy-white flowers.*

DESIGN POINTS

SEASONAL CONTINUITY
This border has a long season of interest. The first flowers appear on the irises and primulas in late spring. The lobelias and the hostas will still be blooming in early autumn. The flowers of the hostas are also finely scented.

SHIFTING PATTERNS
The reflection of light on water can have a dramatic effect on a planting such as this. On a sunny day, ripples of green and bronze make endlessly changing patterns on the undersides of the leaves.

REGAL BEAUTY
The royal fern, *Osmunda regalis*, may take time to settle, but it is worth persevering with. It is an exceptionally handsome, tall fern with bright green fronds, and has flowering spikes covered in dark spores, which look like the dried heads of the astilbes.

A LUSH POOLSIDE

LEAFINESS IS THE KEYNOTE of this border with plenty of plants that do not depend solely on flowers for their effect. Foliage and water are as naturally compatible as Laurel and Hardy, but for the best effect you must make sure that the scale of the planting is in keeping with the size of the pool or stream.

This scheme is designed with a smallish pool in mind. If you are planting beside large stretches of water, you need correspondingly larger plants: giant gunnera with leaves large enough to picnic under in a rainstorm, big stands of willow.

FINE FOLIAGE COLLECTION
The permanently damp conditions of a poolside border encourage lush leaf growth, and here there is a rich interplay of foliage shapes, too: solid swords of the variegated water iris, *Iris pseudacorus* 'Variegata', the hand-shaped leaves of rodgersias, the intricate parallel fronds of ferns. The leaves of the rodgersias are made up from a series of leaflets arranged like the spokes of a wheel, radiating out at right angles to the central stalk. When they emerge in spring, they are richly suffused with bronze. Their warm foliage provides an excellent backdrop for grassy clumps of Bowles' golden sedge, *Carex elata* 'Aurea'. In a strict botanical sense, the sedges are not grasses, but they look and behave like ornamental grasses, and they have the added advantage of doing best in damp soils. They are ideal for a boggy poolside area. They are evergreen, or rather evergold, a bonus in this scheme where most of the plants dive underground for the winter.

ACCENTS OF YELLOW AND RED
The brightest colour comes from the magenta-red heads of *Primula japonica* and the yellow flowers of the iris. The flowers seem almost to suck their yellow from the leaves, for after the plant blooms in early summer, the foliage loses much of its striped greeny-yellow variegation.

You will need to be careful in your choice of astilbes. Some are a particularly vicious shade of pink. As this scheme contains a good deal of clear yellow and bronze, choose astilbes in brick colours or play safe with white.

THE SCHEME IN HIGH SUMMER
As the primulas fade, the ligularias and eupatoriums come into bloom. Rodgersia aesculifolia is in flower now with thick, buff-pink sprays the texture of plush.

GIANT COWSLIP
Primula florindae produces several stems of yellow flowers arising from each leafy clump.

LOBELIA
Flourishing in damp, heavy soils, *Lobelia syphilitica* has erect stems set with clear, blue flowers.

PLANTING PLAN

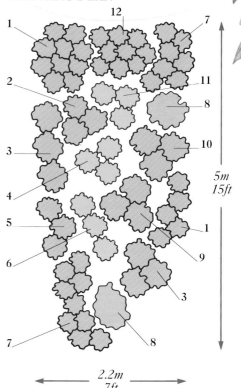

PLANT LIST

1 *Primula florindae* (Giant cowslip) x 16
2 *Astilbe* x *arendsii* x 3
3 *Hosta plantaginea* x 6
4 *Osmunda regalis* (Royal fern) x 3
5 *Lobelia syphilitica* x 3
6 *Rodgersia aesculifolia* x 3

7 *Primula japonica* (Japanese primrose) x 16
8 *Carex elata* 'Aurea' (Bowles' golden sedge) x 2
9 *Ligularia przewalskii* x 3
10 *Eupatorium rugosum* x 3
11 *Rodgersia podophylla* x 3
12 *Iris pseudacorus* 'Variegata' x 9

ASTILBE
Crimson-bronze and amber cover the spring shoots of *Astilbe* x *arendsii*, the colour echoed in the dried mahogany stems of winter.

Iris pseudacorus 'Variegata'

ROYAL FERN
The royal fern, *Osmunda regalis*, is the largest fern that can be grown outdoors in temperate countries.

LATE SPRING
Clumps of Iris pseudacorus 'Variegata' *and* Primula japonica *add bright touches of colour to a tapestry of different leaf shapes and textures.*

IRIS
Iris pseudacorus 'Variegata' contributes cheerful splashes of bright yellow.

JAPANESE PRIMROSE
Candelabra primulas such as *Primula japonica* hold their heads high above rosettes of leaves.

Primula japonica

JAGGED RODGERSIA
Big, jagged leaves are the trademark of *Rodgersia podophylla*, bronze when young, turning green as they mature.

EUPATORIUM
Flat, fluffy heads of white flowers are produced in late summer on the slender, branching stems of *Eupatorium rugosum*.

LIGULARIA
Elegant, deeply fingered leaves provide the underpinning for narrow spires of clear yellow flowers in *Ligularia przewalskii*.

HORSE-CHESTNUT RODGERSIA
Broad, crinkled leaves, similar to those of a horse-chestnut tree, characterize the foliage plant *Rodgersia aesculifolia*.

HOSTA
Showy, white flowers that smell of lilies are the surprise that *Hosta plantaginea* provides in early autumn.

BOWLES' GOLDEN SEDGE
Although not always easy to establish, Bowles' golden sedge, *Carex elata* 'Aurea', is worth including for the arresting colour of its leaves.

PLANTS *for a* POOLSIDE BORDER

BEFORE YOU EMBARK on this kind of planting, make sure that your bog has the right kind of underpinning. Flood water must be able to escape without dislodging the plants. In a long, dry summer, will the bog retain the right level of bogginess? An underlay of thick plastic, similar to a pool liner, may be necessary.

The iris can be planted in the water, if need be, or at the water's edge in the boggiest part of the ground. If you are planting in the water, you will need to sink the roots in a plastic basket, weighted down with a stone.

Iris pseudacorus 'Variegata' *Rhizomatous perennial with striped foliage and yellow flowers. H to 2m (6ft), S indefinite.*

Primula japonica (Japanese primrose) *Perennial with reddish-pink flowers. H 60cm (2ft), S 30cm (12in).*

CARE AND CULTIVATION

SPRING
Plant irises in full sun – if in water, no more than 15cm (6in) deep. Plant rodgersias with crowns just below the soil surface, osmundas with crowns at soil level, and lobelias in the shade of a neighbouring plant. Remove dead stems from carex. Protect emerging hostas against slugs. Top-dress all plants with humus-rich material.

SUMMER
Dead-head irises after flowering. Divide and replant clumps every three years, immediately after flowering. Remove faded flower stems of rodgersias in late summer.

AUTUMN
Plant astilbes now, and carex, ligularias, eupatoriums, hostas, and primulas now or in spring. Cut established astilbes down to ground level, and lift and divide clumps once every three years. Cut down stems of eupatoriums after flowering, and cut back osmunda foliage, leaving the brown flowering spikes.

WINTER
Cut ligularias down to ground level.

Primula florindae (Giant cowslip) *Perennial with heads of bell-shaped, yellow flowers. H 1m (3ft), S 60cm (2ft).*

Astilbe x arendsii *Perennial with fern-like foliage and feathery flower plumes. H 90cm (3ft), S 45cm (18in).*

Rodgersia podophylla *Clump-forming perennial with large leaves and cream flowers in summer. H 1.2m (4ft), S 1m (3ft).*

Eupatorium rugosum *Perennial that bears flat heads of white flowers in late summer. H 1.2m (4ft), S 45cm (18in).*

Hosta plantaginea *Perennial with glossy leaves and fragrant flowers in late summer–autumn. H 60cm (2ft), S 1.2m (4ft).*

Rodgersia aesculifolia *Perennial with crinkled, bronze-green foliage, and plumes of flowers in mid-summer. H and S 1m (3ft).*

Lobelia syphilitica *Perennial with blue flowers on tall spikes in late summer and autumn. H 1m (3ft), S 23cm (9in).*

Osmunda regalis (Royal fern) *Deciduous fern with broad fronds and rusty flower spikes when mature. H 2m (6ft), S 1m (3ft).*

Ligularia przewalskii *Perennial with deeply cut leaves and yellow flower spikes from mid-summer. H 2m (6ft), S 1m (3ft).*

Carex elata 'Aurea' (Bowles' golden sedge) *Evergreen perennial with grass-like leaves. H 40cm (16in), S 15cm (6in).*

ALTERING *the* PLANTING SCHEME

THERE ARE MANY WAYS to change the emphasis of your planting plan. You can alter the colour scheme, for example, perhaps cooling down the warm colours of the original plan by introducing more white-flowered plants. If the pool is in a prominent position, you may want to extend the season of the border's interest with plants that star in winter and early spring.

Zantedeschia aethiopica **'Crowborough' (Arum lily)** *Early to mid-summer-flowering tuber with white, goblet-like spathes and deep green leaves. H 1m (3ft), S 45cm (18in).*

CREATING A COOLER MOOD

Some gardeners are particularly fastidious in the matter of yellow flowers. Diehards of the anti-yellow brigade may prefer to omit the offending colour and cool down this planting by using white and silvery plants instead. Substitute pale silver-variegated *Iris laevigata* for the carex, white, waxy arum lilies for the flag irises, and white bugbane for the ligularias. This combination of plants will be less cheerful but more serene. It looks particularly effective at dusk.

Iris laevigata **'Variegata'** *Perennial with striped leaves. It often flowers a second time in autumn after its first show in early to mid-summer. H 25cm (10in), S indefinite.*

Cimicifuga simplex (Bugbane) *Upright perennial with glossy, divided leaves. In autumn, arching flower spikes wave above the foliage. Each spike is made up of tiny, slightly fragrant, star-shaped flowers. H 1.5m (5ft), S 60cm (2ft).*

PLANTING FOR WINTER AND SPRING

To extend the season of this border, choose a dogwood such as *Cornus alba* 'Elegantissima' for its bare red winter stems, later clothed in variegated foliage. For the best colour, cut it back hard in late winter and feed it to stimulate new, young growth. Use skunk cabbage for its brilliant yellow spathes. The angelica adds height and drama, with its large, divided leaves and its tall, proud stems crowned with domed, greenish flowerheads.

Cornus alba **'Elegantissima' (Dogwood)** *Variegated shrub with creamy-white flowers in late spring followed by white fruits. H and S 1.5m (5ft).*

Lysichiton americanus (Skunk cabbage) *Vigorous, deciduous perennial with fascinating, stiff, bright yellow spathes in early spring followed by cabbagey, fresh green leaves. H to 1m (3ft), S 75cm (2½ft).*

Angelica archangelica *Statuesque perennial, usually grown as a biennial, with lush, divided leaves, and heads of white or green flowers in late summer. H 2m (6ft), S 1m (3ft).*

BRIGHT BERRIES *for* AUTUMN

PLANT THIS CURVING BORDER alongside the driveway to your house for a warm welcome home in autumn and winter, or along a boundary to provide shelter or blot out an unwanted view. It needs little in the way of maintenance and is packed with plants that generously pay their rent twice a year – with a mass of spring flowers and a colourful display of autumn fruits.

ROSY BLUSH
The conical fruits of Malus *'John Downie' are a deep yellow, flushed with red. They can be made into an excellent translucent jelly.*

DESIGN POINTS

— 🐚 —

COLOUR REVIVAL
This border provides interest when much of the garden may be at a low ebb.

SUBSTANTIAL SHRUBS
Trees and shrubs provide height and substance as well as contributing shelter and screening.

MELLOW SHADES
Rich, russet tones from autumn leaves and fruits add warmth and vitality.

SPLASH OF WHITE
Snowdrops and daffodils add a cheering dash of light and colour in late winter.

The rose, crab apple, rowan, and spindle all provide a rich crop of berries and hips, while shiny sealing-wax berries hang from the viburnum. In spring, the same plants froth with blossom: creamy-white heads on the viburnum, clusters of china pink and white petals along the branches of the crab apple, and wide, heavy heads on the rowan. The rose comes later with single flowers of clear, paintbox red.

FRUITS AND BERRIES FOR COLOUR
The crab apple *Malus* 'John Downie' makes a neat, well-balanced tree, covered in brilliant fruits. In regions where fire blight is a problem, choose *M. floribunda*. Where space is tight, try 'Golden Hornet' or 'Red Sentinel' instead.

Spindles, *Euonymus europaeus*, have striking autumn fruit – pink seed capsules that split

open to show orange berries, an astonishing colour combination. 'Red Cascade' has arching branches thickly covered with red seed capsules. The leaves also turn scarlet in a dramatic last display before the onset of winter.

The rowan *Sorbus* 'Joseph Rock' grows in an upright, compact way. It has bunches of cream flowers in late spring and glossy, green-toothed leaves that turn russet red in autumn. In autumn, too, there are pale yellow berries that darken to amber as they age. If you want this scheme to fit a larger area, choose the taller Korean mountain ash *S. alnifolia*, which has attractive, egg-shaped, orange fruits.

The holly used here is a female and will produce berries only if there is a male holly somewhere within reach of pollinating insects. This does not have to be in your own garden.

PLANT LIST

1 *Lunaria annua* 'Variegata' (Honesty) x 16
2 *Euonymus europaeus* 'Red Cascade' (Spindle) x 1
3 *Galanthus nivalis* (Snowdrop) x 170
4 *Helleborus foetidus* (Stinking hellebore) x 10
5 *Rosa moyesii* 'Geranium' x 2
6 *Narcissus* 'Thalia' (Daffodil) x 55
7 *Callicarpa bodinieri* x 2
8 *Ilex aquifolium* 'Argentea Marginata' (Holly) x 1
9 *Iris foetidissima* (Stinking iris) x 15
10 *Viburnum opulus* 'Compactum' x 1
11 *Sorbus* 'Joseph Rock' (Rowan) x 1
12 *Malus* 'John Downie' (Crab apple) x 1

A BLAZE OF BRILLANT COLOUR
In autumn, many of the plants are encrusted with bead-like berries or colourful hips. The fiery combination of reds, oranges, and yellows is complemented by the changing autumn colours of the leaves.

SPINDLE
Particularly good on lime or chalk soils, the spindle, *Euonymus europaeus* 'Red Cascade', is weighed down by its abundant autumn fruits.

HONESTY
Once established, honesty, including this variegated one, *Lunaria annua* 'Variegata', will seed itself about the border.

PLANTING PLAN

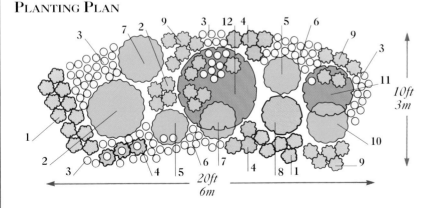

Helleborus foetidus

20ft
6m

10ft
3m

WINTER AND SPRING BEAUTY

This border provides a long season of interest. The snowdrops are first on the scene, set off by the brilliant seed pods of the iris and the handsome foliage of the hellebore. By the time the snowdrops are fading, the hellebores are in flower, followed by the daffodils. After these, the honesty will take over the scene until it is time for the explosion of blossom in the trees above it.

CALLICARPA
An entirely new colour is introduced into this scheme with the purple berries of *Callicarpa bodinieri*.

CRAB APPLE
All the crab apples make excellent small trees but *Malus* 'John Downie' has the largest and showiest fruits.

LATE SPRING DISPLAY
Although planned for autumn interest, this border offers treats at other times, too. In late spring, the hellebores will still be flowering when the pale, creamy bells of the daffodils open, creating a flower show in green and white.

SNOWDROP
Always eagerly awaited in early spring, snowdrops – *Galanthus nivalis* – slowly spread to make carpets beneath trees and shrubs.

DAFFODIL
Narcissus 'Thalia' carries three or more milk-white flowers on each stem.

STINKING HELLEBORE
Handsome, black-green leaves provide a foil for the pale spring flowers of *Helleborus foetidus*.

ROSE
The flowers of this rose, *Rosa moyesii* 'Geranium', tell you what to expect in its hips: both are a clear, singing red.

ROWAN
At their best in moist climates, rowans, like this *Sorbus* 'Joseph Rock', provide an excellent display of autumn fruit.

HOLLY
The broad-leaved silver-variegated holly, *Ilex aquifolium* 'Argentea Marginata', grows very slowly but makes a stately contribution to any garden.

VIBURNUM
Viburnum opulus 'Compactum' is the best cultivar of this species; it is very free with both its flowers and its berries.

STINKING IRIS
The flowers of *Iris foetidissima* are not at all showy but the bright red seed pods compensate.

41

PLANTS *for an* AUTUMN BORDER

THE KEY PLANTS IN THIS SCHEME are the trees and shrubs and it is vital to give them a good start in life. Enrich the soil with compost or well-rotted manure before planting. Deciduous species such as the rowan and the crab apple are best planted in autumn or early winter so they can settle their roots well before having to produce leaves in spring.

Select bare-root trees, if possible, as they usually have better developed root systems than those grown in containers. If choosing a container-grown tree, slide the rootball out of the pot before buying to check that the roots are not tightly coiled.

CARE AND CULTIVATION

SPRING
Plant snowdrops, preferably "in the green" just after they have finished flowering. Plant the holly. Mulch the crab apple and roses with well-rotted manure. Prune roses hard the first spring after planting, thereafter remove only dead or diseased branches. Dead-head daffodils, and remove dead leaves and seed pods on irises.

SUMMER
Sow honesty in early summer. Water newly established trees and shrubs, if necessary, and mulch around them to conserve moisture.

AUTUMN
Plant the deciduous trees and shrubs. Plant irises about 30cm (12in) apart, and daffodils 15cm (6in) deep. Site hellebores in shade when planting them. Transplant the honesty to flowering positions in early autumn.

WINTER
Cut previous year's growth of callicarpas back to young wood in late winter and, in exposed areas, protect the base of young plants with bracken or straw.

Helleborus foetidus (Stinking hellebore) *Evergreen, clump-forming perennial with green flowers. H and S 45cm (18in).*

Iris foetidissima (Stinking iris) *Rhizomatous perennial with seed pods of scarlet fruits. H 1m (3ft), S indefinite.*

Euonymus europaeus 'Red Cascade' (Spindle) *Deciduous shrub or tree with red fruits. H and S 2.5m (8ft).*

Malus 'John Downie' (Crab apple) *Deciduous tree with white flowers borne amid bright green foliage in late spring, and attractive fruits in autumn. H 9m (28ft), S 5m (15ft).*

Sorbus 'Joseph Rock' (Rowan) *Deciduous tree with white spring flowers then yellow autumn berries. H and S to 15m (50ft).*

Lunaria annua 'Variegata' (Honesty) *Biennial with round, silvery seed pods. H 75cm (2½ft), S 30cm (12in).*

Rosa moyesii 'Geranium' *Vigorous rose with large, red hips in autumn. H to 3m (10ft), S 2.5m (8ft).*

Ilex aquifolium 'Argentea Marginata' (Holly) *Evergreen tree with cream-edged, dark leaves. H to 14m (45ft), S 5m (15ft).*

Galanthus nivalis (Snowdrop) *Bulb with green-tipped, white flowers and strap-shaped leaves. H 15cm (6in), S 8cm (3in).*

Narcissus 'Thalia' (Daffodil) *Bulb bearing graceful, milky-white flowers in mid-spring. H to 38cm (15in), S to 20cm (8in).*

Callicarpa bodinieri *Deciduous shrub bearing small, lilac flowers in mid-summer, then violet berries. H 3m (10ft), S 2.5m (8ft).*

Viburnum opulus 'Compactum' *Dense, deciduous shrub with white flowers in spring, then red berries. H and S 1.5m (5ft).*

ALTERING *the* PLANTING SCHEME

IF YOU WANT TO BEEF UP THE SUMMER DISPLAY, include more shrub roses in the scheme. Choose those with attractive hips and colourful autumn foliage for an extended period of interest.

If you have an acid soil, your choice of plants is widened considerably. You can grow all sorts of heathers, and lime-hating shrubs such as pernettya, hamamelis, and various acers.

ROSES FOR SUMMER GLORY

All the Rugosa roses are first-class shrubs that never suffer from rust or black spot. *Rosa rugosa* 'Frau Dagmar Hartopp' has single flowers of pale pink that continue over a long season. The last flowers appear with the first hips: showy red fruits, the size of small tomatoes, finished off with a flurry of elegant sepals. *R. virginiana* is a smaller, suckering shrub rose with orange hips.

Rosa virginiana
Wild rose with glossy foliage and open, pink flowers. The leaves colour well in autumn. H to 1.5m (5ft), S 1m (3ft).

Rosa rugosa 'Frau Dagmar Hartopp'
Vigorous rose with flowers followed by large, red hips. H and S 2m (6ft).

Clematis macropetala
Hardy climber with divided leaves, and small, bell-shaped flowers produced in spring. H 3m (10ft), S 1.5m (5ft).

ACID-LOVING SHRUBS

On acid soil, replace the irises with pink heather as winter-flowering ground cover. While the callicarpa in the original scheme provides only purple berries, pernettya gives you a choice of colours from white through pink to deep purple and it is evergreen. The witch hazel has flowers like drunken spiders but they come when they are most welcome in the dark days of late winter. They smell wonderful, too.

Pernettya mucronata 'Mulberry Wine' *Bushy, evergreen shrub with white flowers in spring–summer, and magenta to purple berries. H and S 1.35m (4½ft).*

Hamamelis x intermedia **'Arnold Promise' (Witch hazel)** *Deciduous shrub with yellow flowers in winter. H 4m (12ft), S 3m (10ft).*

Erica x darleyensis **'Ghost Hills' (Heather)** *Shrub with needle-like foliage, cream-tipped in spring, and pink flowers in winter. H 45cm (18in), S 1m (3ft).*

PERFECTLY PLUMP
*A key plant in this scheme is
an exquisite peony –
Paeonia 'Sarah
Bernhardt'. It produces
wonderfully plump blooms,
packed with soft tissue
petals of pale pink.*

COTTAGE-GARDEN BORDER

DREAMS OF THE COUNTRY are usually more comfortable than the reality. The idea of a cottage garden conjures up an idealized image of gentle disorder, with roses tumbling round the door – and no mud. But unchecked charm can easily turn into unfettered chaos. A gardener's skill lies in balancing on the tightrope between the two.

It is one of the ironies of gardening that the old-fashioned, cottage style is so in vogue with affluent, urban thirty-somethings. The style is based not on historical accuracy but on artifice – a contemporary, romantic view of country gardens of the past. It should have an air of spontaneity, but you will have to act as referee, to make sure that hefty plants, such as the peonies, do not knock out more delicate ones, such as the columbines.

PLANTS WITH OLD-FASHIONED STYLE
Peonies, with columbines and fat double daisies, are classic ingredients of an old-fashioned country border. *Paeonia* 'Sarah Bernhardt' has outrageous powder-puff blooms, apple-blossom pink and scented. The deeply divided foliage sometimes turns a warm, foxy red in autumn.

The columbines, for preference, should be the stubby kind sometimes called granny's bonnets, rather than those with long spurs. Any kind of double daisy will be charming and, although the plants are short-lived, they will perpetuate themselves by self-seeding. The columbines will self-seed too, often putting themselves in places that you would never have thought of yourself. You can learn from that. Sometimes, you may even find a new colour strain arising in a seedling, which is a great thrill. And, by nurturing the novelty, you will be carrying on in the best traditions of the cottage garden.

Use a scented daphne, such as the semi-evergreen *Daphne* x *burkwoodii*, which flowers in spring, or the evergreen *D. bholua*, which brightens up the dull days of winter.

PLANT LIST

1 *Viola labradorica*
  'Purpurea' (Purple-leaved violet) x 12
2 *Bellis perennis* 'Pomponette'
  (Double daisy) x 23
3 *Camassia leichtlinii*
  (Quamash) x 16
4 *Aquilegia vulgaris*
  (Columbine) x 12

5 *Daphne* x *burkwoodii*
  'Somerset' x 1
6 *Geranium pratense*
  'Flore-pleno' x 3
7 *Paeonia* 'Sarah Bernhardt'
  (Peony) x 3
8 *Salvia sclarea* var.
  turkestanica (Vatican sage) x 5

9 *Thalictrum delavayi*
  (Meadow rue) x 5
10 *Campanula lactiflora*
  'Prichard's Variety' x 5
11 *Gypsophila paniculata*
  'Bristol Fairy' (Baby's breath) x 3
12 *Lychnis coronaria* x 7

PLANTING PLAN

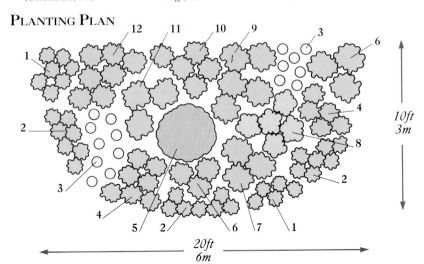

10ft
3m

20ft
6m

LYCHNIS
Grey leaves
the texture
of flannel
make a clump
from which rise
the magenta flowers
of *Lychnis coronaria*.

QUAMASH
A native American
plant, *Camassia leichtlinii*
bears slender stems of
starry flowers in summer.

DOUBLE DAISY
The fat double daisy, *Bellis
perennis* 'Pomponette', flowers
generously and will self-seed.

A RELAXED APPROACH

The original creators of this style could not afford the luxury of agonizing over the exact shade of blue for their campanulas. Nor should you. If you try too hard, you will have lost the point. Borders such as this work as often as not because of something you didn't do rather than something you did.

COLOUR HARMONIES

At the height of summer, the border froths with flower – soft mounds of blues, mauves, and pinks, given an edge by the sharp, clear magenta of the Lychnis coronaria.

CAMPANULA
Campanula lactiflora 'Prichard's Variety' is one of the taller campanulas with spires of violet-blue flowers.

***Daphne* x *burkwoodii* 'Somerset'**

BABY'S BREATH
Tiny, star flowers make a cloud of white over the grey leaves of *Gypsophila paniculata* 'Bristol Fairy'.

LATE SPRING DISPLAY

In late spring, the peonies are the main focal point, backed by the pink daphne and complemented by the airy columbines.

COLUMBINE
Pretty, nodding, purple flowers hang from the upright stems of *Aquilegia vulgaris*.

DAPHNE
Daphne x *burkwoodii* 'Somerset' brings fragrance to the border in late spring.

PEONY
The peony, *Paeonia* 'Sarah Bernhardt', has splendid flowers of pale blush pink.

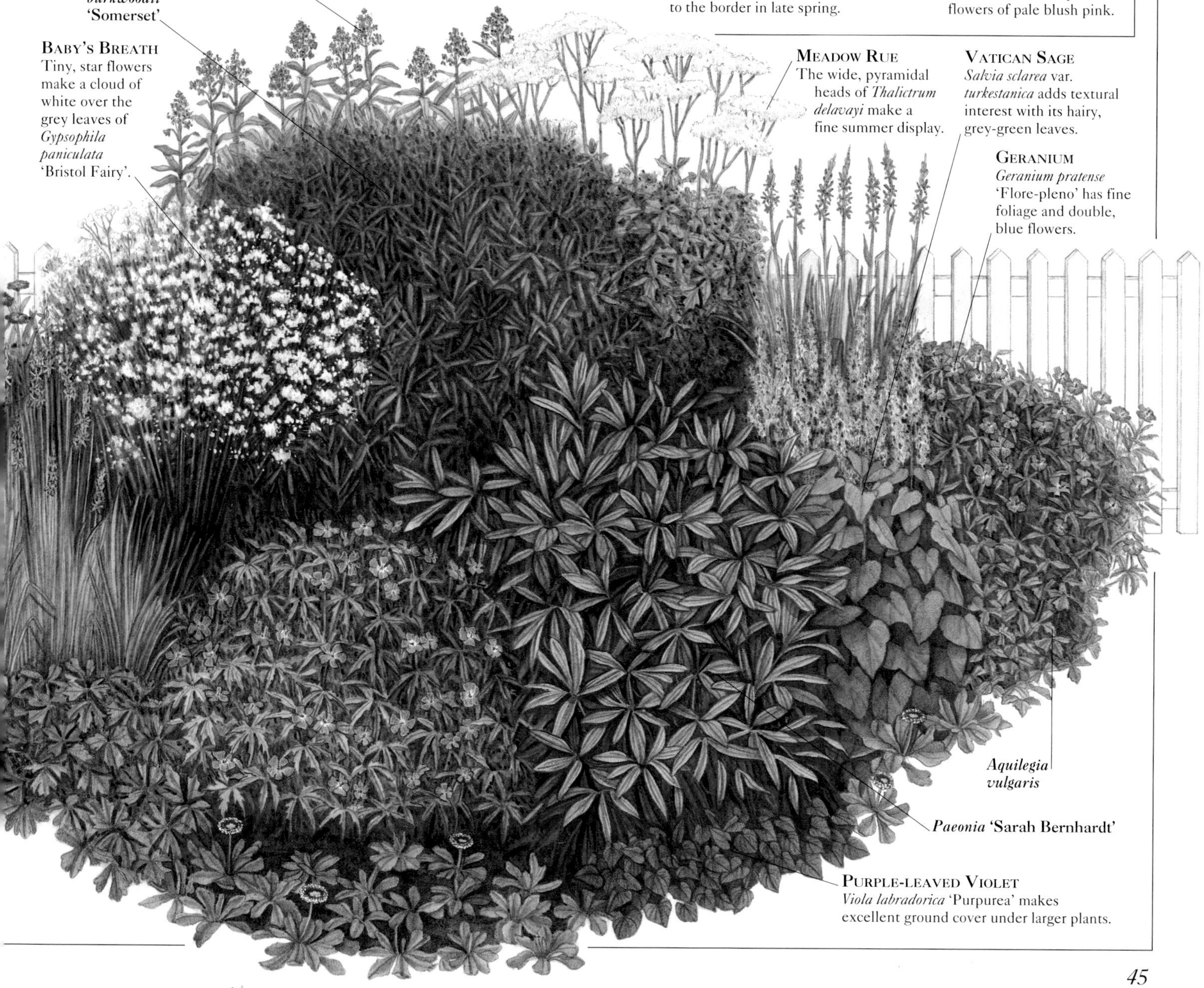

MEADOW RUE
The wide, pyramidal heads of *Thalictrum delavayi* make a fine summer display.

VATICAN SAGE
Salvia sclarea var. *turkestanica* adds textural interest with its hairy, grey-green leaves.

GERANIUM
Geranium pratense 'Flore-pleno' has fine foliage and double, blue flowers.

Aquilegia vulgaris

Paeonia 'Sarah Bernhardt'

PURPLE-LEAVED VIOLET
Viola labradorica 'Purpurea' makes excellent ground cover under larger plants.

FREE PLANTING *for an* UNPLANNED EFFECT

AS SEVERAL OF THESE PLANTS – the Vatican sage, the columbines, and the daisies– are enthusiastic self-seeders, they will soon make a nonsense of any pre-ordained planting plan. Let them. This is not a border that prides itself on its pristine neatness. In any case, the sage needs to self-seed to survive because it is a biennial.

You will have to be decisive about the position of the peonies, though. They resent being transplanted, and as a result may refuse to flower again for several years, so it is important to site them carefully at the outset. Planting them too deeply also prevents them from flowering: a little soil – about 2.5cm (1in) – on top of the crown is enough.

CARE AND CULTIVATION

SPRING
Plant thalictrums, staking if necessary. Plant pot-grown columbines and gypsophila. Plant out Vatican sage in late spring. Mulch peonies and thalictrums with well-rotted manure. Cut back straggly growths of daphne after flowering.

SUMMER
Sow columbines and double daisies in a row in early summer. Stake campanulas before they are fully grown. Dead-head peonies and lychnis, and cut back stems of geraniums after flowering. Split and replant congested clumps of camassias after flowering.

AUTUMN
Cut down old, flowered stems of columbines and campanulas. Plant camassias, and set columbines and double daisies in their permanent positions in early autumn. Plant peonies, adding plenty of bone meal, and violas, geraniums, campanulas, lychnis, and daphne now or in spring.

WINTER
Cut back peonies, gypsophila, thalictrums, and lychnis. Tidy up clumps of geraniums.

Campanula lactiflora 'Prichard's Variety' *Perennial flowering in early summer–late autumn. H 1.2m (4ft), S 60cm (2ft).*

Thalictrum delavayi (Meadow rue) *Perennial that flowers in mid-summer. H 1.5–2m (5–6ft), S 60cm (2ft).*

Daphne x burkwoodii 'Somerset' *Semi-evergreen shrub bearing scented flowers in late spring. H 1.5m (5ft), S 1.2m (4ft).*

Salvia sclarea var. turkestanica (Vatican sage) *Erect biennial with aromatic leaves. H 75cm (2½ft), S 30cm (12in).*

Geranium pratense 'Flore-pleno' *Blue-flowered perennial with bronze autumn leaves. H to 75cm (30in), S 60cm (24in).*

Paeonia 'Sarah Bernhardt' (Peony) *Clump-forming perennial that bears large, fragrant flowers. H and S to 1m (3ft).*

Lychnis coronaria *Perennial, often grown as a biennial, bearing bright magenta flowers on branched, felted, grey stems from mid- to late summer. H 45–60cm (18–24in), S 45cm (18in).*

Gypsophila paniculata 'Bristol Fairy' (Baby's breath) *Perennial with small, dark green leaves and wiry, branching stems covered with a froth of tiny, double, white flowers in summer. H 60–75cm (2–2½ft), S 1m (3ft).*

Camassia leichtlinii (Quamash) *Bulb that has star-shaped, white or violet-blue flowers. H 1.5m (5ft), S 30cm (12in).*

Aquilegia vulgaris (Columbine) *Perennial with divided leaves and nodding flowers. H 75cm (2½ft), S 50cm (20in).*

Bellis perennis 'Pomponette' (Double daisy) *Perennial with double flowers in spring. H and S 15–20cm (6–8in).*

Viola labradorica 'Purpurea' (Purple-leaved violet) *Spring-flowering perennial. H 12cm (5in), S indefinite.*

ALTERING *the* PLANTING SCHEME

THERE ARE MANY WAYS of shifting the balance of colour in the scheme. If you choose deep red peonies, purple columbines, and red lychnis, the effect will be far richer than if you use the same flowers in pink, blue, and white. Here, the alternative planting concentrates on other priorities: scaling up the plan for a larger area, and making it more fit for heavy, damp soils.

A SUBSTANTIAL DESIGN FOR A LARGER PLOT

If you are adapting the plan for a larger area, add different varieties and colours of the same plants or include other old-fashioned plants such as pinks (*Dianthus*), poppies (*Papaver rhoeas*), biennial stocks (*Matthiola*), and sweet williams (*Dianthus barbatus*). Or introduce some shrubs to give bulk and height to the scheme. Choose those with an upright habit, or they will tangle with the plants around them. By using fragrant philadelphus and honeysuckle, you can also intensify the degree of scent in the border.

In soils that are heavy and damp, both the gypsophila and the Vatican sage will sulk and possibly rot away altogether. In these conditions, substitute Japanese anemones – in tones of pink and white – with a scattering of gently coloured primulas.

***Clematis* 'Perle d'Azur'** *Deciduous climber that bears a profusion of large, open, azure-blue flowers during summer. H 3m (10ft), S 1m (3ft).*

***Lonicera periclymenum* 'Belgica' (Early Dutch honeysuckle)** *Bushy climber with richly perfumed blooms in late spring–early summer. H to 7m (22ft).*

***Philadelphus* 'Belle Etoile' (Mock orange)** *Deciduous, arching shrub smothered with scented, white blooms in late spring–early summer. H and S to 3m (10ft).*

***Anemone* x *hybrida,* syn. *A. japonica,* 'Honorine Jobert'** *Vigorous perennial that has open, pure white flowers in late summer– autumn. These are carried on wiry stems above deeply divided, dark green leaves. H 1.5m (5ft), S 60cm (2ft).*

***Primula vulgaris* 'Gigha White'** *Low-growing primrose with yellow-eyed white flowers. H and S 15–20cm (6–8in).*

AN AUTUMN–WINTER DISPLAY

WINTER IS USUALLY THE ORPHAN of the garden scene. Spring and summer get all the best clothes, while winter has to make do with second-hand cast-offs from other seasons. But the garden does not disappear with the first dark days of winter. It is still there outside the windows, and not all winter days are so miserable that we want to spend them entirely inside.

WINTER WELCOME
In the depths of winter, the delicate, cup-shaped flowers of Helleborus lividus *subsp.* corsicus *are a welcome sight.*

DESIGN POINTS

CONTINUITY OF INTEREST
A low-maintenance border with evergreen plants continuing to provide good form and foliage through the whole year.

FOLIAGE FEATURES
Handsome leaves are a strong feature of the mahonia, the cyclamen, the ivy, and both hellebores.

SHADE LOVERS
Suitable for a site shadowed by overhanging trees, as all the plants in this scheme thrive in shade.

One of the main attractions of this winter border is its display of evergreen foliage, which provides an altogether more sustaining diet in the garden than flowers. The whole purpose of a flower is instant seduction; foliage, however, works in a more subtle way, continuing to give quiet pleasure long after the accompanying flowers have withdrawn their offers.

SCENTED SHRUBS
Many winter-flowering shrubs such as viburnum, daphne, chimonanthus, corylopsis, hamamelis, osmanthus, as well as the mahonia that forms the focal point of this winter planting, have the added advantage of scent. This is one of the most elusive of pleasures in the garden. A single waft of perfume from a particular flower can open up a whole Pandora's box of emotions. And in winter, when there is less in the garden to distract the senses, a scented flower seems much more precious than it would do in summer.

FINE FOLIAGE AND FLOWERS
The advantage of using the mahonia, rather than any other of the scented shrubs of winter, is its form. Tall and craggily handsome, evergreen, uncompromising, it never falters. The leaves are pinnate, each one made up of a series of leaflets arranged in matching pairs along the leaf's rib, with a terminal flourish of a leaflet at the end. Some species have as many as twenty pairs of leaflets arranged along the midrib. If you choose *Mahonia* x *media* 'Charity', the peak season will be early winter when the shrub bears its upright, terminal spikes of lemon-yellow flowers, smelling of lily-of-the-valley.

The two groups of hellebores flower in succession. The pale green-white clusters of *Helleborus lividus* subsp. *corsicus* often appear by Christmas. The Lenten rose, *H. orientalis*, with flowers in a wide range of colours from freckled white to rich plummy-black, follows on in late winter and early spring. Both have excellent foliage, new leaves emerging before the old have quite given up, so there is never a bare patch.

PLANT LIST
1 *Helleborus orientalis* (Lenten rose) x 7
2 *Cyclamen coum* subsp. *coum* x 20
3 *Cyclamen hederifolium* x 20
4 *Erythronium dens-canis* (Dog's-tooth violet) x 24
5 *Galanthus nivalis* (Snowdrop) x 100
6 *Hyacinthoides hispanica* (Spanish bluebell) x 30
7 *Helleborus lividus* subsp. *corsicus* (Hellebore) x 3
8 *Phyllitis scolopendrium* (Hart's tongue fern) x 5
9 *Mahonia* x *media* 'Charity' x 1
10 *Hedera helix* 'Adam' (Ivy) x 3

PLANTING PLAN

WINTER CYCLAMEN
Snub-nosed flowers, either pink or white, appear among the shiny leaves of *Cyclamen coum* subsp. *coum* in late winter.

LENTEN ROSE
The flowers of *Helleborus orientalis* vary widely in colour, dark or pale, plain or freckled.

AUTUMN CYCLAMEN
Long lasting, marbled foliage is as much of an asset of *Cyclamen hederifolium* as its autumn flowers.

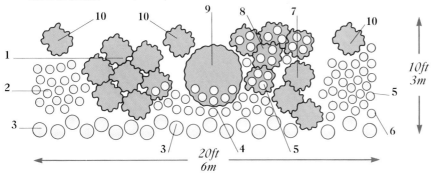

COLOURFUL GROUND COVER

The rest of the planting fills in at ground level, creating a continuity of colour and texture for many months. The bright fronds of the evergreen fern, the marbled leaves of *Cyclamen hederifolium*, and the variegated ivy continue to provide interest in this border long after winter has given way to spring. The cyclamen rest, leafless, in early summer before producing masses of tiny shuttlecock flowers, miniature versions of *C. persicum*, the popular houseplant. *C. hederifolium* is followed by *C. coum* subsp. *coum*, which carries flowers from mid-winter to early spring. Pink is the usual colour, but both species also produce white flowers.

Snowdrops will flower with the first of the Lenten hellebores. Other bulbs such as dog's-tooth violets and Spanish bluebells add colour and extend the season through into late spring.

THE JOYS OF SPRING
In late spring, the Spanish bluebells and dog's-tooth violets come into flower, adding clumps of fresh colour against the substantial mass and contrasting textures of the evergreen planting.

SPANISH BLUEBELL
Hyacinthoides hispanica has more upright flower spikes than the wild bluebell.

DOG'S-TOOTH VIOLETS
Erythronium dens-canis need to be left undisturbed in cool, rich soil.

SCHEME FOR A COOL SEASON
In late winter, both hellebores are at their best, with elegant flowers offset by a backcloth of dark leaves. The mahonia makes a striking centrepiece all year round.

IVY
Hedera helix 'Adam' has neat, variegated leaves and can easily be controlled.

MAHONIA
A shrub with magnificent foliage, *Mahonia × media* 'Charity' also has scented, umbrella-like spikes of flowers in winter.

HART'S TONGUE FERN
Broad, undulating, strap-shaped fronds are the trademark of the evergreen hart's tongue fern, *Phyllitis scolopendrium*.

HELLEBORE
Helleborus lividus subsp. *corsicus* has the most beautiful leaf of any hellebore, veined and edged with fine prickles.

SNOWDROP
With its flowers of purest white, the snowdrop, *Galanthus nivalis*, is a welcome sight at the beginning of the year.

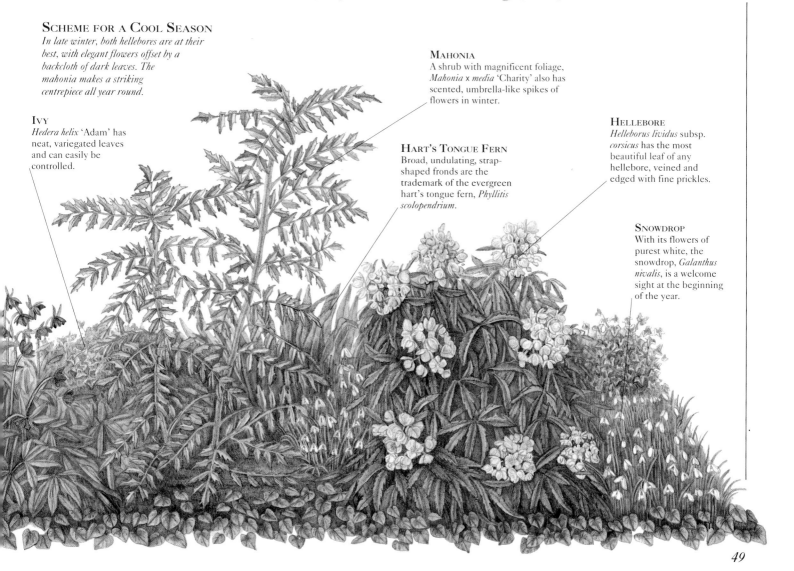

LOW-MAINTENANCE PLANTS *for* WINTER INTEREST

LEFT TO ITSELF, the mahonia will reach for the sky until its terminal spikes of flowers are way beyond nose level. Curb this tendency by cutting a few of its stems back by half each winter. The habit of the mahonia is sternly upright, so you can easily grow other plants beneath it. The mahonia, as well as the other plants used here, will cope in a position shaded by overhanging trees. This kind of shade is often slightly dry and you need to compensate for this by feeding all the plants liberally with compost or by mulching around them with a bulky manure.

The ground-cover plants in this scheme need very little attention, but encourage the ivies to spread in the direction you want by pegging down long growths with wire hoops. The cyclamen seed themselves about with magnificent abandon. Fortunately, this is one of the few plants you can never have too many of, so let them spread where they will.

CARE AND CULTIVATION

SPRING
Plant the mahonia and ivies now or in autumn. Once established, the mahonia needs little attention, apart from a regular, deep mulch. Plant snowdrops "in the green" as soon as they have finished flowering. Cut out old, flowered stems of *Helleborus lividus* subsp. *corsicus* and mulch round new growth.

SUMMER
Plant dog's-tooth violets as soon as available in late summer, also ferns, keeping them well watered until established. Before cyclamen start to flower, feed them with a scattering of bone meal and a layer of leaf mould about 2.5cm (1in) thick.

AUTUMN
Plant hellebores. They resent disturbance, so once they are settled leave them alone. Plant cyclamen in early autumn, barely covering the corms with soil. Plant Spanish bluebells, setting them about 10cm (4in) deep.

WINTER
Cut back old leaves of *Helleborus orientalis* when new flower stems start to show through. Cut out dying fronds of ferns.

Hedera helix 'Adam' (Ivy) *Spreading, evergreen creeper with small, light green leaves edged with creamy-yellow. H 1.2m (4ft), S 1m (3ft).*

Phyllitis scolopendrium (Hart's tongue fern) *Fully hardy, evergreen fern with bright green, leathery, tongue-shaped fronds. H 45–75cm (18–30in), S to 45cm (18in).*

Hyacinthoides hispanica (Spanish bluebell) *Bulb with blue, white, or pink, bell-like flowers in spring. H to 30cm (12in), S 10–15cm (4–6in).*

Helleborus orientalis (Lenten rose) *Evergreen perennial with white, pink, or purple flowers in winter–spring. H and S 45cm (18in).*

Mahonia x *media* 'Charity' *Evergreen shrub with dark green leaves and slender, yellow flower spikes. H 3m (10ft), S 2.5m (8ft).*

Helleborus lividus subsp. *corsicus* (Hellebore) *Evergreen perennial with greenish-white flowers in winter–spring. H and S to 60cm (2ft).*

Galanthus nivalis (Snowdrop) *Bulb with pendent, white flowers in winter–spring, and strappy leaves. H 10–15cm (4–6in), S 5–8cm (2–3in).*

Cyclamen coum subsp. *coum* *Tuber with bright pink flowers in winter. H to 10cm (4in), S 5–10cm (2–4in).*

Erythronium dens-canis (Dog's-tooth violet) *Tuberous perennial with attractively mottled, pointed leaves and nodding, pink, purple, or white flowers in spring. H 15–25cm (6–10in), S 8–10cm (3–4in).*

Cyclamen hederifolium *Tuber with patterned leaves, and pink flowers in autumn. H to 10cm (4in), S 10–15cm (4–6in).*

ALTERING *the* PLANTING SCHEME

FEW OTHER WINTER-FLOWERING shrubs can match the mahonia for year-round interest, but in areas where there are doubts about its hardiness, another shrub, such as viburnum, could be used instead. There is plenty of room to experiment with the ground-cover plants, too. Try other ferns and other bulbs, although you must avoid those that need full sun.

SHADES OF PINK

To create a scheme dominated by shades of pink, substitute a winter-flowering viburnum for the mahonia. The growth of *Viburnum* x *bodnantense* 'Dawn' is stiff and upright, the stems covered in mid-winter with clusters of scented, pink-flushed flowers. Disguise its summer dullness with a cloak of clematis, choosing a pale variety such as the pink 'Comtesse de Bouchaud', which flowers in late summer. Choose a clematis that you can cut back each year, so that the viburnum has a chance each season to flex its muscles. Both viburnum and clematis will need a slightly more open situation than the mahonia if they are to flower well.

There are plenty of plants that enjoy life snuffling around at ground level in dappled shade. Use periwinkles in place of the ivies to introduce more flowers, and crinkly-edged hart's tongue ferns instead of the plain ones. Or use the ostrich-feather fern, *Matteuccia struthiopteris*; it is not evergreen, but the drama of its eruption in late spring makes up for that.

Viburnum x *bodnantense* '**Dawn**' *Deciduous shrub carrying clusters of deep pink buds that open to fragrant, pink flowers from late autumn to early spring. H 3m (10ft), S 2.5m (8ft).*

Phyllitis scolopendrium '**Marginatum**' *Fully hardy, evergreen fern with long, upright, bright green, slender fronds that are attractively frilled at the edges. H and S 30–40cm (12–16in).*

Vinca minor '**Argenteovariegata**' (**Lesser periwinkle**) *Evergreen, ground-cover plant, with white-margined leaves and lilac-blue flowers. H 15cm (6in), S indefinite.*

Clematis '**Comtesse de Bouchaud**' *Hardy, strong-growing, deciduous climber. In late summer, it is covered with masses of single, large, mauve-pink flowers with yellow anthers. H 2–3m (6–10ft), S 1m (3ft).*

BORDER *of* MINIATURES

P ROVIDED YOU ALWAYS KEEP IN MIND the sort of conditions that alpine plants thrive in, you can grow them in many different places in the garden: in the cracks between paving stones on a terrace or a patio, in a lawn or scree bed, in shallow troughs and pans, in a cool greenhouse, or, as here, in a raised border.

Abandon any attempts to recreate the Alps in your back garden. Nothing you can do to builder's rubble will ever make it look like an alpine scree. Grow the plants in a raised bed instead and you will be able to enjoy them at close quarters. You could plant the border in a low, retaining wall, perhaps marking the boundary between terrace and lawn, or arrange it to fill in one end of a patio. As well as making it easier for you to admire the plants, siting them in a raised border provides the sharply drained conditions they need to flourish. They will also need sun and an open situation.

COLOURFUL ALPINES AND BULBS
Spring is the peak of the year for alpine plants and the kinds of bulb that fit in well with them, for example fritillaries, scillas, dwarf narcissus, and species tulips and crocuses. Fortunately, many of the spring-flowering plants, such as the saxifrages, are pleasing enough in form and leaf to pay their way all year round.

The saxifrages are a huge and diverse family and, indeed, you could make a whole border using nothing else. But here, with heroic restraint, you will have to restrict yourself to two. One should be a mossy type that will form neat hummocks of green foliage, scattered in spring with short-stemmed flowers. For the other saxifrage, choose *Saxifraga* 'Southside Seedling', which has enormously showy, arching plumes of flower, a mass of white, blotched and spotted with crimson. The rosette of 'Southside Seedling' dies after it has flowered, leaving several satellite rosettes that take a season or

PUTTING ON A SHOW FOR SPRING
In late spring, the hebe, pulsatillas, and mossy saxifrages are covered in flowers, while a dwarf pine and a group of columnar, dwarf junipers add strong shapes and contrasting textures.

CLUMPS OF COLOUR
The distinctive rosettes of Sempervivum tectorum *are suffused with deep red.*

DESIGN POINTS

— ❧ —

SMALL IS BEAUTIFUL
A miniature garden, perfect for a very narrow border, is created using alpines and other compact plants.

— ❧ —

FORM AND CONTRAST
Delicate flowers and bulbs contrast with the robust, architectural shapes of dwarf conifers and the rough texture of gravel and tufa rocks.

PLANT LIST
1 *Convolvulus cneorum* x 1
2 *Sempervivum tectorum* (Houseleek) x 14
3 *Pulsatilla vulgaris* (Pasque flower) x 6
4 *Dianthus gratianopolitanus* (Cheddar pink) x 6
5 *Saxifraga* 'Southside Seedling' (Saxifrage) x 10
6 *Sisyrinchium graminoides* x 5

7 *Campanula carpatica* (Dwarf bellflower) x 6
8 *Saxifraga* 'Sanguinea Superba' (Mossy saxifrage) x 3
9 *Lithodora diffusa* 'Heavenly Blue' x 6
10 *Pinus mugo* 'Humpy' (Dwarf pine) x 1
11 *Hebe pinguifolia* 'Pagei' x 1
12 *Juniperus communis* 'Compressa' (Dwarf juniper) x 3

CONVOLVULUS
Convolvulus cneorum is a pretty silver-leaved plant but not reliably hardy.

PLANTING PLAN

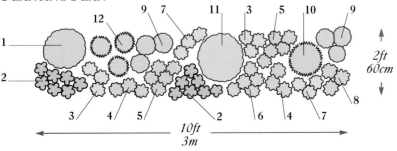

2ft
60cm

10ft
3m

more to build up to flowering size again. Buy half the plants you need one year, half the next. That way, they will not all die out at the same time, and you should always have some in flower.

Include at least one plant to flop over the edge of the retaining wall and soften its hard lines. Some campanulas and dianthus will do this and will extend the flowering season into summer.

STRUCTURAL FRAMEWORK

Include a selection of plants of greater substance and stature to help balance the display. Dwarf conifers are traditional companions for rock plants and provide evergreen bulk all year. There are many upright junipers that will add height and solidity. A pine such as *Pinus mugo* 'Humpy' or *P. pumila* 'Globe' makes a compact, rounded dome, the needles arranged like bottle brushes in whorls round the stubby branches. *P. leucodermis* 'Schmidtii' is another dwarf conifer of character. Before buying, check that the conifers you choose are truly dwarf rather than young plants of larger trees.

THE BORDER IN LATE SUMMER

In summer, the convolvulus, sisyrinchiums, lithodoras, and campanulas come to the fore, displaying a wealth of colourful blooms.

LITHODORA
The spreading, prostrate stems of *Lithodora diffusa* 'Heavenly Blue' are covered in summer with deep blue flowers.

SISYRINCHIUM
Sisyrinchium graminoides has star-shaped flowers held on stiff stems.

DWARF BELLFLOWER
Neat, low mounds of bright green leaves are studded in summer with the blue or white flowers of the dwarf bellflower, *Campanula carpatica.*

DWARF JUNIPER
Juniperus communis 'Compressa' is an excellent dwarf juniper to use with low-growing alpines.

HOUSELEEK
All the houseleeks, varieties of *Sempervivum tectorum*, share the same form, making compact rosettes of fleshy leaves.

HEBE
A low, dense shrub, *Hebe pinguifolia* 'Pagei' has foliage of an intense, glaucous grey.

PASQUE FLOWER
Pulsatilla vulgaris, the Pasque flower, has silky leaves topped with purple flowers.

Sisyrinchium graminoides

SAXIFRAGE
Saxifraga 'Southside Seedling' has a froth of showy, pink and white flowers on foot-long stems.

CHEDDAR PINK
The long-lived Cheddar pink, *Dianthus gratianopolitanus*, fills the air with its sweet scent in early summer.

DWARF PINE
The most compact form of the mountain pine, *Pinus mugo* 'Humpy' grows slowly into a dense, rounded bush.

Campanula carpatica

MOSSY SAXIFRAGE
Saxifraga 'Sanguinea Superba' is a mossy saxifrage with red flowers in spring.

Lithodora diffusa 'Heavenly Blue'

A WELL-DRAINED BORDER *for* MINIATURE PLANTS

DRAINAGE IS THE KEY to success here. Use a compost specially modified for alpine plants, or make up your own by adding extra grit to a loam-based mixture. The compost will settle after you have filled your raised bed, so be generous. A mulch of gravel chippings is also invaluable. It makes a fast-draining layer round the necks of alpine plants, keeps down weeds, and cuts down on the amount of watering needed.

Vary the horizontal plane with lumps of natural tufa. Bury it to at least one-third of its depth so that it is stable and looks settled.

CARE AND CULTIVATION

SPRING
Plant junipers and pinks, adding bone meal to the soil for the latter. Plant campanulas, convolvulus, lithodoras, sempervivums, and sisyrinchiums. Protect campanulas against slugs, and add leaf mould to the soil for lithodoras. Split and reset congested clumps of sempervivums. Cut back leggy growth of hebes if necessary.

SUMMER
Shear off dead flowers of mossy saxifrages. Cut out flowered stems of *Saxifraga* 'Southside Seedling', pinks, and campanulas. Remove dead, flowered rosettes of sempervivums. Dead-head hebes after flowering.

AUTUMN
Plant saxifrages now or in spring, working plenty of grit into the hole, and position pulsatillas in a sunny spot. Cut out dead, flowered stems and leaves of sisyrinchiums. Cut back lithodoras if they encroach on neighbouring plants.

WINTER
Plant the pine in a sunny position now or in spring. Remove fallen leaves from pinks and saxifrages. In wet areas, protect convolvulus with panes of glass or a cloche.

Saxifraga 'Southside Seedling' (Saxifrage) *Evergreen perennial flowering in late spring–early summer. H and S 30cm (12in).*

Lithodora diffusa 'Heavenly Blue' *Evergreen sub-shrub with summer flowers. H 30cm (12in), S 45cm (18in).*

Convolvulus cneorum *Evergreen shrub with silvery leaves, and white flowers in late spring–summer. H and S 75cm (2½ft).*

Hebe pinguifolia 'Pagei' *Evergreen, spreading shrub with glossy leaves, flowering profusely in early summer. H and S 90cm (3ft).*

Pinus mugo 'Humpy' (Dwarf pine) *Dwarf conifer with needle-like, dark green leaves. H and S 25–30cm (10–12in).*

Sempervivum tectorum (Houseleek) *Evergreen succulent with neat, fleshy rosettes. H 15cm (6in), S 20cm (8in).*

Juniperus communis 'Compressa' (Dwarf juniper) *Conifer with aromatic leaves. H 75cm (2½ft), S 15cm (6in).*

Campanula carpatica (Dwarf bellflower) *Perennial with blue or white summer flowers. H 10cm (4in), S 30cm (12in)*

Pulsatilla vulgaris (Pasque flower) *Perennial with red, pink, purple, or white flowers in spring. H and S 23cm (9in).*

Dianthus gratianopolitanus (Cheddar pink) *Evergreen perennial. H 15cm (6in), S 30cm (12in).*

Saxifraga 'Sanguinea Superba' (Mossy saxifrage) *Perennial with reddish-pink flowers. H 10cm (4in), S indefinite.*

Sisyrinchium graminoides *Semi-evergreen perennial with blue summer flowers. H 30cm (12in), S 8cm (3in).*

ALTERING *the* PLANTING SCHEME

DWARF BULBS OF MANY KINDS will complement the other plants in this border, and will also help to extend its season of interest. Growing bulbs in pots to plunge into the bed temporarily makes it easy to change the scheme each season. Choose varieties that are in scale with the rest of the plants; some daffodils look as if they spend their rest time at body-building classes.

BULBS FOR A LONGER DISPLAY

Include cyclamen for a breath of life when many plants are lying low: *Cyclamen coum* subsp. *coum* may produce its flowers in early winter. Colchicums carry the torch at the other end of the season, pushing up sheaves of chequered pink flowers. In spring the choice is enormous: species crocus, scillas, chionodoxas, puschkinias, and *Anemone blanda* all make fine displays. Plant tulips and narcissus in pots, then lift them after flowering and allow the leaves to die down before storing the bulbs until next year.

Colchicum agrippinum *Early autumn-flowering bulb bearing erect, funnel-shaped, pink flowers. H 10–15cm (4–6in), S 10cm (4in).*

Cyclamen coum subsp. ***coum*** *Winter-flowering tuber with rounded, silver-splashed or plain green leaves, and pink flowers. H and S 10cm (4in).*

***Narcissus* 'Hawera'** *Mid-spring-flowering bulb with nodding blooms which are lemon-yellow, with swept-back petals. H and S to 20cm (8in).*

***Iris reticulata* 'Cantab'** *Bulb with pale blue flowers, each fall marked with a blaze of bright yellow. H 10–15cm (4–6in), S 5cm (2in).*

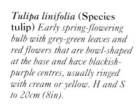

***Tulipa linifolia* (Species tulip)** *Early spring-flowering bulb with grey-green leaves and red flowers that are bowl-shaped at the base and have blackish-purple centres, usually ringed with cream or yellow. H and S to 20cm (8in).*

Crocus tommasinianus *Spring-flowering bulb that produces long, slender, goblet-shaped flowers that may be lilac, deep purple, or violet, occasionally silver outside. It naturalizes well. H to 10cm (4in), S to 8cm (3in).*

ISLAND AND OTHER BEDS

&

*Beds in a garden need to work from more
than one viewpoint. Island beds are particularly
demanding in this respect as there is such a
large proportion of foreground to background.
The shape of the bed may suggest the style of
planting. Symmetrical or geometric-shaped
beds lend themselves to formal schemes, while
informal planting is appropriate for
curving or irregular beds.*

A BED *of* ROSES

F EW PLANTS CAN RIVAL ROSES for their seductive scent and range of colours, whether rich and deep or pale and subtle. In traditional, formal gardens, roses are often grown on their own, but in this formal scheme a tapestry of plants weaves beneath the roses to provide a backcloth of colour and texture.

REPEAT PERFORMANCE
The open blooms of Rosa *'Penelope' are flushed with pink. If dead-headed, this rose will flower through summer and autumn.*

DESIGN POINTS

GEOMETRIC SHAPES
Repeated blocks of colour in the underplanting give a formal structure.

SCULPTURAL CENTRE
The obelisk at the heart of the design adds height and acts as a focal point.

SOFT COLOURS
Co-ordinated groups of lady's mantle, geraniums, anaphalis, and pinks are chosen to complement the colours of the roses.

It is perfectly possible to plant roses that are healthy, that smell good, that give a good display for a long period in summer, that have handsome foliage as well as beautiful flowers, and that grow with form and grace. The difficulty lies in finding a variety that possesses all these characteristics at once.

For individual flower power, nothing can beat the large-flowered bush (Hybrid Tea) roses, which have "Never mind the quality, feel the colour" stamped right through them. But the habit is graceless, the constitution often weak. The old shrub roses have grace, but a short, one-off season of flowering in mid-summer. Somewhere between the two sits the superb race of roses known as Hybrid Musks. These are healthy shrubs with a relaxed habit and, unlike old roses, they continue to flower intermittently through until autumn.

This scheme includes 'Felicia', which has rich pink, fully double flowers, the salmon overtones fading to cream as the flowers age, and the paler 'Penelope' with clusters of cream flowers flushed with pink. Both are sweetly scented. Use these roses in contrasting groups of three in the corners of this formal, diamond-shaped bed.

A CLIMBING CENTREPIECE

Make a centrepiece with a luxuriant climbing rose that you can train through a support. Metal obelisks are long lasting and make handsome pieces of garden sculpture when the roses are dormant.

Avoid wildly vigorous cultivars such as 'Kiftsgate', which will swamp an obelisk with magnificent contempt. Climbing sports of large-flowered bushes are shorter, but have a stiff habit of growth. Look instead for a climber such

PLANT LIST

1 *Dianthus* 'Charles Musgrave' (Pink) x 6
2 *Rosa* 'Penelope' x 6
3 *Geranium endressii* x 6
4 *Stachys macrantha* x 6
5 *Nepeta* 'Six Hills Giant' (Catmint) x 6
6 *Rosa* 'Felicia' x 6
7 *Alchemilla mollis* (Lady's mantle) x 3
8 *Geranium psilostemon* x 6
9 *Hosta fortunei* 'Albopicta' x 10
10 *Iris germanica* x 14
11 *Anaphalis triplinervis* x 6
12 *Rosa* 'Félicité Perpétue' x 1

LATE SUMMER SHOW
With the Hybrid Musk roses in full bloom, the underplanting is deliberately low key. The pinks and anaphalis form mats of soft, grey foliage while blue catmint and pink Geranium endressii *provide clumps of colour.*

PLANTING PLAN

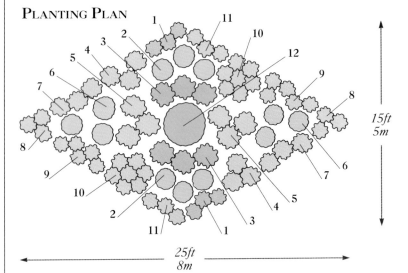

15ft
5m

25ft
8m

GERANIUM
Geranium endressii provides useful, evergreen ground cover and a long succession of silver-pink flowers.

HOSTA
With its sheaves of painted leaves, *Hosta fortunei* 'Albopicta' makes a spectacular spring foliage plant.

as 'Félicité Perpétue', which has no ambitions beyond the 5m (15ft) level. In mild areas, its foliage should be evergreen – an added bonus. The flowers are small, but borne in big clusters, creamy-white, sometimes flushed with pink, and beautifully scented.

If even this seems too much to keep under control, try 'The Garland', one of Gertrude Jekyll's favourite roses, which rarely reaches beyond 3m (10ft). It flowers profusely with masses of tiny, creamy-white blooms borne in clusters and the scent is sweetly pungent, like oranges.

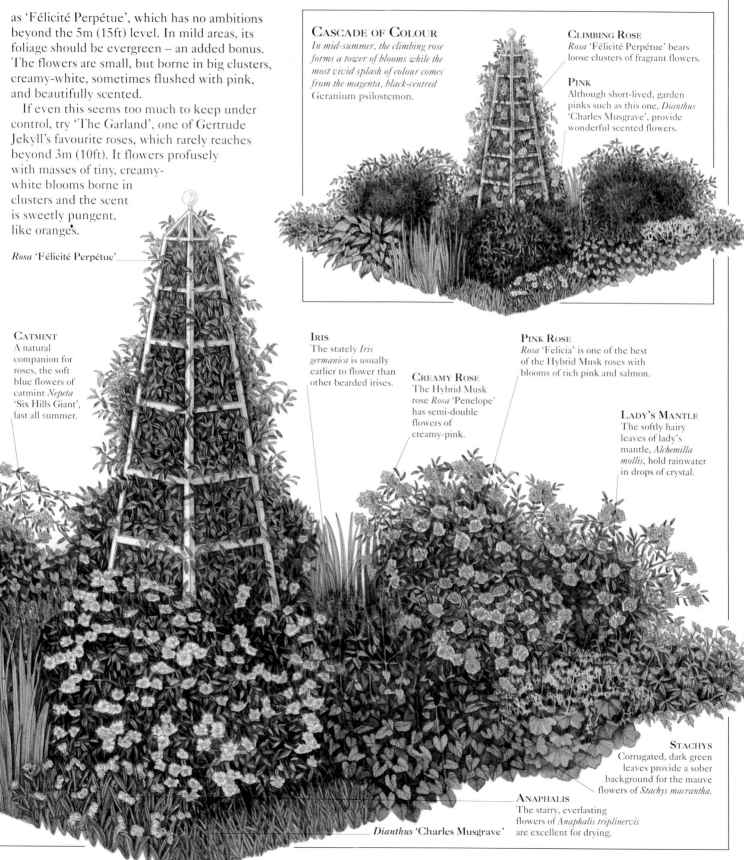

CASCADE OF COLOUR
In mid-summer, the climbing rose forms a tower of blooms while the most vivid splash of colour comes from the magenta, black-centred Geranium psilostemon.

CLIMBING ROSE
Rosa 'Félicité Perpétue' bears loose clusters of fragrant flowers.

PINK
Although short-lived, garden pinks such as this one, *Dianthus* 'Charles Musgrave', provide wonderful scented flowers.

Rosa 'Félicité Perpétue'

CATMINT
A natural companion for roses, the soft blue flowers of catmint *Nepeta* 'Six Hills Giant', last all summer.

IRIS
The stately *Iris germanica* is usually earlier to flower than other bearded irises.

CREAMY ROSE
The Hybrid Musk rose *Rosa* 'Penelope' has semi-double flowers of creamy-pink.

PINK ROSE
Rosa 'Felicia' is one of the best of the Hybrid Musk roses with blooms of rich pink and salmon.

LADY'S MANTLE
The softly hairy leaves of lady's mantle, *Alchemilla mollis*, hold rainwater in drops of crystal.

STACHYS
Corrugated, dark green leaves provide a sober background for the mauve flowers of *Stachys macrantha*.

ANAPHALIS
The starry, everlasting flowers of *Anaphalis triplinervis* are excellent for drying.

Dianthus 'Charles Musgrave'

COMPLEMENTARY PLANTS *for a* ROSE GARDEN

EVEN THE BETTER TYPES OF ROSE, such as the Hybrid Musks, cannot pretend that their foliage is so good that you would make a detour to see it. This makes it doubly important to have plants with pleasing foliage in the rest of the planting. Lady's mantle is a good ally in this respect, though always coming into leaf later than you would wish. It can be invasive so it is a good idea to cut back the flowering stems before it has chance to set seed.

Stachys macrantha has distinctive, corrugated, triangular leaves that spread to make a thick, green mat. It is not as widely planted as its cousin, *S. byzantina*, but is well worth growing.

Geranium endressii
Semi-evergreen, carpeting perennial producing cup-shaped, pink flowers in summer. H 45cm (18in), S 60cm (2ft).

Dianthus 'Charles Musgrave' (Pink)
Spreading perennial with single, white flowers in mid-summer. H 45cm (18in), S 30cm (12in).

Iris germanica
Rhizomatous, bearded iris. Yellow-splashed, violet flowers are produced in late spring and early summer. H to 1.2m (4ft), S indefinite.

Rosa 'Felicia'
Vigorous, Hybrid Musk rose with grey-green foliage and double, scented flowers in summer–autumn. H 1.5m (5ft), S 2.2m (7ft).

Rosa 'Félicité Perpétue' *Semi-evergreen, climbing rose bearing clusters of fully double, blush-pink to white flowers in mid-summer. H 5m (15ft), S 4m (12ft).*

Geranium psilostemon
Clump-forming perennial with cup-shaped, black-centred flowers in mid-summer. The deeply cut leaves have good autumn colour. H and S 1.2m (4ft).

Rosa 'Penelope' *Bushy, Hybrid Musk rose with plentiful, dark green leaves. It bears clusters of scented, double, pinkish-white flowers in summer–autumn. H and S 1m (3ft).*

Nepeta 'Six Hills Giant' (Catmint)
Summer-flowering perennial with narrow, grey-green leaves and spikes of lavender-blue flowers. H and S 60cm (2ft).

Hosta fortunei 'Albopicta' *Clump-forming perennial grown mainly for its cream-splashed foliage. It has pale violet flowers in early summer. H and S 1m (3ft).*

Anaphalis triplinervis
Dwarf, leafy perennial with grey-green foliage and silvery stems. The white flowerheads appear in late summer. H 20–30cm (8–12in), S 15cm (6in).

Stachys macrantha
Clump-forming perennial bearing crinkled, heart-shaped, soft green leaves. In summer, it has whorls of large, rose-purple flowers. H and S 30cm (12in).

Alchemilla mollis (Lady's mantle)
Ground-cover perennial with downy leaves and sprays of greenish-yellow flowers in summer. H and S 50cm (20in).

ALTERING *the* PLANTING SCHEME

THE ORIGINAL SCHEME USES ROSES in soft shades of pale creamy-pink. For an effect that is altogether more sumptuous, substitute some deep magenta Rugosa roses instead. Extend the season of interest in this bed by including spring-flowering bulbs such as hyacinths and tulips. You can plant out hyacinth bulbs that have been forced for an early show indoors.

A RICH DISPLAY OF DEEP PINK AND PURPLE

The Rugosa roses have a very different habit of growth from the Hybrid Musks. They are dense, upright, and vigorous, and the result is a thicket, rather than the loose, open, airy effect of the Hybrid Musks. Rugosas are outstandingly healthy roses, strangers to black spot and mildew. 'Roseraie de l'Haÿ', has large, flat, semi-double flowers of rich magenta. 'Frau Dagmar Hartopp' has paler flowers but compensates with spectacular autumn fruit, the size and colour of cherry tomatoes.

To intensify the rich effect, you could replace the pale climbing rose with a darker one, too. 'Veilchenblau' would be perfect: its flowers are like purple tissue paper left out in the rain, clusters of lavender-purple that fade as they age to a lilac-grey. Avoid bright yellow roses; they would fight to the death with the magenta *Geranium psilostemon*.

Rosa rugosa 'Frau Dagmar Hartopp' *Shrub rose with fragrant, single, pink flowers, then large red hips in autumn.* H 1.5m (5ft), S 1.2m (4ft).

Rosa rugosa 'Roseraie de l'Haÿ' *Vigorous, strongly scented rose with large, double, magenta blooms. H 2m (6ft), S 1.5m (5ft).*

BEAUTIFUL BULBS FOR A SPRING SHOW

As the scheme is planned to peak in summer, a generous planting of bulbs will give it another chance to hog the spotlight earlier in the year. You could plant thick bands of crocus round the edges of the diamond with a cluster of daffodils at the feet of the central rose. Or you could plant random groups of hyacinths (use at least seven in a group), mixed with tulips. Try the raspberry ripple ice-cream colours of the parrot tulip 'Estella Rijnveld' and the earlier flowering, simple, white 'Purissima'.

Tulipa 'Estella Rijnveld' (Parrot tulip) *Late spring-flowering bulb with fantastically frilled, red blooms, streaked with white. H 60cm (2ft), S to 20cm (8in).*

Tulipa 'Purissima' (Fosteriana tulip) *Spring-flowering bulb with white blooms above broad leaves. H 35–40cm (14–16in), S to 20cm (8in).*

Hyacinthus orientalis 'Delft Blue' (Hyacinth) *Winter- or spring-flowering bulb with scented, violet-blue flowers. H 10–20cm (4–8in), S 6–10cm (2½–4in).*

A BOLD DESERT BED

HANDSOME EXOTICS such as yucca, agave, kniphofia, and phormium need to be displayed like pieces of sculpture in a gallery, with plenty of room all round them. This bed would work well in a modern setting alongside a patio, planted in a courtyard with plain, whitewashed walls, or adapted to fit round two sides of a terrace. You could also modify it to suit a conservatory; then, even in cold regions, the scheme would work for twelve months of the year instead of four.

STEELY SUCCULENT
The fleshy, succulent leaves of Agave parryi *form a compact, spiky, steely-blue rosette and help the plant to tolerate long periods of drought.*

DESIGN POINTS

CONTEMPORARY STYLE
Bold, architectural plants complement an unfussy, contemporary setting.

DRY SITE
An ideal scheme for a very dry, well-drained, sunny spot or a bed in a frost-free conservatory.

AFTER DARK DISPLAY
Plants of sculptural form such as those used here look particularly striking if lit up at night.

COLOUR AND FORM
Foliage carries much of the colour in this group: blue-grey and variegated gold in the agave, glaucous grey in the eucalyptus, deep purple in the phormium. The aeoniums look as if they are made of wax, toy trees with succulent rosettes of leaves arranged in perfect symmetry. The surface of the leaves is glossy and slippery, a fine contrast to the dull sheen of the phormium. Even the fuchsia, which is from a family not generally noted for its foliage, has lustrous leaves, darker and silkier than those on ordinary fuchsias.

This scheme uses the alpine snow gum, *Eucalyptus niphophila*, which is smaller and slower growing than the widely planted *E. gunnii*,

though it is equally hardy and wind resistant. The young leaves are a light mahogany and this colour spreads in winter to the twigs which glow glossy red. In spring, they are covered in a blue-white bloom, the same colour as the bark on young trees. Older trees shed their bark, which mutates through cream to grey and reddish-brown.

The phormium makes a strong upright feature in the centre of the group, its evergreen sword leaves very much more important than its flowers. Only the bright yellow gazania (which will grow as a perennial in mild areas) is here chiefly on account of its flowers, which are models of symmetry – yet even the gazania has foliage that is attractively backed with silver.

PLANT LIST

1 *Datura* x *candida* (Angels' trumpets) x 1
2 *Gazania uniflora* x 16
3 *Agave americana* 'Variegata' x 1 and *Agave parryi* x 2
4 *Fuchsia* 'Thalia' x 1
5 *Begonia rex* 'Helen Lewis' x 4
6 *Phormium tenax* 'Purpureum' (New Zealand flax) x 1

7 *Aeonium arboreum* 'Schwarzkopf' x 3
8 *Kniphofia caulescens* (Red hot poker) x 3
9 *Eucalyptus niphophila* (Alpine snow gum) x 1
10 *Crassula falcata* (Aeroplane propeller) x 1
11 *Echeveria gibbiflora* var. *metallica* x 1
12 *Yucca whipplei* x 1

PLANTING PLAN

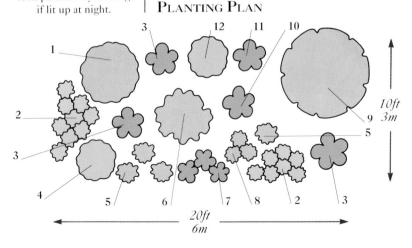

10ft
3m

20ft
6m

SCULPTURAL TABLEAU
The strength of this scheme is its simplicity – plants with strong silhouettes, limited colours, and echoing forms and habits are seen against a textured plane of gravel or shingle.

ANGELS' TRUMPETS
The heavily scented flowers of angels' trumpets, *Datura* x *candida*, are produced over a long period in late summer and autumn.

FUCHSIA
The green leaves of *Fuchsia* 'Thalia' are red beneath and make an excellent foil for the tubular, orange-red flowers.

GAZANIA
Each one a miniature sun, the brilliant flowers of *Gazania uniflora* shine out against the dark foliage.

A SCHEME OF SUN-LOVERS

Few of these plants make any pretence at being hardy. They are sybarites, built for sun and pleasure not frost and torment. In warm areas around the Mediterranean, in Australia, and the southern USA, all the plants could stay out permanently. In regions where winters are cold and winds harsh, they should only be left out in the garden for a temporary summer display. The smaller plants such as the crassula and aeoniums may be grown in clay pots to stand out on the gravel during the summer months. The begonias will also look good in pots and both can then be shifted easily if necessary to overwinter in a frost-free greenhouse.

In all but the coldest areas, the eucalyptus, the spiky yucca, the phormium, and the kniphofia can stay as permanent features. These four on their own will provide effective contrasts of foliage and form.

ALPINE SNOW GUM
Grow *Eucalyptus niphophila*, the Alpine snow gum, as a single trunk tree or coppice it to provide the most handsome foliage.

VARIEGATED AGAVE
Although dangerously sharp, the pointed leaves of this *Agave americana* 'Variegata' add drama in a planting scheme.

BLUE AGAVE
Agave parryi is a scaled-down version of the big American agaves, but its rosettes are no less arresting.

AEROPLANE PROPELLOR
Handle *Crassula falcata* carefully as the bloom easily rubs off its succulent leaves.

YUCCA
Vast panicles of cream bells rise from the grey foliage of *Yucca whipplei* in summer.

BEGONIA
Good-looking leaves rather than flowers are the chief glory of *Begonia rex* 'Helen Lewis'.

AEONIUM
The whorls of leaves on *Aeonium arboreum* 'Schwarzkopf' are wonderfully dark and gleaming.

NEW ZEALAND FLAX
Phormium tenax 'Purpureum' forms a fountain of arching leaves.

RED HOT POKER
Beautiful grey leaves set off the soft coral-red flowers of *Kniphofia caulescens*, the red hot poker.

ECHEVERIA
The succulent leaves of *Echeveria gibbiflora* var. *metallica* are suffused with pink.

PLANTS *for a* DRY, WELL-DRAINED SITE

A DESERT SCHEME such as this needs an open position in full sun. Most of the plants used here need dry, well-drained conditions, particularly the succulents such as the echeveria and aeoniums, which will rot if they are too damp. Cover the ground round the plants with shingle, gravel, or small pebbles. This will set them off well and make them look more natural than if they are surrounded by bare earth. Using shingle has practical advantages, too: it acts as a weed suppressant and also slows down the rate at which water evaporates from the soil.

CARE AND CULTIVATION

SPRING
Plant the yucca, kniphofias, gazanias, and phormium. Repot agaves in gritty, free-draining compost. Pot on begonias, and the echeveria and crassula if necessary, using a compost mixed with coarse sand. Set out the fuchsia once all danger of frost has passed.

SUMMER
Plant the eucalyptus in well-drained soil; water well until the tree is fully established and stake if necessary. Set out agaves. Syringe foliage of begonias with water to maintain a humid atmosphere, and give them a liquid feed every two weeks. Plunge datura in its pot, or plant out, depending on conditions. Set out pots of aeoniums.

AUTUMN
Lift and overwinter mature fuchsia plants or propagate fresh plants from cuttings. Cut down stems of remaining plants after first frosts.

WINTER
Keep the crassula and agaves under cover on the dry side: they rot if they are too damp. In late winter, cut down growths of the datura to within 15cm (6in) of the base.

Eucalyptus niphophila (Alpine snow gum)
Evergreen tree with red-edged, grey-green leaves. H to 10m (30ft), S 6m (20ft).

Echeveria gibbiflora var. **metallica** *Succulent with grey-green, fleshy leaves tinged with pink. H 1m (3ft), S 15cm (6in).*

Gazania uniflora *Mat-forming perennial bearing yellow flowers in early summer. H 45–60cm (18–24in), S 45cm (18in).*

Kniphofia caulescens (Red hot poker) *Autumn-flowering, evergreen perennial. H 1.2m (4ft), S 60cm (2ft).*

Begonia rex 'Helen Lewis' *Evergreen perennial with cream flowers in early summer. H and S to 60cm (2ft).*

Yucca whipplei *Evergreen shrub with slender, blue-green leaves and a tall flower spike. H 1.5m (5ft), S 1m (3ft).*

Aeonium arboreum 'Schwarzkopf' *Perennial succulent with narrow, purple leaves. H to 60cm (2ft), S 1m (3ft).*

Agave americana 'Variegata' *Perennial succulent with stiff, pointed leaves edged with yellow. H and S to 2m (6ft).*

Datura x candida (Angels' trumpets) *Semi-evergreen shrub with scented flowers in summer–autumn. H and S to 3m (9ft).*

Fuchsia 'Thalia' *Tender, deciduous shrub with long, slender flowers and dark foliage. H and S 1m (3ft).*

Phormium tenax 'Purpureum' (New Zealand Flax) *Evergreen perennial with bold leaves. H 2m (6ft), S 1m (3ft).*

Crassula falcata (Aeroplane propeller) *Perennial succulent that has fleshy, twisted, grey leaves. H and S 1m (3ft).*

ALTERING *the* PLANTING SCHEME

THE EFFECT OF THE PURPLE FOLIAGE and the brilliantly coloured flowers in the original scheme is rich and sumptuous but where a lighter, airier effect is required, this can easily be achieved by altering some of the planting.

Use the feathery-leaved albizia instead of the more architectural phormium. Substitute plants with pale flowers of cream, white, and pink for the bright red and yellow flowers of the fuchsia, the kniphofia, and the gazania.

COOLER COLOUR COMBINATIONS

Albizia, the silk tree, is airiness incarnate, a shimmering mirage of grey-green leaflets and, in late summer, preposterous small, pink powder-puff flowers. It is not fully hardy but fortunately will grow in a large pot and can be put under cover if necessary.

Other plants have to be toned down to fit the new mood of this scheme. Use only the steely blue-grey agaves, rather than the variegated one, and switch the red kniphofia for a white one. Plant patches of pink and white busy lizzies instead of the bright gazanias.

Albizia julibrissin (**Silk tree**) *Deciduous tree with large, divided leaves and clusters of frothy, pink flowers in late summer. H and S to 10m (30ft).*

Impatiens 'Accent Pink' (**Busy lizzie**) *Tender perennial, usually grown as an annual, that is covered with pink flowers in summer–autumn. H and S to 38cm (15in).*

Begonia fuchsioides *Evergreen, shrub-like begonia with oval, toothed, dark green leaves and single, red, hanging flowers. H to 1.2m (4ft), S 30cm (12in).*

Echeveria elegans *Clump-forming, perennial succulent with rosettes of pale silvery-blue leaves and a pink flower that shoots above the leaves in summer. H 5cm (2in), S 50cm (20in).*

Kniphofia 'Percy's Pride' *Upright perennial with large, creamy-coloured flower spikes tinged with green, borne on erect stems in autumn. H 1m (3ft), S to 50cm (20in).*

Agave parryi *Perennial succulent with stiff, blue-grey leaves radiating from a basal rosette. Mature plants may produce a tall stem bearing creamy-yellow flowers. H 50cm (20in), S 1m (3ft).*

DESIGN POINTS

LIVING FRAME
A colourful frame of flowers for a slow-growing specimen tree or shrub.

SHORT-TERM PLEASURES
Instant effect from a combination of fast-growing plants.

LONG-TERM EFFECT
Long-term promise in the centrepiece, here the well-known *Magnolia* x *soulangeana*.

OLD AND NEW
A scheme that can be adapted to fit almost any existing specimen tree or shrub in your garden.

INSTANT FLOWERS

ALL GARDENS NEED SHORT-TERM as well as long-term plantings. This bed shows how you can have the best of both worlds. The centrepiece is a magnolia, which will take many years to acquire distinction. While you are waiting, you can use the space around the tree to grow colourful, summer-flowering, short-lived plants.

The principle of creating an instant display around a long-term plant can be adapted to any other tree or shrub that takes a long time to grow into its adult clothes. Where this scheme suggests a magnolia, you could equally well use a mulberry (*Morus*), a tulip tree (*Liriodendron tulipifera*), or a standard wisteria. Choose whatever is most likely to thrive in your own particular situation.

Magnolias grow best on soil that is rich, fertile, moisture retentive, and slightly on the acid side of neutral; the finest magnolias grow in areas that receive at least 70cm (28in) of rain a year, and do not have prolonged droughts in summer. They will grow on alkaline soils, but should not be wasted on poor, thin, chalky ground.

A SILVERY CARPET
The flowery bed under the magnolia includes four big bushes of daisy-flowered argyranthemums. Try and get hold of the fine grey-leaved cultivar with white flowers, known as *Argyranthemum gracile* 'Chelsea Girl'. It flowers non-stop throughout the summer until the first frosts. Few annuals have attractive, bulky foliage and this is what you gain from the argyranthemums as well as the tireless show from its flowers.

Add more body to the scheme by including plants of silver fern, *Senecio maritima* 'Silver Dust'. The leaves and stems are covered with white, woolly hairs; the whole thing looks as though it has been cut from felt. In mild areas, it will overwinter, as it is by nature a shrubby plant, but it is often used like an annual, raised each spring from seed.

ARGYRANTHEMUM
All the argyranthemums are attractive, but 'Chelsea Girl' has intensely blue-grey, needle-fine foliage to set off the white daisy flowers.

A SPECTACLE FOR SUMMER
In summer, the bed is at its best, with gloriously colourful flowers repeated in patches to create a patterned yet luxuriant effect.

SALVIA
The purple-blue flowers of *Salvia farinacea* 'Victoria' are held high on upright stems of the same colour.

TOADFLAX
The neat toadflax, *Linaria maroccana* 'Fairy Lights', bears pretty little flowers, each with a contrasting white throat.

VERBENA
Intense pink flowers appear all through summer on *Verbena* 'Sissinghurst'.

SPLASHES OF COLOUR

When this grey background is in place, you can start adding colour. Edge the bed with the toadflax, *Linaria maroccana* 'Fairy Lights', mixed with some brightly coloured verbena such as the deep pink 'Sissinghurst'. Fill in behind this border and between the argyranthemums with pale pink diascia and the tall, purplish-blue *Salvia farinacea* 'Victoria'. This is often late in working up to its display, but do not let this prejudice you against it. It is agreeable to have something fresh to look forward to and once the salvia has got going, only frost will stop it. Into this mix of pink, blue, grey, and white, throw an unexpected surprise: a few clumps of acid yellow snapdragons. Choose the shade carefully: the best colour will be a yellow with green rather than red overtones.

PLANTING PLAN

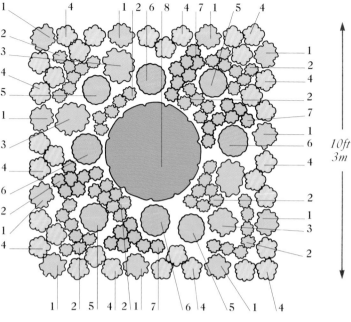

10ft
3m

10ft
3m

MAGNOLIA
Though susceptible to late frosts, the fragrant flowers of *Magnolia* x *soulangeana*, which appear in late spring, are undeniably showy.

SNAPDRAGON
Use an acid-yellow snapdragon such as this *Antirrhinum majus*, rust resistant yellow for a striking colour contrast in this scheme.

PLANT LIST

1 *Verbena* 'Sissinghurst' x 11
2 *Antirrhinum majus*, rust resistant yellow (Snapdragon) x 40
3 *Diascia rigescens* x 3
4 *Linaria maroccana* 'Fairy Lights' (Toadflax) x 27
5 *Argyranthemum gracile* 'Chelsea Girl' x 4
6 *Senecio maritima* 'Silver Dust' (Silver fern) x 4
7 *Salvia farinacea* 'Victoria' x 24
8 *Magnolia* x *soulangeana* x 1

SILVER FERN
By mid-summer, *Senecio maritima* 'Silver Dust' makes low mounds of fern-like, silver-white foliage.

DIASCIA
A plant of low, almost shrubby growth, *Diascia rigescens* has copper-pink flowers that last all summer.

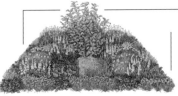

PLANTS *for an* INSTANT DISPLAY

THIS SCHEME MAKES MUCH USE of flowering plants that, although technically classified as perennials or even sub-shrubs, can be used and cultivated as annuals to create an instant effect. The argyranthemums, the verbenas, the diascias, and the salvias all share the cheerful characteristic of flowering continuously right through the season until autumn.

Argyranthemums are not hardy, but you can plunge them in the bed in pots or pot them up before the first frosts and keep them under cover through winter; alternatively, take cuttings in late summer and raise new plants from these to plant out in late spring. The trick with tender plants such as these, as with the true annuals, is to make sure that they do not get such a shock when they are planted out that their growth is checked. If this happens, you will have to wait longer than you need for them to produce flowers. For an early display, make sure that plants reared indoors are properly hardened off before they have to face the harsh world outside. Help them get over the shock of the new by providing plentiful rations of food and water as well.

CARE AND CULTIVATION

SPRING
Plant the magnolia in a sheltered site. In mid-spring, give young magnolias a fertilizer rich in potash, and top-dress the soil each year with leaf mould or compost. Damaged branches can be removed in late spring. Once all danger of frost has passed, plant out verbenas, linarias, snapdragons, diascias, argyranthemums, and senecios.

SUMMER
Dead-head all plants regularly. Give occasional liquid feeds and water during dry spells; in very dry summers, diascias will stop flowering unless well watered. Pinch out leading shoots of verbenas to encourage bushy growth and, in early summer, tips of snapdragons to promote the formation of side shoots. Spray against rust if necessary.

AUTUMN
Lift and pot up argyranthemums if necessary to overwinter in a frost-free place.

WINTER
Protect argyranthemums against frost. Water them sparingly.

Salvia farinacea **'Victoria'** *Perennial with violet flower spikes in summer–autumn. H 45cm (18in), S 30cm (12in).*

Argyranthemum gracile **'Chelsea Girl'** *Sub-shrub with deeply divided leaves and daisy flowers. H and S to 75cm (2½ft).*

Antirrhinum majus, **rust resistant yellow** (Snapdragon) *Bushy, summer-flowering perennial. H and S 45cm (18in).*

Linaria maroccana **'Fairy Lights'** (**Toadflax**) *Annual with snapdragon-like flowers in summer. H and S 20cm (8in).*

Diascia rigescens *Perennial bearing salmon-pink flowers in summer and early autumn. H 23cm (9in), S 30cm (12in).*

Verbena **'Sissinghurst'** *Mat-forming perennial with brilliant pink flowers in summer. H 20cm (8in), S 45cm (18in).*

Magnolia x *soulangeana* *Deciduous tree or shrub bearing large, pink-flushed, white flowers in mid-spring. H and S 6m (20ft).*

Senecio maritima **'Silver Dust'** (**Silver fern**) *Evergreen, bushy sub-shrub, usually grown as an annual, with finely divided, matt, silver leaves. Small, daisy-like, yellow flowerheads appear in summer but are best removed. H and S 30cm (12in).*

Altering *the* Planting Scheme

Shift the balance of colour in this scheme by substituting a different selection of annuals and tender perennials. Replace the pinks and purples of the verbenas, diascias, and linarias with a crisp, white and blue combination of Swan River daisies, lobelias, and *Osteospermum* 'Whirlygig'. The osteospermum has superbly lunatic daisy flowers, each petal neatly pinched in near the centre so that it makes a spoon shape. The flowers are white, washed with dark blue on their backs. The centres are rich, deep blue. Replace the acid yellow snapdragons with rich butter-coloured rudbeckias; these will match the bright yellow centres of the Swan River daisies.

Fresh Blues and Yellows for a Sunny Effect

Use lobelias to edge the bed in the same way that the linarias were used in the main scheme. 'Crystal Palace' has lustrous, dark foliage that is a perfect foil for its flowers and, like all lobelias, is tolerant and free-flowering. The spider plants replace the senecios, warming up the foliage element of the scheme. They are fast growing and their fountains of foliage will make a pleasing contrast with the dumpy annuals. Use the blue Swan River daisies and the yellow rudbeckias in groups around the centre of the bed. The rudbeckias will be later into flower than the daisies as their timetable matches that of the salvias.

Chlorophytum comosum 'Vittatum' (Spider plant) *Tufted, tender perennial with distinctive, green and white-striped leaves. H and S 30cm (12in).*

Rudbeckia hirta 'Marmalade' (Coneflower) *Erect perennial bearing golden-orange flowers with black centres in summer and early autumn. H 45cm (18in), S 30cm (12in).*

Brachycome iberidifolia (Swan River daisy) *Bushy annual with small, fragrant, daisy-like flowers in summer and early autumn. H and S 45cm (18in).*

Osteospermum 'Whirlygig' *Clump-forming, tender, evergreen perennial with grey-green foliage and a lax habit. During summer, it is covered with a mass of bluish-white flowers with deep blue centres. H 60cm (2ft), S 30–45cm (12–18in).*

Lobelia erinus 'Crystal Palace' *Compact annual with bronze leaves and deep blue flowers throughout summer. H 20cm (8in), S 15cm (6in).*

A YEAR-ROUND DISPLAY

ALL-YEAR INTEREST in a garden is a concept that should be carefully appraised. A dozen dwarf conifers in a bed will certainly furnish the space for twelve months of the year, but will your spirits lift when you look at them? Will the plants have sufficient contrast in foliage and form? Will you feel that this is the most exciting, imaginative way to fill the space available?

SPRING BLOSSOM
Prunus 'Tai Haku' is a stunning sight in spring, covered with clusters of white flowers. The blossom contrasts strongly with the young foliage, which is suffused with bronze.

DESIGN POINTS

CONTINUITY AND CHANGE
Evergreens provide continuity and substance throughout the year, while other plants shift the focus of the scheme as the seasons change.

FRESH FLOWERS
Different lilies can be used each year to alter the colour balance and add extra variety.

You certainly need a fair proportion of evergreens in any bed that is planted for winter as well as summer interest, but they need not be dull. There are plenty of plants that will give you abundant opportunity to play with contrasts of shape and texture. Imagine the blood red stems of a dogwood, *Cornus alba*, set against the upright, glossy foliage of *Choisya ternata*, the Mexican orange blossom. Imagine the sculptural, whorled stems of the massive spurge, *Euphorbia characias* subsp. *wulfenii*, soaring above the fine, evergreen foliage of epimediums snuffling round its feet.

PLANT LIST

1 *Epimedium pubigerum* x 6
2 *Cornus alba* 'Elegantissima' (Dogwood) x 1
3 *Bergenia ciliata* x 8
4 *Polystichum setiferum* 'Densum' x 3
5 *Lilium* 'Black Beauty' (Lily) x 16
6 *Cyclamen hederifolium* x 14
7 *Choisya ternata* (Mexican orange blossom) x 1

8 *Tellima grandiflora* 'Purpurea' x 5
9 *Pennisetum villosum* (Feather top) x 3
10 *Prunus* 'Tai Haku' (Great white cherry) x 1
11 *Polystichum setiferum* (Soft shield fern) x 5
12 *Euphorbia characias* subsp. *wulfenii* (Spurge) x 1

PLANTING PLAN

SEASONAL SPLENDOURS
Even a bed with pretensions to a non-stop show should include some plants that peak strongly in one particular season. These accents change the flavour of the bed, as spring moves into summer, autumn into winter. You need this flow of special events in a garden. A bed planted with too many rigid, static plants becomes as tedious as a video stuck on freeze-frame. In spring you need blossom. The choice is enormous: crab apples, amelanchier, hawthorn, and, of course, cherries. This scheme uses the great white cherry 'Tai Haku', but in a small garden you might go for a more compact variety. Make sure that it contributes another special effect in autumn. 'Tai Haku' has leaves that turn a clear, buttery shade of yellow before they fall.

10ft
3m

15ft
5m

THE SCENE IN SPRING
In spring, statuesque, lime-green flowers of the euphorbia rise from mounds of foliage, while abundant, white blossom comes from the cherry and the choisya.

Cornus alba 'Elegantissima'

POLYSTICHUM
Polystichum setiferum 'Densum' is one of the most elegant of the family with finely divided fronds.

EPIMEDIUM
Although the least ornamental in flower, *Epimedium pubigerum* has excellent, smooth, evergreen foliage.

AUTUMN COLOUR
The golden leaves of the cherry lift the scheme in autumn, while strong shards of red come from the bare stems of the dogwood, seen against the green mass of the choisya. The seedheads of the pennisetum are soft and feathery, wonderful to touch.

DOGWOOD
The stems of the dogwood, *Cornus alba* 'Elegantissima', are seen most clearly after leaf fall.

LILY
The mahogany-red petals of *Lilium* 'Black Beauty' curve back to reveal striking black-tipped stamens.

FEATHER TOP
Pennisetum villosum is not fully hardy but bears superb, tufted flowerheads.

GREAT WHITE CHERRY
Where there is space to grow it, *Prunus* 'Tai Haku' – the great white cherry – is the showiest of spring-flowering cherries.

SPURGE
Imposing clumps of winter foliage are joined in spring by the lime-green flowers of the spurge, *Euphorbia characias* subsp. *wulfenii.*

MEXICAN ORANGE BLOSSOM
The luxuriant greenery of *Choisya ternata*, the Mexican orange blossom, makes a handsome backdrop for its pure white flowers.

SOFT SHIELD FERN
The soft shield fern, *Polystichum setiferum*, is tolerant of dry conditions and will thrive almost anywhere.

TELLIMA
Tellima grandiflora 'Purpurea' makes fine, evergreen ground cover and has sprays of creamy bells.

BERGENIA
Bergenia ciliata is only evergreen in the mildest areas, but it has superb, rounded, hairy leaves.

Pennisetum villosum

CYCLAMEN
Leaves and flowers appear separately on *Cyclamen hederifolium*, the foliage providing ornamental winter ground cover.

CARE AND CULTIVATION

SPRING

Plant the choisya, dogwood, pennisetums, and ferns, siting the ferns in a semi-shaded spot. In subsequent years, mulch the choisya and remove any frost-damaged shoots. Cut the dogwood back hard. Remove old foliage of epimediums in early spring before new growth begins. Top-dress epimediums and lilies with sifted compost.

SUMMER

Cut back old, flowered stems of the euphorbia and tellimas. Water ferns in dry spells. Lilies may require staking.

AUTUMN

Plant the cherry, staking it if in an exposed site. Plant euphorbia, choosing a small specimen, and bergenias; congested clumps will need replanting. Plant cyclamens, barely covering the tubers with soil. In subsequent years, top-dress them with sifted leaf mould after flowering. Plant epimediums, tellimas, and – as soon as available – lilies.

WINTER

No routine care is needed in winter.

PLANTS *for* ALL-YEAR INTEREST

THE CORE PLANTS in this scheme provide structure and substance over a long period and need little maintenance. The ferns' elegant new fronds start to unfurl in late spring ready to replace the previous season's foliage; by now this may be rather battered and can be cut away. The choisya needs no regular pruning, but you can cut back any straggly growth after flowering.

In winter, the brightest splash of colour comes from the stems of the dogwood. The fresh, young growth has the strongest colour, so cut it back hard each spring to stimulate a new flush of stems. Give the bed a fresh image each year by changing the variety of lily. You can raise lilies in pots then simply plunge them in the bed for the summer season.

Epimedium pubigerum *Evergreen, carpeting perennial grown for its heart-shaped foliage and creamy-white or pink flowers in spring. H and S 45cm (18in).*

Euphorbia characias subsp. *wulfenii* **(Spurge)** *Evergreen, upright shrub with grey-green leaves and fat spikes of acid green flowers. H to 1.5m (5ft), S 75cm (2½ft).*

Prunus 'Tai Haku' (Great white cherry) *Deciduous, spreading tree with large, single, white flowers in mid-spring. H 8m (25ft), S 10m (30ft).*

Lilium 'Black Beauty' (Lily) *Summer-flowering bulb bearing green-centred, very deep red flowers with curved back petals. H 1.5–2m (5–6ft).*

Cornus alba 'Elegantissima' (Dogwood) *Vigorous, deciduous shrub. Young stems are bright red in winter. H and S 2m (6ft).*

Choisya ternata (Mexican orange blossom) *Evergreen shrub with fragrant, white blooms in late spring. H 2.5m (8ft), S 2.2m (7ft).*

Tellima grandiflora 'Purpurea' *Semi-evergreen perennial with reddish-purple leaves and pinkish-cream flowers in late spring. H and S 60cm (2ft).*

Bergenia ciliata *Clump-forming perennial with large, rounded leaves. In spring, it bears white flowers that age to pink. H 30cm (12in), S 50cm (20in).*

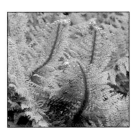

Polystichum setiferum 'Densum' *Evergreen fern with soft-textured, spreading fronds, clothed with white scales as they unfurl. H 60cm (2ft), S 45cm (18in).*

Cyclamen hederifolium syn. *C. neapolitanum* *Tuber with pale to deep pink flowers in autumn and silvery-green, ivy-shaped leaves. H to 10cm (4in), S 10–15cm (4–6in).*

Pennisetum villosum (Feather top) *Herbaceous, tuft-forming, perennial grass covered in fluffy, creamy-pink plumes that fade to pale brown in autumn. H to 1m (3ft), S 50cm (20in).*

Polystichum setiferum (Soft shield fern) *Evergreen fern with finely divided, moss-like fronds that are covered with white scales as they open. H 60cm (2ft), S 45cm (18in).*

Altering *the* Planting Scheme

In areas that have long winters with hard frosts and cutting winds, several plants in the scheme might freeze to death. The choisya, euphorbia, bergenias, cyclamen, and pennisetums will need to be replaced with plants of a more rugged disposition.

Plants for Cold Areas

The biggest loss will be the euphorbia, a child of the balmy Mediterranean. The hellebore used in its place is hardier, but not as dramatic. Its deeply divided foliage eventually makes a handsome, but sober dome. Like many quiet plants, it grows on you. Another hardier euphorbia is used to replace the bergenia. Its foliage is less appealing than the bergenia's, but it is crowned with flowers of an intense acid green.

The pyracantha will provide white blossom a little later than the choisya, with the added benefit of brilliant red berries in winter. Grow a late summer-flowering clematis over it to bridge the gap between flowers and fruit.

Low mats of cool colour come from the textured mass of a blue juniper and the silver leaves of a creeping dead nettle.

Pyracantha x wateri
Glossy-leaved, evergreen shrub bearing white flowers in summer and bright red berries in autumn.
H and S 2.5m (8ft).

Euphorbia cyparissias
(Spurge) *Leafy perennial with grey-green foliage, and lime-green flowers in late spring. H and S 30cm (12in).*

Clematis viticella
'Purpurea Plena Elegans'
Climber with rose-purple flowers in summer–autumn.
H to 4m (12ft), S 1.5m (5ft).

Juniperus squamata 'Blue Star' (Juniper) *Clump-forming, dwarf conifer with dense, grey-blue foliage. H 50cm (20in), S 60cm (2ft).*

Lamium maculatum 'White Nancy' (Dead nettle)
Silver-leaved perennial with white flowers in spring–summer.
H 15cm (6in), S 1m (3ft).

Helleborus foetidus
(Stinking hellebore)
Evergreen perennial with pale green flowers in late winter–spring. H and S 45cm (18in).

A FORMAL HERB DESIGN

THERE IS AN IRRESISTIBLE URGE in a herb garden to classify, sort, and arrange: all mints here; all sages there; all culinary herbs in one corner; all medicinal herbs in another. This may suit the tidy minded but will not necessarily result in a good-looking display. You must decide how much you are prepared to bend the rules.

CONSTANT DISPLAY
The glossy, aromatic foliage of bay, Laurus nobilis, *is a constant feature of the herb garden, staying green all year round. Bay may be clipped to shape.*

DESIGN POINTS

FORMAL LINES
Geometric shapes and a strong, simple pattern create a well-ordered, formal effect.

COLOUR CONTRASTS
Foliage plants such as purple sage and golden hop provide distinctive blocks of colour.

STYLISH SUPPORTS
The climbers can be supported by smart trellis obelisks or simple wigwams of poles. Let the style be dictated by the wider garden setting.

Herb gardens are popular because they can be fitted into the tiniest of spaces. Formality suits them, but the design should not be too intricate. Some herbs flop about a good deal and may upset the finer points of your well-planned symmetry.

Four pyramids of bay mark the inside corners of these herb beds, echoing the tall pyramids of hop on the outside edges. Borders of parsley and chives, invaluable in cooking, surround patches of purple sage, sweet cicely with ferny foliage and edible seeds, and sweet woodruff with leaves that smell of new-mown hay when dried. A herb garden is usually at its peak for just a month in mid-summer. If you want your patch to work harder than that, plant tulips for an early

display among the emerging herbs, and include colourful plants such as nasturtiums or heliotropes to keep the show going in late summer.

PLANT PYRAMIDS FOR HEIGHT

Unless you want a low, Persian carpet effect of thyme, marjoram, chervil, parsley, and mint, you will also need to add some plants to give height. The golden hop, *Humulus lupulus* 'Aureus', is a climber that you can train up tall pyramids in the

GOLDEN HOP
Less vigorous than the plain green hop, this golden variety, *Humulus lupulus* 'Aureus', is easier to contain on a support.

PLANT LIST

1 *Tulipa* 'Orange Favourite' (Parrot tulip) x 60
2 *Laurus nobilis* (Bay) x 4
3 *Eschscholzia californica* (Californian poppy) x 60
4 *Petroselinum crispum* (Parsley) x 48
5 *Allium christophii* x 60
6 *Salvia officinalis* 'Purpurascens' (Purple sage) x 4

7 *Galium odoratum* syn. *Asperula odorata* (Sweet woodruff) x 12
8 *Clematis* 'Jackmanii Superba' x 4
9 *Humulus lupulus* 'Aureus' (Golden hop) x 4
10 *Myrrhis odorata* (Sweet cicely) x 12
11 *Tanacetum parthenium* 'Aureum' (Golden feverfew) x 28
12 *Allium schoenoprasum* (Chives) x 48

PLANTING PLAN

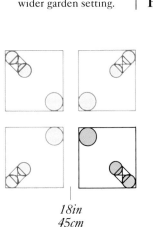

18in
45cm

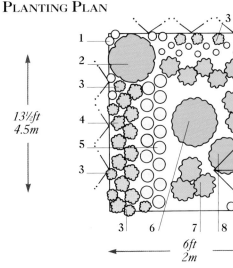

13½ft
4.5m

6ft
2m

6ft
2m

outside corner of each bed. Add some early and late-flowering clematis to make up for the hops' own lack of flowers. For a more formal effect, use standard roses instead of the hop pyramids.

COLOUR CONTRASTS AND HARMONIES

The greenish-yellow of the hops is echoed in the finely cut foliage of the ground-hugging feverfew. Contrasting in colour is the dull purple foliage of the aromatic sage, which grows in a low, sprawling mound. If you think the orange of the parrot tulip, *Tulipa* 'Orange Favourite', makes too violent a contrast with this, choose a dark purple cultivar such as 'Queen of the Night' instead. Add extra colour for summer by scattering seeds of bright annuals such as Californian poppies over any bare patches.

GOLDEN DAYS OF SUMMER

At the height of summer, the golden hops seem to reflect the sunlight back onto the Californian poppies and daisy-like feverfews about their feet. But the whole scheme is not dominated by yellows: the purple clematis, the blue-flowered sage, and the mauve, pompom heads of the chives make a cool contrast.

SPRING SURPRISE

Tulips are not the first thing you would expect to see in a herb bed, but when space needs to be filled in spring, they do the job admirably. The foliage of some herbs tends to be slow coming through and a blast of colour from the bulbs helps to prevent the bed from looking bare.

PARROT TULIP

Tulipa 'Orange Favourite' is a showy parrot tulip, orange-red, feathered with apple-green.

CALIFORNIAN POPPY

Eschscholzia californica has tissue-paper flowers of orange, red, yellow, and cream.

BAY

Laurus nobilis makes a dense, evergreen pyramid, and responds well to being clipped into geometric forms.

CLEMATIS

Few clematis are as generous with their flowers as 'Jackmanii Superba', an old cultivar raised in the middle of the 19th century.

SWEET CICELY

Myrrhis odorata is a charming self-sower, which thrives in sun or shade.

GOLDEN FEVERFEW

The foliage of golden feverfew, *Tanacetum parthenium* 'Aureum', makes bright splashes of colour early in the year and it is a useful self-seeder.

CHIVES

The grassy leaves of chives, *Allium schoenoprasum*, have a more delicate flavour than onions and the pretty, edible flowers may be added to salads.

PURPLE SAGE

The greyish-purple leaves of *Salvia officinalis* 'Purpurascens' combine well with a wide variety of other plants.

PARSLEY

Petroselinum crispum, either curled or flat-leaved parsley, is one of the most useful of all culinary herbs.

ALLIUM

A blown-up version of the common chive, *Allium christophii* has showy, drumstick heads of purple flowers.

SWEET WOODRUFF

In the wild, sweet woodruff, *Galium odoratum*, is found in dappled, wooded areas but adapts easily to most places in the garden.

EDIBLE EDGING *for a* HERB BED

TRADITIONAL HERB GARDENS have box-edged beds. In design terms, this is an advantage: the lines are clearly marked out. In a small space, however, box is unproductive and greedy.

Chives and parsley are both good, edible alternatives; in this scheme, the edging plants follow the lines of the paths, chives in one direction, parsley in the other. Unfortunately, chives dive underground in the winter, but do not hold that against them. The pinkish-purple lollipop flowers on the green stems in summer make up for that. Parsley is a biennial and will need renewing every couple of years. The curly-leaved parsley makes the prettiest edging, but the flat-leaved type has the best flavour.

If necessary, paths in the herb garden can be very narrow, just wide enough to shuffle along for picking and weeding. Bricks, laid on edge, have a more interesting texture than concrete slabs. If the ground is not too sticky, leave the paths as plain beaten earth.

Humulus lupulus 'Aureus' (Golden hop) *Twining climber with greenish-yellow, divided foliage. H to 6m (20ft).*

Galium odoratum syn. **Asperula odorata (Sweet woodruff)** *Perennial with white flowers in summer. H 15cm (6in), S 30cm (12in).*

Clematis 'Jackmanii Superba' *Vigorous climber producing single, purple flowers in mid-summer. H 3m (10ft), S 1m (3ft).*

Salvia officinalis 'Purpurascens' (Purple sage) *Semi-evergreen shrub with purple, aromatic foliage. H 60cm (2ft), S 1m (3ft).*

Myrrhis odorata (Sweet cicely) *Perennial with fragrant, white flowers in early summer. H 1m (3ft), S 60cm (2ft).*

Eschscholzia californica (Californian poppy) *Annual with red, orange, or yellow flowers in summer. H 30cm (12in), S 15cm (6in).*

Allium christophii *Summer-flowering bulb with spherical, purplish-violet flowerheads. H 40cm (16in), S 20cm (8in).*

Petroselinum crispum (Parsley) *Biennial with ornamental, curly-edged, bright green leaves. H and S 30cm (12in).*

Tulipa 'Orange Favourite' (Parrot tulip) *Spring-flowering bulb with orange-red blooms. H to 60cm (2ft), S to 20cm (8in).*

Tanacetum parthenium 'Aureum' (Golden feverfew) *Perennial with greenish-gold foliage. H and S 20–45cm (8–18in).*

Allium schoenoprasum (Chives) *Clump-forming bulb with pink or mauve flowers in summer. H 25cm (10in), S 10cm (4in).*

Laurus nobilis (Bay) *Dense, evergreen tree with glossy, tough, aromatic leaves. H to 12m (40ft), S to 10m (30ft).*

ALTERING *the* PLANTING SCHEME

EVERYONE HAS THEIR OWN FAVOURITE HERBS and the plan below shows how you can substitute other herbs of your choice in the bed; those used here are good for cooking. You could also add a large, decorative terracotta pot to the scheme, placing it as a centrepiece where the two paths cross. Scented-leaved pelargoniums would fit in well with the theme of the bed; the aromatic leaves borrow their scents from other plants like peppermint, lemon, pine, and even roses. Surround the pelargoniums with *Convolvulus sabatius*, planted to tumble over the side of the pot. For a hotter effect, use trailing nasturtiums; as well as being attractive, their colourful flowers and peppery leaves make an unusual, edible addition to salads.

Coriandrum sativum (**Coriander**) *Annual with aromatic, scalloped leaves and pale flowers in summer, followed by edible seeds. H 60cm (2ft), S 30cm (12in).*

CULINARY HERBS WITH A FOCAL POINT

Instead of the hops, use bronze fennel to give height at each corner of bed. Its fine, filigree foliage is topped with flat heads of flowers. Substitute coriander for the sweet cicely: its leaves are essential for cooking Indian-style. It is easy to grow from seed, but some varieties quickly leap up into flower without much leaf. The flowers eventually turn into seeds, which are also useful in cooking, but if it is leaves you want, choose your variety with care.

For extra colour, add scented-leaved pelargoniums in a large pot. In very mild areas, they may overwinter outside. In cool regions, take cuttings or move the plants under cover until spring.

Pelargonium tomentosum (**Peppermint-scented geranium**) *Tender, evergreen, bushy perennial with strongly scented, velvety, grey-green leaves and clusters of small, white flowers. H 30–60cm (12–24in), S to 1m (3ft).*

Convolvulus sabatius *Trailing perennial with purplish-blue, flat trumpet flowers throughout summer. It is not hardy and should be overwintered in a greenhouse. H 15–20cm (6–8in), S 30cm (12in).*

Foeniculum vulgare '**Purpureum**' (**Bronze fennel**) *Tall, upright perennial with finely divided, feathery, bronze leaves, which have an aniseed fragrance, and heads of golden flowers. H 2m (6ft), S 45cm (18in).*

FLOWERS *and* FRUITS

A SINGLE FRUIT TREE can scarcely be called an orchard but in a small garden where every plant has to work hard for its living, one is better than none. A fruit tree is as beautiful to look at in spring as any purely ornamental tree and twice as useful in autumn when you can gather in your own home-grown fruit.

ROSY CHEEKS
The fruits of the pear
Pyrus communis
'Marguerite Marillat'
*are flushed with warm
coppery-red.*

DESIGN POINTS

ADDING HEIGHT
The upright form of the pear tree allows planting beneath it and lends height and structure to the scheme.

REPEAT PATTERNS
Using the same plant several times, such as the London pride here, creates a degree of patterning that pulls mixed plantings together.

A PEAR OF GRACEFUL STATURE
This scheme is built around a pear, but you could adapt the planting to fit around a tree that you already have in your garden. If buying a tree, choose a half-standard – one that has 1.2–1.5m (4–5ft) of clean, straight trunk below its branches. This will make a far more graceful and long-lived tree than a dwarf type and will also give a pleasant feeling of permanence to a new and perhaps rather bare garden.

Your pear will need a partner to help it set fruit, a pollinator not more than a bee's hop away. Bees hop surprisingly long distances, so the pollinator need not be in your own garden, but you should check with a specialist fruit nursery which varieties are compatible with your chosen pear before you buy.

AN ISLAND PLANTING
Use the pear as the off-centrepiece of an island planting with a crambe to take over the starring role in summer. When the pear blossoms in spring, the crambe will be nothing more than a low mound of leaves. Then in early summer it erupts, with huge clouds of tiny, white flowers held on towering stems. The crambe has large, heavy leaves; do not be tempted to plant other perennials too close to it. In spring there may seem to be spare space. Fill it with bulbs that can get their act over before the crambe gets into its stride.

Beneath the pear, grey-leaved senecio provides bulk and winter furnishing. For this scheme, dominated by pinks and mauves, you should cut off its yellow flowers as they open. Wherever you can find room, push in a few alpine strawberry plants. The leaves are decorative, and the small, succulent fruits provide a welcome reward during summer weeding sessions.

PLANTING PLAN

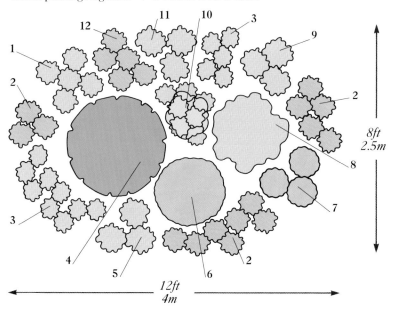

8ft
2.5m

12ft
4m

PLANT LIST
1 *Fragaria vesca* (Alpine strawberry) x 5
2 *Saxifraga* × *urbium* (London pride) x 15
3 *Viola* 'Nellie Britton' and 'Primrose Dame' x 14
4 *Pyrus communis* 'Marguerite Marillat' (Pear) x 1
5 *Geranium* 'Johnson's Blue' x 3
6 *Senecio* 'Sunshine' x 1
7 *Helianthemum* 'Wisley Pink' (Rock rose) x 3
8 *Crambe cordifolia* x 1
9 *Geranium psilostemon* x 3
10 *Digitalis purpurea* 'Suttons Apricot' (Foxglove) x 7 and *Cleome hassleriana* 'Colour Fountain' (Spider flower) x 7
11 *Sedum spectabile* 'Brilliant' (Ice plant) x 3
12 *Pulmonaria saccharata* (Lungwort) x 5

ALPINE STRAWBERRY
As well as delicious fruits, *Fragaria vesca* has attractive, rounded leaves.

Saxifraga × *urbium*

YELLOW VIOLA
Viola 'Primrose Dame' flowers from mid-spring through until early autumn.

BLUE GERANIUM
Elegant, divided leaves make dense ground cover over which *Geranium* 'Johnson's Blue' sends up stems of fine china blue flowers.

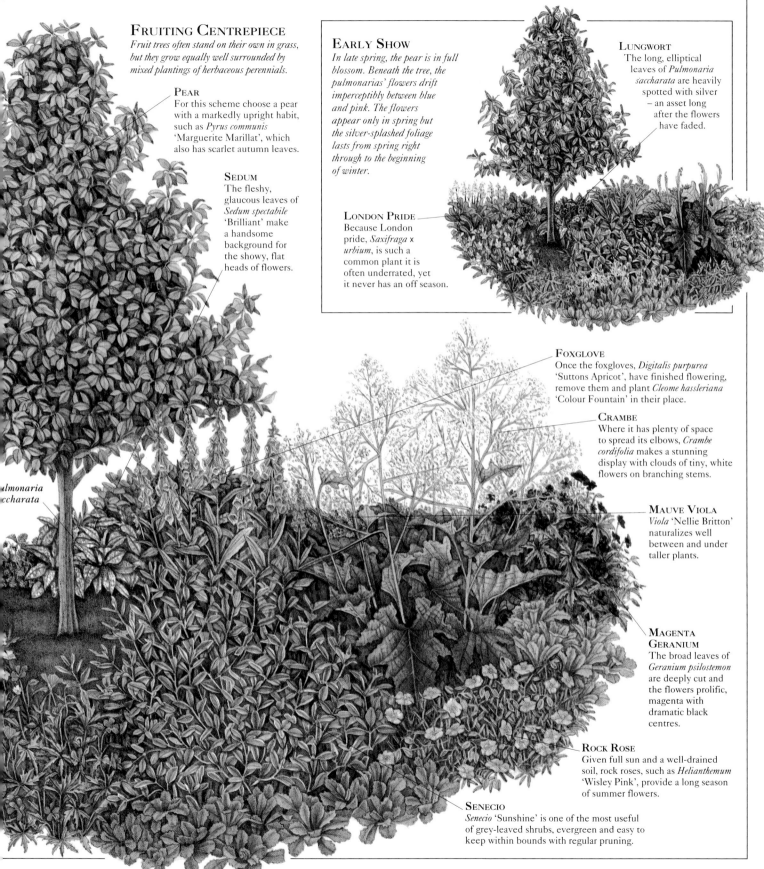

FRUITING CENTREPIECE
Fruit trees often stand on their own in grass, but they grow equally well surrounded by mixed plantings of herbaceous perennials.

PEAR
For this scheme choose a pear with a markedly upright habit, such as *Pyrus communis* 'Marguerite Marillat', which also has scarlet autumn leaves.

SEDUM
The fleshy, glaucous leaves of *Sedum spectabile* 'Brilliant' make a handsome background for the showy, flat heads of flowers.

EARLY SHOW
In late spring, the pear is in full blossom. Beneath the tree, the pulmonarias' flowers drift imperceptibly between blue and pink. The flowers appear only in spring but the silver-splashed foliage lasts from spring right through to the beginning of winter.

LONDON PRIDE
Because London pride, *Saxifraga* x *urbium*, is such a common plant it is often underrated, yet it never has an off season.

LUNGWORT
The long, elliptical leaves of *Pulmonaria saccharata* are heavily spotted with silver – an asset long after the flowers have faded.

Pulmonaria saccharata

FOXGLOVE
Once the foxgloves, *Digitalis purpurea* 'Suttons Apricot', have finished flowering, remove them and plant *Cleome hassleriana* 'Colour Fountain' in their place.

CRAMBE
Where it has plenty of space to spread its elbows, *Crambe cordifolia* makes a stunning display with clouds of tiny, white flowers on branching stems.

MAUVE VIOLA
Viola 'Nellie Britton' naturalizes well between and under taller plants.

MAGENTA GERANIUM
The broad leaves of *Geranium psilostemon* are deeply cut and the flowers prolific, magenta with dramatic black centres.

ROCK ROSE
Given full sun and a well-drained soil, rock roses, such as *Helianthemum* 'Wisley Pink', provide a long season of summer flowers.

SENECIO
Senecio 'Sunshine' is one of the most useful of grey-leaved shrubs, evergreen and easy to keep within bounds with regular pruning.

FLOWER FILLERS *for* LATE SUMMER

TO KEEP THIS BORDER going through the second half of summer, you will need to replace the foxgloves with later-flowering annuals. Cleomes have the necessary height and will flower until the first frosts with large heads of pink and white. Pull up the foxgloves when they have finished but leave one to set and ripen seed. Shake the stem over the earth where you want the next batch of plants to grow and save yourself the bother of raising fresh plants in seed trays. Alternatively, buy plants in early spring which will flower at the beginning of summer.

CARE AND CULTIVATION

SPRING
Protect young growths of the crambe against slugs. Tidy up dead leaves and stems of geraniums. Remove dead flower stems from pulmonarias and mulch around the plants. Stake sedums if necessary.

SUMMER
Replace foxgloves after flowering with cleomes. Clip flowerheads from the senecio as they appear. Cut back flower stems of geraniums to encourage a second show and shear over helianthemums after flowering. Dead-head all plants as necessary. Shear off straggly growths of violas in late summer.

AUTUMN
Plant the pear in late autumn or early winter, staking it firmly in position. Cut sedum flowers for drying.

WINTER
Cut down flowering stems of the crambe and cut back sedums.

Sedum spectabile 'Brilliant' (Ice plant) *Perennial with pink flowers in late summer–autumn. H and S to 45cm (18in).*

Geranium psilostemon *Summer-flowering perennial with black-centred, magenta flowers. H and S 75cm (2½ft).*

Fragaria vesca (Alpine strawberry) *Perennial bearing small, sweetly flavoured fruits. H 30cm (12in), S 45cm (18in).*

Pulmonaria saccharata (Lungwort) *Spring-flowering perennial with leaves blotched with silver. H 30cm (12in), S 60cm (2ft).*

Digitalis purpurea 'Suttons Apricot' (Foxglove) *Perennial grown as a biennial. H to 1.5m (5ft), S 60cm (2ft).*

Cleome hassleriana 'Colour Fountain' (Spider flower) *Pink- or white-flowered annual. H 1.2m (4ft), S 45cm (18in).*

Viola 'Nellie Britton' *Perennial with brownish-mauve flowers in spring and summer. H and S 15cm (6in).*

Pyrus communis 'Marguerite Marillat' *Upright, deciduous tree with edible fruits. H 4–5.5m (12–18ft), S 3m (10ft).*

Crambe cordifolia *Perennial with fragrant, white flowers in summer above large, crinkled leaves. H to 2m (6ft), S 1.2m (4ft).*

Geranium 'Johnson's Blue' *Perennial with deep lavender-blue flowers borne throughout summer. H 30cm (12in), S 60cm (2ft).*

Senecio 'Sunshine' *Evergreen, mound-forming shrub with grey leaves and clusters of yellow flowers. H 75cm (2½ft), S 1.5m (5ft).*

Saxifraga x urbium (London pride) *Evergreen perennial with small flowers in late spring. H 30cm (12in), S indefinite.*

Helianthemum 'Wisley Pink' (Rock rose) *Evergreen shrub with pale pink summer flowers. H and S 30cm (12in) or more.*

ALTERING *the* PLANTING SCHEME

BULBS ARE WHAT YOU NEED to bring this bed to life in early spring, when only the pulmonarias will be in flower. Bulbs are the garden's buried treasure and the best thing about them is that so often you forget you have planted them. Suddenly in spring, there they are, beaming and bountiful.

A PATCHWORK PLANTING OF BULBS

A good spring display requires forethought and a dedicated autumn planting session. Bulbs should be put in after perennials, otherwise you are in danger of digging up the one while planting the other. Use daffodils around the pear tree, with crocuses around the crambe. The crocuses will be up, out, and over before the crambe even starts to heave itself out of its winter bed. Another patch of early crocuses can fill in between the violas and the geraniums, with De Caen Group anemones to fill in any other spaces. Use bulbs to boost the display at the end of the season, too, putting in galtonias and nerines for extra colour in late summer and autumn.

Anemone coronaria
De Caen Group *Spring-flowering, tuberous perennial with white, blue, or red flowers, each surrounded by a neat, green ruff. H 15–30cm (6–12in).*

Crocus tommasinianus
Early spring-flowering corm with lilac-purple blooms. H to 10cm (4in), S 2.5–8cm (1–3in).

Galtonia candicans
(Summer hyacinth) *Late summer-flowering bulb with fleshy, strap-shaped leaves and spikes of hanging, white flowers. H to 1.2m (4ft), S 20cm (8in).*

Narcissus **'Pheasant's Eye'**
(Daffodil) *Bulb bearing pure white flowers with stubby, orange-red trumpets in late spring. H 45cm (18in), S to 20cm (8in).*

Crocus **'Snow Bunting'**
Spring-flowering corm bearing fragrant, funnel-shaped, white flowers with mustard-yellow centres. H to 10cm (4in), S 2.5–8cm (1–3in).

Nerine bowdenii *Autumn-flowering bulb bearing a head of glistening, pink flowers with frilled petals. It is a tender plant that may suffer in severe winters. H 45–60cm (18–24in), S 12–15cm (5–6in).*

A LOW-MAINTENANCE SCHEME

DECIDUOUS AZALEAS IN RICH SHADES of yellow and orange are the dominant feature of this bed, planned for plants that like acid soil. These vibrant colours are set off by the cool tones of an evergreen rhododendron and the restrained foliage of a Korean fir. The fir is like a sober-suited chaperone, keeping an eye on a gaggle of artless ingenues, out in their new spring clothes.

SPRING SHOW
The glorious blooms of Rhododendron *'Frome'* bring a brilliant splash of fiery colour to the bed in spring.

DESIGN POINTS

❧

GOING WILD
An informal scheme perfect for a semi-wild or wooded area.

❧

EASY CARE
Suitable for a site where access is awkward, such as a bank, as little maintenance is needed.

Schemes that are composed mainly of shrubs, as this one is, generally require a lot less maintenance than beds of mixed perennials. These plants do not need lifting or dividing. They do not need pruning. They are hardy and grow in sun or shade, although a site that gives them a bit of both is what they like best. In the wild, rhododendrons often grow in woodland; this informal bed would sit particularly well near the perimeter of a garden where there are trees beyond, echoing the rhododendrons' natural habitat.

COLOUR FOR SPRING AND AUTUMN
Spring will be the most eye-catching season for this bed, with a succession of flowers – yellow, orange, greenish-white, and blue from the azaleas. The evergreen *Rhododendron hippophaeoides* will provide the first spring flowers in this scheme, appearing sometimes six weeks before the heavily scented blooms of *Rhododendron luteum*.

In autumn, the gentian starts its searing display with flowers a more vivid blue than any artist would ever dare use. These will lap round the feet of the fir and make a brilliant pool in front of the acer, alight in its autumn leaves. The yellow azaleas used in this bed are all deciduous. What you lose in winter you gain in autumn, however, for the leaves, before they fall, turn rich, burnished shades of bronze, red, and orange.

EVERGREEN CONTINUITY
For evergreen steadfastness you can depend on the fir, which grows slowly to make a broadly conical tree. This handsome conifer has the obliging habit of growing fir cones while it is still young. You can expect them on trees no more than 1m (3ft) high. The cones stand upright, like fat candles on a Christmas tree, borne usually along the topmost branches. They are an astonishing shade of violet blue, almost the same colour as the blue azalea.

The arbutus is the chief, long-term landscape feature in this scheme. In the *really* long term, you may have to dispense with the fir. There will not be room for them both, but since both take a very long time to reach maturity, you need not lose sleep over this at the outset.

PLANTING PLAN

15ft
5m

15ft
5m

PLANT LIST
1 *Gentiana sino-ornata* (Gentian) x 12
2 *Rhododendron luteum* (Azalea) x 1
3 *Polypodium vulgare* (Polypody) x 10
4 *Acer palmatum* 'Dissectum' (Japanese maple) x 1
5 *Rhododendron* 'Frome' (Azalea) x 1
6 *Rhododendron* 'Narcissiflorum' (Azalea) x 1
7 *Rhododendron hippophaeoides* x 1
8 *Arbutus unedo* (Strawberry tree) x 1
9 *Hosta* 'Royal Standard' x 5
10 *Rhododendron* 'Palestrina' (Azalea) x 1
11 *Abies koreana* (Korean fir) x 1

A WEALTH OF BRIGHT BLOOMS
In late spring, the bed is ablaze with the yellow and orange flowers of the azaleas. Cool contrasts are provided by the mass of the Korean fir and the pale green leaves of the acer.

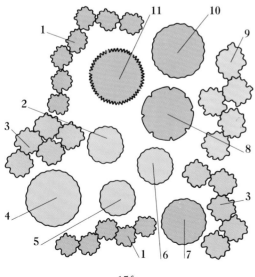

POLYPODY
Polypodium vulgare provides ornamental ground cover with its deeply cut leaves.

JAPANESE MAPLE
Japanese maples, such as *Acer palmatum* 'Dissectum', are very slow-growing, eventually forming low mounds wider than they are high.

AUTUMN TINTS
The brilliant colours of the acer and the bronze tones of the deciduous azaleas give the scheme a second season of interest.

STRAWBERRY TREE
Arbutus unedo bears flowers and fruits together in early autumn.

GENTIAN
Gentiana sino-ornata is covered in autumn by azure-blue trumpet flowers.

FRAGRANT AZALEA
The double, pale-yellow flowers of *Rhododendron* 'Narcissiflorum' are sweetly scented and grow on a vigorous, upright bush.

Arbutus unedo

WHITE AZALEA
Rhododendron 'Palestrina' is a compact, evergreen azalea with funnel-shaped, white flowers.

HOSTA
Broad, heart-shaped leaves set off the late blooms of the fine *Hosta* 'Royal Standard'.

ORANGE AZALEA
Rhododendron 'Frome', a deciduous azalea of shrubby habit, bears orange-yellow flowers.

YELLOW AZALEA
The only European native azalea, *Rhododendron luteum* has yellow, sweetly scented flowers that appear before the leaves.

RHODODENDRON
Rhododendron hippophaeoides, one of the hardiest and most easily grown of the dwarf rhododendrons, bears flowers of a cool lavender-blue.

KOREAN FIR
The sparse, dark green leaves of *Abies koreana* have bright silvery undersides.

Gentiana sino-ornata

83

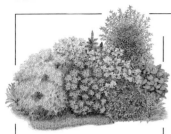

ACID-LOVING PLANTS *for* DAPPLED SHADE

IF YOU CHOOSE A SITUATION under trees for this scheme, it is a good idea to enrich the soil at planting time with leaf mould and bone meal. Ground in which trees are growing is often starved and, although none of these plants is outstandingly greedy, all will grow better with the benefit of special rations.

Do not be tempted to grow rhododendrons if your soil is very alkaline. However hard you try, it will be difficult to make them happy. The leaves will mope, becoming blotchy yellow instead of glossy green. Flowering will be sparse. The plants will look at you accusingly each time you pass, reminding you that they were made for a better kind of life than you will ever be able to give them.

Like most of its kind, the little polypody fern is happiest out of full sun; taller plants growing nearby can provide the necessary shade. Cut down the old fronds in spring so that you can take full advantage of the drama of the bright green new ones unfurling.

CARE AND CULTIVATION

— ❧ —

SPRING

Plant the fir in mid-spring in a lightly shaded position that will give protection from late spring frosts. Choose a plant with a single, strong leading shoot; if a secondary shoot appears, prune it out flush with the trunk. In late spring, feed the fir and rhododendrons, and mulch. Arbutus needs no regular pruning but cut straggly shoots flush with the main stem in mid-spring. Protect emerging shoots of hostas from slugs. Divide and replant congested clumps if necessary. Plant ferns, setting the rhizomes just beneath the soil surface; anchor them with small stones if necessary. Cut down old fronds of ferns.

— ❧ —

SUMMER

Pinch out dead rhododendron flowers.

— ❧ —

AUTUMN

Plant the acer and arbutus in positions sheltered from wind. Plant gentians and hostas, enriching the soil with leaf mould. Plant rhododendrons.

— ❧ —

WINTER

Protect young arbutus with bracken or straw. Clear dead leaves and flower stems of hostas.

***Gentiana sino-ornata* (Gentian)** *Evergreen perennial with rich blue flowers in autumn. H 5cm (2in), S to 30cm (12in).*

***Arbutus unedo* (Strawberry tree)** *Evergreen, spreading tree or shrub. White flowers appear in autumn–winter as previous season's strawberry-like fruits ripen. H and S 7m (22ft).*

***Rhododendron* 'Palestrina' (Azalea)** *Compact, evergreen shrub bearing white flowers. H and S to 1.2m (4ft).*

***Polypodium vulgare* (Polypody)** *Evergreen fern with herringbone-like, narrow fronds. H and S 25–30cm (10–12in).*

***Rhododendron luteum* (Azalea)** *Deciduous shrub with yellow flowers and richly coloured autumn leaves. H and S 1.5–2.5m (5–8ft).*

***Abies koreana* (Korean fir)** *Slow-growing conifer with violet-blue cones. Needles have silver undersides. H to 10m (30ft), S 1.5m (5ft).*

***Hosta* 'Royal Standard'** *Clump-forming perennial with broadly oval, pale green leaves. H 60cm (2ft), S 1.2m (4ft).*

***Acer palmatum* 'Dissectum' (Japanese maple)** *Deciduous shrub with finely divided foliage. H 1m (3ft), S 1.5m (5ft).*

***Rhododendron* 'Frome' (Azalea)** *Spring-flowering, deciduous shrub with colourful autumn foliage. H and S to 1.5m (5ft).*

***Rhododendron* 'Narcissiflorum' (Azalea)** *Deciduous shrub with scented flowers. H and S 2m (6ft).*

Rhododendron hippophaeoides *Evergreen shrub with grey-green leaves and lavender-blue flowers in spring. H and S 1.5m (5ft).*

ALTERING *the* PLANTING SCHEME

THIS SCHEME SUBSTITUTES rich crimson, magenta, and pale pink shades for the bright yellow and slate blue of the original scheme. The two Kurume azaleas are more compact than the yellow ones they replace and you may find that the scheme fits into a smaller planting space. These substitutes will change the character as well as the colour of the bed.

The plants are lower, denser, less wild looking. Here, the emphasis is still on azaleas, but you could include a camellia instead of one of the azaleas in order to extend the season of interest. The camellia will bloom in early spring, two months ahead of the azaleas. A sturdy, weatherproof variety such as *Camellia* x *williamsii* 'Brigadoon' would be a good choice.

Eucryphia glutinosa
Deciduous tree with leaves that turn orange-red in autumn and scented, white flowers in summer. H to 10m (30ft), S 6m (20ft).

COMPACT PLANTS IN PINK AND WHITE

These, of course, are acid-loving shrubs and must have lime-free soil to grow happily. The eucryphia likes the same kind of conditions as the arbutus, but it is deciduous and does not grow as big.

The Kurume azaleas flower most freely in warm, sunny areas. In wet regions, they sometimes become straggly and may need careful cutting back. *Rhododendron yakushimanum* can take any amount of rain, for its home is in the windy, sodden mountains of Yakushima Island in Japan. Its strength is its foliage. The leaves curve down slightly at the edges and are covered underneath with rich rust-coloured felting. The new leaves are powdered with silver.

Rhododendron 'Strawberry Ice' (Azalea) *Deciduous, bushy shrub. In spring it bears deep pink buds that open to flesh-pink blooms with yellow throats. H and S 1.5–2.5m (5–8ft).*

Rhododendron 'Hatsugiri' (Kurume azalea) *Compact, evergreen shrub that bears a mass of small, bright crimson-purple flowers in spring. H and S 60cm (2ft).*

Rhododendron 'Hinodegiri' (Kurume azalea) *Compact, evergreen shrub that bears abundant, small, funnel-shaped, bright crimson flowers in late spring. Thrives in sun or light shade. H and S 1.5m (5ft).*

Rhododendron yakushimanum *Slow-growing, compact, evergreen shrub. Oval leaves are silvery at first, maturing to deep green. In late spring, pale pink flowers appear and gradually fade to white. H 1m (3ft), S 1.5m (5ft).*

CORNER SITES

&.

Corners provide special opportunities in gardens, whether open and sunny, dark and mysterious, or even awkward and narrow. Sometimes a sheltered corner will give just enough extra protection to a plant of borderline hardiness to see it through the winter. Some corners call for dramatic focal plants, placed to attract your attention. The positioning of these will depend on how you approach and view your corner.

TACTILE PLEASURE
It is hard to pass by the pleated, downy leaves of Alchemilla mollis, *lady's mantle, without reaching out to touch them. After a shower, raindrops cling to the leaves like beads of mercury.*

DESIGN POINTS

SURFACE CONTRASTS
Woolly willow contrasts with waxy euphorbia and the gleaming leaves of hebe.

BALANCED FORMS
Plants of differing habit are used to create balance and variety – softly rounded mounds of hostas and alchemillas are balanced by sternly upright irises and veratrums and fountain-like dieramas.

WATERY IMAGES
Wands of pink-flowered dierama arch over the water, creating intriguing reflections.

WATERSIDE TEXTURES

THE TEXTURE OF A PLANT'S LEAVES is one of those quiet pleasures that you take for granted, like the softness of wool or the shininess of a well-polished table. It is a less immediately eye-catching attribute than the leaf's colour and shape, but leaves too may be woolly or smooth, shiny or matt. Their surfaces may be prickly or silky soft, crinkled or plain, waxy, sticky, or slippery as an ice cube.

Touching leaves is just like feeling different kinds of fabric: silk, satin, linen, angora, felt, wool. *Veratrum nigrum*, in this scheme grouped around a formal pool, has leaves like permanently pleated silk. Use it with mounds of alchemilla and domes of evergreen hebe. The form of these leaves differs markedly, which is a good reason for using them together, but the effect is enhanced by the contrasts in texture: pleated silk veratrum, alchemilla with the texture of brushed cotton, and dull satin hebe.

Often a plant's botanical name will give you a clue as to its outstanding characteristic. The *nigrum* of *Veratrum nigrum* refers to the purple-black flowers. A woolly texture is often signalled by the word *lanata*. The well-known lamb's tongue, *Stachys lanata* (now renamed *Stachys byzantina*), sprawls over the apex of the corner. The woolly willow, *Salix lanata*, is set off by the iris and the waxy-textured leaves of a large hosta.

CONTRASTING FORMS
In a scheme where you want to see beyond the planting to another feature such as a pool, you need to keep most of the plants low, but the tall, sword leaves of iris and dierama will add vertical emphasis. The dieramas will surge dramatically out of the textured carpet, but are airy enough to see through. The habit of the dierama is best explained by its common name, angel's fishing rod. Its wiry stems arch from the centre of the clump, exploding into a shower of pink bells. The flowers are attached to the stems by a thread so fine they look as though they are suspended, magically, in space.

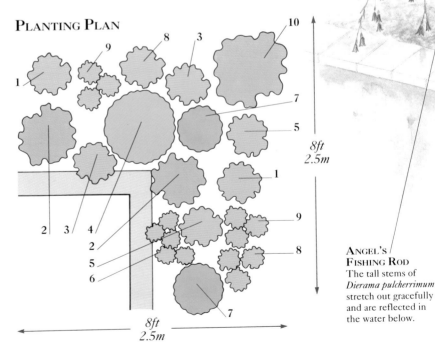

PLANT LIST
1 *Salvia argentea* x 2
2 *Dierama pulcherrimum* (Angel's fishing rod) x 2
3 *Hosta sieboldiana* var. *elegans* x 2
4 *Salix lanata* (Woolly willow) x 1
5 *Alchemilla mollis* (Lady's mantle) x 2
6 *Iris ensata* 'Alba' (Japanese flag) x 5
7 *Hebe albicans* x 2
8 *Euphorbia seguieriana* (Spurge) x 4
9 *Veratrum nigrum* (Black false hellebore) x 6
10 *Stachys byzantina* syn. *S. lanata* (Lamb's tongue) x 1

PLANTING PLAN

8ft 2.5m

8ft 2.5m

ANGEL'S FISHING ROD
The tall stems of *Dierama pulcherrimum* stretch out gracefully and are reflected in the water below.

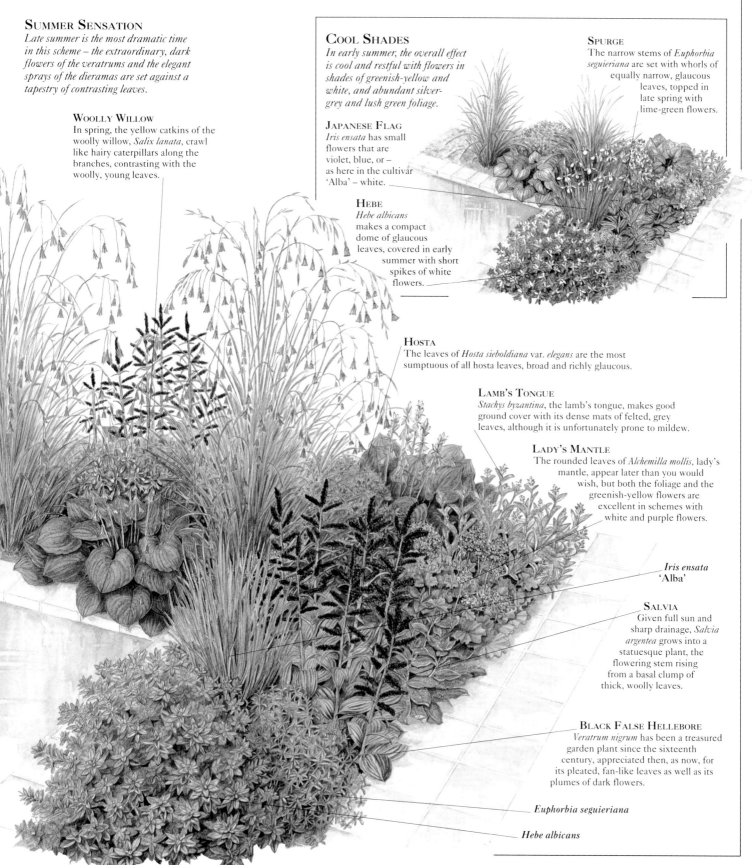

SUMMER SENSATION
Late summer is the most dramatic time in this scheme – the extraordinary, dark flowers of the veratrums and the elegant sprays of the dieramas are set against a tapestry of contrasting leaves.

WOOLLY WILLOW
In spring, the yellow catkins of the woolly willow, *Salix lanata*, crawl like hairy caterpillars along the branches, contrasting with the woolly, young leaves.

COOL SHADES
In early summer, the overall effect is cool and restful with flowers in shades of greenish-yellow and white, and abundant silver-grey and lush green foliage.

JAPANESE FLAG
Iris ensata has small flowers that are violet, blue, or – as here in the cultivar 'Alba' – white.

HEBE
Hebe albicans makes a compact dome of glaucous leaves, covered in early summer with short spikes of white flowers.

SPURGE
The narrow stems of *Euphorbia seguieriana* are set with whorls of equally narrow, glaucous leaves, topped in late spring with lime-green flowers.

HOSTA
The leaves of *Hosta sieboldiana* var. *elegans* are the most sumptuous of all hosta leaves, broad and richly glaucous.

LAMB'S TONGUE
Stachys byzantina, the lamb's tongue, makes good ground cover with its dense mats of felted, grey leaves, although it is unfortunately prone to mildew.

LADY'S MANTLE
The rounded leaves of *Alchemilla mollis*, lady's mantle, appear later than you would wish, but both the foliage and the greenish-yellow flowers are excellent in schemes with white and purple flowers.

Iris ensata
'Alba'

SALVIA
Given full sun and sharp drainage, *Salvia argentea* grows into a statuesque plant, the flowering stem rising from a basal clump of thick, woolly leaves.

BLACK FALSE HELLEBORE
Veratrum nigrum has been a treasured garden plant since the sixteenth century, appreciated then, as now, for its pleated, fan-like leaves as well as its plumes of dark flowers.

Euphorbia seguieriana

Hebe albicans

PLANTS *for* FOLIAGE EFFECTS

THE MASSIVE VARIATION IN THE TEXTURE of plants is not a show put on solely for our tactile delight, but is usually their response to a particular set of growing conditions or problems. For example, the hairs that give woolly plants their distinctive appearance protect them from the intense light of high altitudes and insulate them from extremes of temperature; many woolly plants grow in deserts or freezing upland steppes. The ones used in this planting scheme mostly do best in soil that never dries out.

The salvias need good drainage. They are best grown as biennials and may need to be replaced every couple of years. The leaves of the first year – silvery, thickly furred rosettes – are very much better than the flowers of the second.

The rhizomes of the veratrums do best in moist, light soil in a semi-shaded position. Applying a thick mulch in late spring will help to create the kind of conditions they most enjoy. Unfortunately, slugs love them, so – like the hostas – they must be well protected.

CARE AND CULTIVATION

SPRING
Plant dieramas, salvias, and stachys. Clear damaged leaves from plants before new growth starts. Protect hostas against slugs. Plant irises, euphorbias, and hebes. Hebes need no regular pruning, but cut back winter-damaged growth now. Do not let soil dry out round veratrums; mulch if necessary in late spring. Congested iris clumps will occasionally need to be divided.

SUMMER
Dead-head hebes. Cut out flowered stems of euphorbias. Cut back stems of alchemillas as flowers fade and shear over foliage to encourage fresh growth.

AUTUMN
Plant hostas in soil enriched with compost or leaf mould. Plant veratrums in a moist, slightly shaded position. Plant alchemillas. Cut down stems of dieramas as flowers fade. In very cold areas, lift corms and overwinter under cover.

WINTER
Cut down stems of veratrums.

Euphorbia seguieriana (Spurge) *Perennial with narrow leaves and clusters of yellowish-green flowers. H and S 45cm (18in).*

Hosta sieboldiana var. **elegans** *Clump-forming perennial with bluish-grey, ribbed leaves. H 1m (3ft), S 1.5m (5ft).*

Stachys byzantina syn. **S. lanata** (Lamb's tongue) *Perennial with woolly, grey foliage. H to 38cm (15in), S 60cm (2ft).*

Salvia argentea *Rosette-forming perennial with woolly, silver foliage, and white flowers in summer. H to 1m (3ft), S 45cm (18in).*

Salix lanata (Woolly willow) *Slow-growing shrub with thickly textured, grey leaves. H and S to 1.2m (4ft).*

Hebe albicans *Dense, evergreen shrub with blue-grey foliage, and small, white flowers from early summer. H and S 1.5m (5ft).*

Dierama pulcherrimum (Angel's fishing rod) *Evergreen perennial with strap-like leaves, and deep pink flowers in summer. H 1.5m (5ft), S 30cm (1ft).*

Alchemilla mollis (Lady's mantle) *Clump-forming perennial with downy leaves and greenish-yellow flowers. H and S 50cm (20in).*

Iris ensata 'Alba' *Rhizomatous perennial with white flowers and leaves with a prominent midrib. H to 1m (3ft), S indefinite.*

Veratrum nigrum (Black false hellebore) *Erect perennial with oval leaves, and dark purple flowers from late summer. H 2m (6ft), S 60cm (2ft).*

ALTERING *the* PLANTING SCHEME

MANY EVERGREEN SHRUBS, SUCH AS HOLLY, choisya, fatsia, and camellia, have shiny foliage that provides an excellent foil for grey-leaved plants, but some could grow too large for this situation. Instead, increase the winter interest by using hart's tongue ferns, with their highly polished fronds. Introduce extra spring colour with carpets of low-growing species tulips.

STRENGTHENING THE WINTER INTEREST

Evergreen hart's tongue ferns, with a spreading, horizontal juniper, and clumps of cyclamen will all give this poolside more winter weight. Unlike the stachys, which it replaces, the juniper is as handsome in mid-winter as it is in the more promising days of summer.

The cyclamen will liven up the juniper, providing a touch of frippery with its late summer or autumn flowers. Its foliage echoes the tones of the juniper – both on the blue side of green. The cyclamen's leaves are more complex, marbled in silver in patterns as varied as fingerprints.

Juniperus horizontalis **'Turquoise Spreader' (Juniper)** *Dwarf, evergreen conifer that spreads slowly to form a thick mat of glaucous, turquoise-green foliage. H to 50cm (20in), S 1.5m (5ft) or more.*

Cyclamen hederifolium *Autumn-flowering tuber. Silver-patterned leaves appear with or after pink flowers and last until spring. H to 10cm (4in), S 10–15cm (4–6in).*

Phyllitis scolopendrium **(Hart's tongue fern)** *Evergreen fern with bright green, leathery, tongue-like fronds. H 45–75cm (18–30in), S to 45cm (18in).*

A SWATHE OF SPRING TULIPS

Increase the impact of spring which, apart from the upright catkins on the willow, is rather short of special effects, by filling the spaces between the other plants with species tulips. These are not as showy, nor as large, as the ordinary garden tulips, but are the original blueprints from which all garden varieties have been developed. They come into bloom earlier than the larger tulips and the scale of their flowers, used among low-growing plants, also seems more appropriate.

Tulipa tarda **(Species tulip)** *Bulb that bears yellow flowers in spring, with each pointed petal neatly tipped in white. H to 15cm (6in), S to 10cm (4in).*

Tulipa turkestanica **(Species tulip)** *Early spring-flowering bulb, producing starry, white flowers with yolk-yellow centres. H 10–30cm (4–12in), S to 20cm (8in).*

Tulipa saxatilis **(Species tulip)** *Bulb bearing fragrant, lilac-pink flowers with yellow centres in early spring among shiny, pale green leaves. H 15–45cm (6–18in), S to 20cm (8in).*

COLOURED FOLIAGE

GOLD FOLIAGE placed in a gloomy corner of the garden can instantly transform it from a pit of despair into a place of pilgrimage. A gold-leaved robinia lights up this group of shrubs that might fill an awkward corner. Although yellow is shunned by some extremely finely tuned gardeners, it is a cheerful colour to have about. Purple foliage adds depth and density, while grey provides a cool contrast.

GLEAMS OF GOLD AND YELLOW

Colour in this scheme comes mostly from leaves rather than flowers. The golden robinia is an outstanding foliage tree, the colour clear and bright, the leaves like short strings of flat, yellow beads. If you can arrange a dark background for it, so much the better: a simple backing of ivy or pyracantha would be ideal. The branches of the robinia are rather brittle so do not plant it where it will be exposed to gale force winds.

Gold and yellow foliage tends to be less stable than purple. The robinia starts with a fresh golden glow in spring, but is far less bright by leaf fall in autumn. Its companion, the golden philadelphus, also fades as the season advances.

PLANT LIST

1 *Robinia pseudoacacia* 'Frisia' (False acacia) x 1
2 *Berberis thunbergii* f. *atropurpurea* (Barberry) x 1
3 *Senecio* 'Sunshine' x 1
4 *Origanum vulgare* 'Aureum' (Golden marjoram) x 3
5 *Nepeta* 'Six Hills Giant' (Catmint) x 2
6 *Sedum spectabile* (Ice plant) x 1
7 *Geranium cinereum* 'Ballerina' (Cranesbill) x 1
8 *Philadelphus coronarius* 'Aureus' (Mock orange) x 1
9 *Alchemilla mollis* (Lady's mantle) x 3
10 *Euphorbia characias* subsp. *wulfenii* (Spurge) x 1
11 *Phlomis fruticosa* (Jerusalem sage) x 1

PLANTING PLAN

Despite this, the philadelphus is a useful and easy-going shrub, and its cream flowers have the swooniest smell you could desire.

PATCHES OF PURPLE AND GREY

Purple foliage may be more difficult to use in a garden than gold. It looks lovely in spring, but can sometimes seem heavy as summer wears on. This is more of a problem with large-leaved trees than with the neat berberis used here. Its leaves are the rich colour of good port and, in autumn, turn a blazing red before they fall.

By far the most restful of the three types of coloured foliage included here is the grey – too restful if used all on its own, as it sometimes is. An unrelieved expanse of grey foliage has rather less allure than last week's laundry. Here, contrasted with the golden robinia and philadelpus and the rich, vinous tones of the berberis, it acts as a useful buffer.

Both senecio and phlomis bear yellow flowers in early summer, but the flowers are nowhere near as important as the leaves – the senecio's painted with palest silver on the undersides, those of the phlomis greyish-green and roughly textured. Both have the advantage of staying on during winter. They continue to provide interest when the other shrubs are "resting", as actresses say. Similarly, the euphorbia, which constantly renews itself with fresh growth, never leaves a gap in the planting.

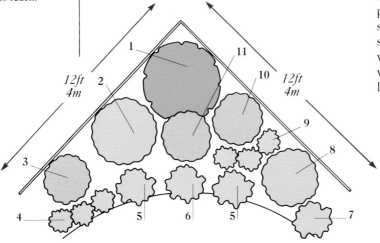

SENECIO
Senecio 'Sunshine' is a sprawling shrub wider than it is high, bearing branching heads of brilliant yellow, daisy flowers in early summer.

GOLDEN MARJORAM
The aromatic leaves of *Origanum vulgare* 'Aureum' are as useful for cooking as those of the plain green marjoram and make thick patches of colour in the front of a bed.

COLOUR CONTRASTS AND ECHOES
*The golds of the marjoram and the philadelphus
echo the colour of the robinia and add zest to the
dark berberis and the cool senecio, creating
a cheerful mid-summer display.*

FALSE ACACIA
The fast-growing *Robinia pseudoacacia* 'Frisia'
has the brightest foliage of any gold-leaved tree.

JERUSALEM SAGE
The stems of *Phlomis fruticosa* are stiff and,
like the leaves, covered in greyish-green felt.

CATMINT
Nepeta 'Six Hills Giant',
as its name implies,
is a giant form of
catmint, twice as
large as the normal
Nepeta x *faassenii*.

SPURGE
All the various types of *Euphorbia characias*,
including this one, *E. c.* subsp. *wulfenii*, make
dramatic clumps of upright stems, clothed with
whorls of evergreen foliage.

MOCK ORANGE
The foliage of *Philadelphus coronarius*
'Aureus' grows at its best in light
shade, where the lime-green leaves
will not scorch.

BARBERRY
Berberis thunbergii
f. *atropurpurea*
has purple
leaves that
turn bright
red in autumn.

LADY'S MANTLE
Common, but always welcome,
Alchemilla mollis, lady's mantle, has
flowers of a peculiar lime-green that
make a brilliant foil for purple foliage.

ICE PLANT
The succulent foliage of *Sedum
spectabile* makes a fine background
for its flat flowerheads, which turn
from green to pink then rusty red.

CRANESBILL
Geranium cinereum is an alpine
species, native to the Balkans.
This cultivar, 'Ballerina', has purplish-pink
flowers with deep purple veins.

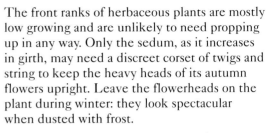

PLANTS *for a* LOW-MAINTENANCE SCHEME

ONCE ESTABLISHED, the shrubs in this scheme will need little attention to keep them looking good. They will put up with thin, poor soil reasonably well, but will of course perform better if given a reasonable diet. The robinia needs sun, so do not consider this scheme for a position that is overhung by taller trees or in shade for most of the day.

The front ranks of herbaceous plants are mostly low growing and are unlikely to need propping up in any way. Only the sedum, as it increases in girth, may need a discreet corset of twigs and string to keep the heavy heads of its autumn flowers upright. Leave the flowerheads on the plant during winter: they look spectacular when dusted with frost.

CARE AND CULTIVATION

SPRING
Plant marjorams, nepetas, and alchemillas, also the geranium and sedum. Cut down dead sedum flower stems before new growth begins.

SUMMER
Dead-head the phlomis and senecio and shorten any overlong shoots. Thin out some old wood from the philadelphus after flowering. Cut down flowered stems of the euphorbia. Remove faded flowers of alchemillas to prevent self-seeding. Shear over alchemillas and the geranium in late summer to produce fresh foliage.

AUTUMN
Plant the robinia, staking it until it is well rooted. Plant the berberis, phlomis, philadelphus, and senecio. Plant a small euphorbia specimen: large plants are difficult to establish. Cut back marjorams by two-thirds before plants die down in winter. Cut down nepetas.

WINTER
Cut back straggly berberis growths in late winter. Rejuvenate old shrubs by cutting out some old stems at ground level.

Senecio 'Sunshine'
Summer-flowering shrub that forms a mound of evergreen foliage with silvery undersides. Leaves are silvery-grey when young. H and S 1m (3ft).

Berberis thunbergii f. atropurpurea (Barberry) *Deciduous, arching shrub grown for its reddish-purple foliage and autumn berries. H to 2m (6ft), S 3m (10ft).*

Robinia pseudoacacia 'Frisia' (False acacia)
Fast-growing, deciduous tree with golden foliage that turns orange-yellow in autumn. H to 15m (50ft), S to 7.5m (25ft).

Philadelphus coronarius 'Aureus' (Mock orange)
Deciduous shrub bearing fragrant flowers in late spring and early summer. H 2.5m (8ft), S 1.5m (5ft).

Nepeta 'Six Hills Giant' (Catmint)
Perennial with grey-green leaves and lavender-blue flowers in summer. H and S 60cm (2ft).

Euphorbia characias subsp. *wulfenii* (Spurge)
Evergreen, architectural shrub with large heads of yellow-green flowers in spring. H and S 1.5m (5ft).

Alchemilla mollis (Lady's mantle)
Perennial with velvety leaves, and greenish-yellow flowers in summer. H and S 50cm (20in).

Origanum vulgare 'Aureum' (Golden marjoram) *Perennial with aromatic, yellow leaves and tiny, mauve summer flowers. H 8–45cm (3–18in), S indefinite.*

Phlomis fruticosa (Jerusalem sage)
Evergreen shrub with yellow flowers in summer, amid sage-like, grey-green foliage. H and S 1m (3ft).

Sedum spectabile (Ice plant) *Fleshy-leaved, clump-forming perennial with flat heads of pink flowers in late summer–autumn. H and S 45cm (18in).*

Geranium cinereum 'Ballerina' (Cranesbill)
Spreading perennial bearing pink flowers with purple veins in late spring and summer. H 10cm (4in), S 30cm (12in).

ALTERING *the* PLANTING SCHEME

PURPLE AND YELLOW MAKE a strong contrast. If this is not to your taste, use a quieter shrub in place of the berberis. Choose one with good foliage – you can always add extra flowers by training clematis up one or two of the shrubs. Celebrate the arrival of spring by adding low bulbs in the foreground, letting them weave in and out of the alchemilla, nepeta, and geranium.

Astrantia major **'Sunningdale Variegated' (Masterwort)** *Clump-forming perennial with deeply divided, variegated leaves. In summer, it bears greenish-white flowers touched with pink. H 60cm (2ft), S 45cm (18in).*

VARIEGATED FOLIAGE FOR A LIGHTER EFFECT

Using a pale-variegated shrub such as *Cornus alba* 'Elegantissima' instead of the berberis will lighten the whole effect. In winter, its bare stems will shine out like red neon strips, a brilliant contrast to the soft greys of the phlomis and senecio around it.

Let this variegation echo in the foreground of the scheme by using an astrantia with creamy-yellow leaves instead of the plain, pink geranium. Replace the sedum with a different geranium, such as the blue-flowered *Geranium himalayense*. A straight swap between the astrantia and the sedum would put both variegated plants on the same side of the scheme, which might unbalance it.

Cornus alba **'Elegantissima' (Dogwood)** *Vigorous, deciduous shrub with white-margined leaves. The stems are bright red in winter. H and S to 2m (6ft).*

A SWATHE OF SPRING BULBS

Dwarf bulbs, such as crocuses, scillas, chionodoxas, and puschkinias, are ideal for filling bare spring ground that will be covered later by the spread of perennial plants. Bulbs are opportunists. They bob up and get their act over while everything else is hovering in the wings, wondering whether it is the right time to go on or not. Then, even more obligingly, they dive underground, letting us off the dreary sight of their foliage languishing for the rest of the year.

There is scarcely any dwarf crocus that is not a delight. They increase lavishly, too, if they are in a position where the sun can get at them to ripen the corms.

Geranium himalayense **(Cranesbill)** *Summer-flowering perennial with violet-blue flowers borne above a dense mound of intricately cut leaves. H 30cm (12in), S 60cm (2ft).*

Scilla siberica **'Atrocoerulea'** *Early spring-flowering bulb that has nodding bells of startlingly clear blue flowers and strap-shaped, glossy leaves. H 10–15cm (4–6in), S 5cm (2in).*

Crocus **'E.A. Bowles'** *Corm bearing scented, deep yellow flowers in spring. The petals are stained with bronze on the outside near the base. H 10cm (4in), S 5–8cm (2–3in).*

A Scheme *for* Scent

POOLS OF AROMATIC THYME border this corner planting, placed so that you will tread on them, liberating the characteristic spicy perfume each time you pass up and down the paths on either side. Scent in the garden is an elusive delight, but a powerful one. This scheme uses a wide variety of plants noted for their perfume.

SWEET PERFUME
The madonna lily, Lilium candidum, *is crowned with graceful, pure white funnels, each one filled with heady fragrance.*

DESIGN POINTS

— ❧ —

SCENTS FOR THE SUN
A richly perfumed medley of plants for a sunny corner site.

— ❧ —

FRAGRANT FOLIAGE
Foliage plays as important a part as flowers, with scented-leaved pelargoniums, aromatic thymes, and rosemary.

Some plants, such as jonquils and Madonna lilies, release their scent uninhibitedly, pouring out great quantities of their perfume to intoxicate the world at large. Other plants are more reticent. You need to reach out and crush the foliage of the rosemary or the pelargonium to let loose their essential oils.

The daphne gives perfume early in the year, its small, waxy flowers sending out a smell strong enough to draw you in like a bloodhound. The evergreen species *Daphne odora* is the one to go for, especially the cultivar 'Aureomarginata', which has leathery leaves edged thinly in cream.

Spring- and summer-flowering bulbs add colour to this scheme, but both are also richly scented. The jonquils are among the last of the daffodil family to flower, with brilliant yellow blooms among grassy foliage. What they lack in stature they more than make up for in smell. Madonna lilies are at their best when dusk falls in summer, sending out siren music to the moths from their wide, white trumpets.

AROMATIC HERBS

A spire of rosemary provides the centrepiece here. Choose a naturally upright variety, and, as it grows, tie it in to make a neat column.

Lavender has been grown in gardens from late medieval times, and the essential oil used for perfumes. The oil is a powerful, natural antiseptic. Perhaps this is why the Romans used it in their baths; its name comes from the Latin verb *lavare*, meaning to wash. 'Hidcote' is a neat, compact, silver-leaved variety with particularly dark purple flowers.

Choose an upright thyme such as *Thymus* x *citriodorus*, which will release its lemony scent when you brush past it. Around the edges, plant low-growing thymes, such as *Thymus serpyllum*, that will creep across the paths to make scented mats under your feet. When the flowers are out, bumblebees roll around between them, drunk with the smell.

PLANTING PLAN

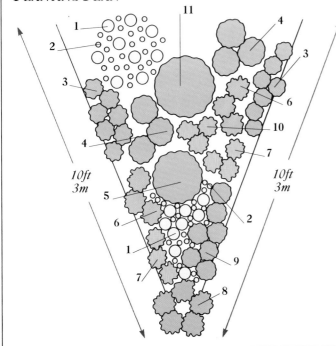

10ft
3m

10ft
3m

PLANT LIST

1 *Lilium candidum* (Madonna lily) x 18
2 *Narcissus jonquilla* (Jonquil) x 50
3 *Thymus* x *citriodorus* 'Silver Queen' (Lemon thyme) x 14
4 *Lavandula angustifolia* 'Hidcote' (Lavender) x 6
5 *Rosmarinus officinalis* 'Miss Jessopp's Upright' (Rosemary) x 1
6 *Pelargonium* 'Mabel Grey' x 6
7 *Iris graminea* syn. *I. colchica* x 6
8 *Dianthus* 'Prudence' (Pink) x 5
9 *Thymus serpyllum* (Wild thyme) x 7
10 *Hemerocallis citrina* (Daylily) x 3
11 *Daphne odora* 'Aureomarginata' x 1

CO-ORDINATED COLOURS

Undulating mats of pinks, irises, pelargoniums, and thymes merge together to create a wave of summer colour in many shades of mauve, pink, and violet-blue. The accent plants are the madonna lilies, adding a distinctive splash of white.

LEMON THYME
The elegant, variegated *Thymus* x *citriodorus* 'Silver Queen' is more tender than the plain version but has the same tangy lemon scent.

PELARGONIUM
The scented leaves of pelargoniums such as 'Mabel Grey' add a distinctive aroma in a perfumed garden.

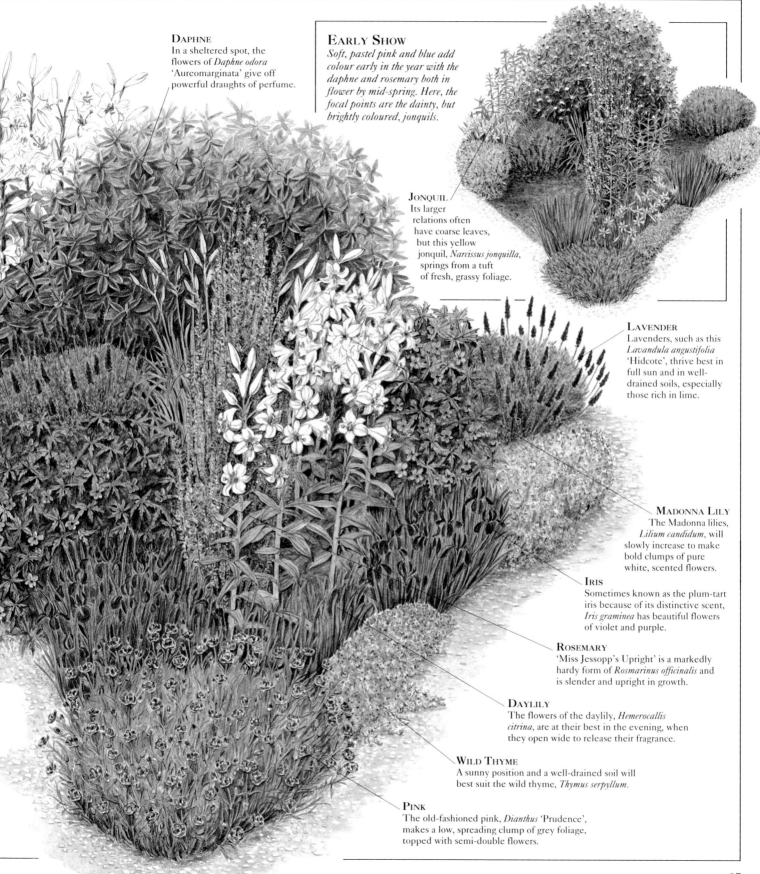

DAPHNE
In a sheltered spot, the flowers of *Daphne odora* 'Aureomarginata' give off powerful draughts of perfume.

EARLY SHOW
Soft, pastel pink and blue add colour early in the year with the daphne and rosemary both in flower by mid-spring. Here, the focal points are the dainty, but brightly coloured, jonquils.

JONQUIL
Its larger relations often have coarse leaves, but this yellow jonquil, *Narcissus jonquilla*, springs from a tuft of fresh, grassy foliage.

LAVENDER
Lavenders, such as this *Lavandula angustifolia* 'Hidcote', thrive best in full sun and in well-drained soils, especially those rich in lime.

MADONNA LILY
The Madonna lilies, *Lilium candidum*, will slowly increase to make bold clumps of pure white, scented flowers.

IRIS
Sometimes known as the plum-tart iris because of its distinctive scent, *Iris graminea* has beautiful flowers of violet and purple.

ROSEMARY
'Miss Jessopp's Upright' is a markedly hardy form of *Rosmarinus officinalis* and is slender and upright in growth.

DAYLILY
The flowers of the daylily, *Hemerocallis citrina*, are at their best in the evening, when they open wide to release their fragrance.

WILD THYME
A sunny position and a well-drained soil will best suit the wild thyme, *Thymus serpyllum*.

PINK
The old-fashioned pink, *Dianthus* 'Prudence', makes a low, spreading clump of grey foliage, topped with semi-double flowers.

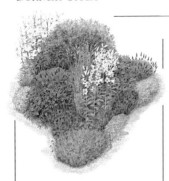

PLANTS *for a* WELL-DRAINED CORNER

ALL THE AROMATIC HERBS in this scheme need well-drained soil round their feet and plenty of sun on their heads. Winter damp is almost more of a problem than winter cold for Mediterranean plants. Dig in grit if necessary to ensure good drainage in heavy soils. Set the pinks and creeping thymes close to the edge of the bed so that they can disguise the edges of the paths.

Lavender is not by nature a very long-lived plant and will need replacing when it becomes woody and unproductive. Persuade it to produce plenty of new growth by cutting it back quite hard each spring. For more unusual flowers, arranged in two-tone plumes, choose the French lavender, *Lavandula stoechas*, but bear in mind that it is not as hardy as 'Hidcote'.

CARE AND CULTIVATION

SPRING
Plant the daphne, the rosemary, thymes, and lavenders. Plant pelargoniums when all danger of frost has passed. Cut back straggly shoots of the daphne in early spring. Plant pinks, burying as little as possible of the stems. Mulch lilies with compost or leaf mould. Dead-head jonquils but leave stems and leaves to die down naturally.

SUMMER
Tie in growths of the rosemary to form a slim spire and clip away ragged shoots. Shear off dead flowers of thymes and lavenders.

AUTUMN
Plant lilies, setting bulbs just beneath the soil surface. Remove flower stems only when totally dry. Plant jonquils, daylilies, and irises. Lift pelargoniums before the first frost, cut them back, and overwinter in a frost-free place, or take cuttings for next year.

WINTER
Remove dead leaves and other debris from clumps of pinks and thymes.

***Thymus x citriodorus* 'Silver Queen' (Lemon thyme)** *Evergreen shrub with aromatic, silver-marked foliage. H and S 10–25cm (4–10in).*

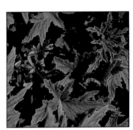

***Pelargonium* 'Mabel Grey'** *Tender, evergreen perennial with diamond-shaped, lemon-scented leaves and small, mauve flowers. H to 60cm (2ft), S 30–45cm (12–18in).*

***Rosmarinus officinalis* 'Miss Jessopp's Upright' (Rosemary)** *Evergreen shrub with aromatic, needle-like leaves and small, blue flowers. H and S 2m (6ft).*

***Daphne odora* 'Aureomarginata'** *Variegated, evergreen shrub with pink and white flowers in mid-winter to spring. H and S 1.5m (5ft).*

***Lavandula angustifolia* 'Hidcote' (Lavender)** *Evergreen shrub with dark purple flower spikes and aromatic, silver-grey leaves. H and S 60cm (2ft).*

***Hemerocallis citrina* (Daylily)** *Vigorous perennial with rich lemon-yellow flowers, each lasting only a night, in mid-summer. H and S 75cm (2½ft).*

Iris graminea* syn. *I. colchica *Rhizomatous iris with plum-scented, purple flowers that have heavily veined, violet-blue falls. H 20–40cm (8–16in), S indefinite.*

***Dianthus* 'Prudence' (Pink)** *Spreading perennial with intricately mottled purple-pink and white flowers in mid-summer. H 30–45cm (12–18in), S 30cm (12in).*

***Lilium candidum* (Madonna lily)** *Summer-flowering bulb bearing upright, elegant stems of white, funnel-shaped, scented blooms. H 1–2m (3–6ft), S 30cm (12in).*

***Thymus serpyllum* (Wild thyme)** *Low, creeping, evergreen shrub with small, scented leaves and mauve-pink flowers. H 8cm (3in), S indefinite.*

***Narcissus jonquilla* (Jonquil)** *Bulb with dark, shining leaves and, in spring, graceful, yellow flowers that have a fine fragrance. H 30cm (12in), S to 20cm (8in).*

ALTERING *the* PLANTING SCHEME

THERE ARE SEVERAL WAYS of increasing the flower power of this corner planting without sacrificing any of its capacity to please the nose. Roses are an obvious choice to replace the rosemary and the daphne, though none of them has much to offer in winter. Scented annuals and biennials will also introduce more colour. You could use any combination of sweet williams, tobacco plants, heliotropes, sweet peas, night-scented stocks, verbenas, sweet sultans, and wallflowers.

BLOOMS FOR COLOUR AND SCENT

Add an air of formality to this scheme by using a standard rose to replace the low-growing daphne. Standard roses always look as if they have wandered into the garden from a child's picture book, the flowers all perched in a rounded head balanced on top of a tall, clear stem. 'The Fairy' would be an excellent choice here. It is not the most heavily scented of roses, but it is one of the prettiest with large trusses of small flowers smothering a wide head of foliage.

A miniature cluster-flowered or patio rose mixes easily with the pelargoniums and thymes. Not all the new patio roses are well endowed with scent, so sniff before you choose. Pick a colour that will blend in with the misty effect of the neighbouring plants.

Although usually treated as annuals, wallflowers are short-lived perennials and they acquire great character if you can persuade them to linger on for more than a year. Let them loll on their elbows over the path.

Sweet sultans provide a long show of flowers in shades of pink, white, purple, or a surprising lemon-yellow, the same tone as the daylilies. Scatter the seed and sift some compost on top. Thin out seedlings growing too close together.

Rosa 'The Fairy' *Dwarf, cluster-flowered bush rose, grown here as a standard, that bears pale pink, double blooms in late summer and autumn. H 1.2–2m (4–6ft), S 60cm (2ft).*

Centaurea moschata (**Sweet sultan**) *Annual with fragrant, fluffy flowerheads in pink, white, purple, or yellow, from summer to early autumn, and greyish-green leaves. H 45cm (18in), S 20cm (8in).*

Cheiranthus 'Bredon' (**Wallflower**) *Short lived, semi-evergreen perennial that produces spikes of bright mustard-yellow flowers in late spring. H 30–45cm (12–18in), S 45cm (18in).*

Rosa 'Regensberg' *Low-growing patio rose that bears fragrant, pale pink flowers with white centres for a long period in summer. H 45cm (18in), S 30cm (12in).*

PLANTING *by the* SEA

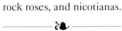

BLOSSOM AND BERRIES
The hawthorn, Crataegus laciniata, *provides a showy explosion of spring blossom and bright winter berries.*

DESIGN POINTS

❦

YEAR-ROUND DISPLAY
Evergreen escallonias and sculptural phormiums continue to provide interest in winter.

❦

A FEAST OF FLOWERS
A long succession of flowers comes from roses, rock roses, and nicotianas.

❦

AUTUMN FRUITS
Autumn brings tomato-red hips on one of the roses and yellow-flushed berries on the hawthorn.

WIND AND SALT are the chief difficulties of gardening near the sea, but there are blessings, too. The sea acts as a gigantic eiderdown, keeping the temperature of coastal regions higher than those inland. Frosts are rare. Spring comes early, winter late. Choose plants that will be undaunted by the conditions: these will survive where many others would struggle – in an exposed corner of a seaside garden.

SHELTER AND SCREENING
The most important task is to create a first line of defence: a sacrificial offering of trees and shrubs to absorb the worst of the wind and shield the plants cowering behind. In large coastal gardens, the Monterey pine and the Monterey cypress are good for screening. Plants with tough, leathery leaves, such as griselinia, or minimal foliage, such as tamarisk, are also well adapted to the vagaries of seaside weather. Here, a hawthorn is used to protect the other plants in the group. As it grows, the hawthorn will probably take on the sculpted appearance of an overgrown bonsai tree, bent into a smooth curve by the prevailing wind.

Tough escallonias, hardy fuchsias, and Rugosa roses are ranged either side of the hawthorn. Use a mixture of Rugosas so you can enjoy the best flowers ('Roseraie de l'Haÿ') and the best hips ('Frau Dagmar Hartopp').

A wattle fence or some other filtering barrier around the corner will be a great help in protecting the plants while they are still finding their feet. Solid enclosures are less effective than perforated ones: when the wind bumps its nose against a solid wall, it drives turbulently over the top and creates extra mayhem on the other side. Slatted screens slow the wind down instead, and avoid inciting it to riot.

PLANTS FOR A SHIELDED SPOT
Once the artificial or natural barriers are in place, you can start filling in the protected space inside the shield. Low-growing shrubs, such as rock roses, are less at the mercy of the wind than tall ones. The rock roses, natives of hot, dry sites around the Mediterranean, also have tough foliage, naturally adapted to resist loss of water from the leaves. The papery flowers are not long lasting, but there are plenty of them, borne in succession through early summer.

Use two kinds of phormium, one a monster towards the back, the other a shorter type at the front, where you can admire the stripes of colour down the leaves.

At the end of summer, the crinums send up stout stems crowned with trumpet flowers that smell like lilies. They flare open in succession to reveal a complex arrangement of stamens.

PLANTING PLAN

1Oft
3m

PLANT LIST
1. *Crataegus laciniata* (Hawthorn) x 1
2. *Phormium tenax* 'Dazzler' x 3
3. *Rosa rugosa* 'Roseraie de l'Haÿ' x 1
4. *Rosa rugosa* 'Frau Dagmar Hartopp' x 2
5. *Crinum* x *powellii* x 3
6. *Escallonia* 'Iveyi' x 2
7. *Nicotiana langsdorfii* x 14
8. *Cistus* x *corbariensis* (Rock rose) x 3
9. *Polygonum campanulatum* x 3
10. *Phormium tenax* 'Maori Sunrise' x 3
11. *Phlomis russeliana* x 1
12. *Fuchsia magellanica* 'Versicolor' x 1

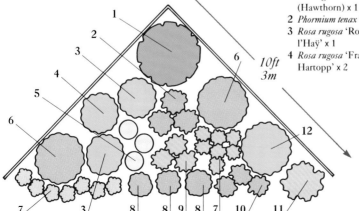

ESCALLONIA
The dark, glossy foliage of *Escallonia* 'Iveyi' provides an excellent backdrop to the large panicles of white flowers.

FLOWERS AND FOLIAGE
In mid-summer, the roses take centre stage, complemented by the striking sword leaves of the two phormiums. The nicotianas begin flowering in early summer and continue into the first few weeks of autumn. Above their heads, the escallonias froth with white flowers.

CRINUM
The bold trumpet flowers of *Crinum* x *powellii* can be either white or pink.

PINK ROSE
The silver-pink flowers of *Rosa rugosa* 'Frau Dagmar Hartopp' appear on a bush that is usually wider than it is tall.

AUTUMN BOUNTY
In early autumn, the hips on the hawthorn and one of the roses add warmth and colour while the large phormium, the fuchsia, and the crinums provide striking flowers.

FUCHSIA
The crimson and purple flowers of *Fuchsia magellanica* 'Versicolor' are beautifully set off against the grey, green, and pink tones of the foliage.

HAWTHORN
The deeply lobed leaves of *Crataegus laciniata* are often toothed at the tip, setting off the white spring blossom and the red autumn fruit.

CRIMSON ROSE
Rosa rugosa 'Roseraie de l'Haÿ' has strongly scented, semi-double flowers of rich crimson-purple, but rarely produces hips.

DAZZLING PHORMIUM
Phormium tenax 'Dazzler' is aptly named for it has the brightest foliage of all its family.

POLYGONUM
The tiny, pink bell flowers of *Polygonum campanulatum* are set on elegant, branching heads.

NICOTIANA
Nicotiana langsdorfii has smaller flowers than those on other tobacco plants but they are an eye-catching lime green.

Fuchsia magellanica 'Versicolor'

ROCK ROSE
Cistus x *corbariensis* is one of the hardiest of the rock roses, bearing a long succession of white flowers in summer.

PHLOMIS
The rough leaves of *Phlomis russeliana* make excellent ground cover even when the whorls of soft, hooded flowers are not in evidence.

STRIPY PHORMIUM
Phormium tenax 'Maori Sunrise' has striped, sword-like leaves that grow slowly into a dramatic clump.

SPRING

Mulch round shrubs and the hawthorn. Plant phormiums and the fuchsia. In cold areas, the fuchsia may be cut to the ground each year, but will sprout again from the base. Plant rock roses in full sun. Plant crinums, setting the bulbs 30cm (12in) deep. Sow nicotianas and plant out in late spring.

SUMMER

The hawthorn needs no regular pruning but may be trimmed to shape after flowering. Remove flowering shoots from escallonias as they fade.

AUTUMN

Plant the hawthorn, phlomis, roses, and escallonias in late autumn or early winter. Plant polygonums in light shade. The phlomis may become invasive: cut it back hard if necessary. Remove dead flower stems from phormiums.

WINTER

Rugosa roses need no regular pruning but twiggy growths may be thinned out occasionally and old stems taken out at ground level. Cut down stems of polygonums and phlomis.

CARING *for* SEASIDE PLANTS

THE WINDS AND SALT SPRAY of a coastal location can be hard on even the toughest plants. Be patient with the plants in your scheme. It will take them a little time to settle in hostile conditions. Choose small plants – they will transplant more easily than large specimens. Planting in autumn will give the hawthorn, roses, and escallonias time to find their feet before they need to think about flowering. Stout stakes, certainly for the hawthorn and possibly for the escallonias as well, will help to prevent wind rock. Mulching the ground at the base of trees and shrubs will help to conserve moisture in the soil around the roots. In cold areas, it may be necessary to protect early growth of the phormiums and crinums against frost.

Crataegus laciniata (Hawthorn) *Deciduous tree with dark green, lobed leaves, and white flowers in spring or early summer. H and S 6m (20ft).*

Rosa rugosa 'Roseraie de l'Haÿ' *Dense, vigorous rose with strongly scented, magenta flowers in summer–autumn. H 2m (6ft), S 1.5m (5ft).*

Rosa rugosa 'Frau Dagmar Hartopp' *Shrub rose with fragrant, single, pink flowers, then large, red hips in autumn. H 1.5m (5ft), S 1.2m (4ft).*

Escallonia 'Iveyi' *Evergreen shrub with dark green, glossy leaves, and fragrant, white flowers in mid- to late summer. H and S to 3.5m (11ft).*

Nicotiana langsdorfii *Erect perennial, grown as an annual, with hanging, pale green to yellow-green flowers in summer. H to 1.5m (5ft), S 30cm (12in).*

Crinum × powellii *Late-summer or autumn-flowering bulb with fragrant, funnel-shaped, pink flowers. H to 1m (3ft), S 60cm (2ft).*

Cistus × corbariensis (Rock rose) *Evergreen, bushy shrub with masses of white flowers in late spring–summer. H 75cm (2½ft), S 1.2m (4ft).*

Polygonum campanulatum *Mat-forming perennial with oval leaves and bell-shaped, pink or white flowers in summer. H and S 1m (3ft).*

Phormium tenax 'Dazzler' *Evergreen perennial with pointed leaves in tones of orange-red and bronze, and panicles of red flowers in summer. H to 2m (6ft), S 1m (3ft).*

Phormium tenax 'Maori Sunrise' *Evergreen, upright perennial with stiff, pointed leaves margined with cream. H to 3m (10ft), S to 2m (6ft).*

Phlomis russeliana *Evergreen perennial with large, heart-shaped leaves. Butter-yellow flowers appear on stout stems in summer. H 1m (3ft), S 60cm (2ft).*

Fuchsia magellanica 'Versicolor' *Deciduous shrub with strikingly variegated foliage. Slender, red and purple flowers are borne in late summer. H 3m (10ft), S 2m (6ft).*

ALTERING *the* PLANTING SCHEME

THERE IS PLENTY OF OPPORTUNITY to juggle with different combinations of colour in this group of plants. The hawthorn, roses, escallonias, fuchsia, rock roses, and crinum can all offer white flowers as well as a cornucopia of pink. This alternative scheme suggests ways that you can swing the colour balance from pink towards yellow, grey, and lime green. This is a more recessive, subtle combination of colours, which retains the white-flowering rock rose from the original scheme and builds on the acid green introduced by the nicotiana.

PALE COLOURS FOR A COASTAL SPOT

In place of the escallonias and the fuchsia, spread the Rugosa roses all around the boundary to make an informal hedge. Use only white-flowered varieties such as 'Alba' and 'Blanc Double de Coubert'.

The homely hawthorn is replaced by a eucalyptus, which will change the whole character of the planting. Eucalyptuses are ghost trees, bark and foliage both bleached to phantom shades of grey.

Olearia replaces the phormium at the back, while a slow-growing pine is used instead of the phormium in the foreground. The tree lupin is covered all summer with yellow flowers that will scent this whole corner.

Eucalyptus coccifera (Tasmanian snow gum) *Evergreen tree with aromatic, grey-green leaves and blue-grey and white bark. H to 18m (60ft), S to 6m (20ft).*

***Rosa rugosa* 'Alba'** *Vigorous rose with fragrant, white flowers in summer–autumn, followed by large, tomato-shaped hips. H and S 1–2m (3–6ft).*

Lupinus arboreus (Tree lupin) *Semi-evergreen shrub with scented, yellow flowers above hairy, pale green leaves. H 1m (3ft), S 75cm (2½ft).*

Bupleurum fruticosum (Shrubby hare's ear) *Evergreen shrub bearing small, yellow flowers from summer to early autumn. H and S 2m (6ft).*

Olearia* x *haastii (Daisy bush) *Bushy, evergreen shrub with small, oval, glossy leaves. In mid- to late summer it bears masses of scented, white, daisy-like flowers. The dense habit of this shrub makes it a good choice for hedging. H and S 2m (6ft).*

***Pinus mugo* 'Humpy'** (Dwarf pine) *Low, spreading, shrubby conifer with needle-like leaves and egg-shaped cones. H 45cm (18in), S 60cm (2ft).*

SUNNY YELLOWS *and* BLUES

ROSES DO NOT HAVE TO BE CONSIGNED to beds on their own, like patients in an isolation ward. Shrub roses, particularly, make graceful centrepieces in a sunny corner site, surrounded by complementary shrubs, perennials, and bulbs. Here, a pale gold rose holds together a scheme of yellow and blue with a phlomis providing a cool mound of felted, grey foliage. Blue and white hyacinths sit stiffly between clumps of blue-flowered brunnera, echoing the crisp, clean effect of willow pattern china.

SUMMER DAYLILIES
The daylily used here, Hemerocallis 'Marion Vaughn', *has upright stems crowned with scented, trumpet flowers of lemon-yellow, each lasting for a single day.*

THE GLORY OF A GOLDEN ROSE
This scheme is suitable for a corner backed by a wall or fence, where you see the plants from the front only. Use a rose such as 'Frühlingsgold' that holds itself well. Large-flowered (Hybrid Tea) types would not be suitable: they are too stiff, too awkward. 'Frühlingsgold' has large, almost single flowers of clear yellow, fading to creamy-primrose. The stamens are particularly beautiful, peppering the blooms with *pointilliste* touches of gold and brown. It is vigorous and upright, rather than spreading, making it a friendly neighbour, and easy to plant under.

A HOST OF HANDSOME COMPANIONS
Roses are not generally endowed with good foliage, but you can compensate with other plants. The phlomis makes a rounded dome of evergrey foliage, and so covers up the bare stems at the base of the rose. Daylilies and irises form vertical punctuation marks among the soft humps of the other plants. The irises' foliage spears through the ground in bright, fresh green. The daylilies also have good spring foliage – juicy enough to eat. They are often among the first herbaceous plants to poke through in those chill winter days when you are anxiously looking for signs of life. For this scheme use a yellow variety, rather than an orange or terracotta one. Look for 'Marion Vaughn', 'Cartwheels', or 'Hyperion'.

The ceratostigma comes into its own in late summer, when it is covered with brilliant blue flowers, and in autumn, when the foliage is tinged with rich, lustrous red.

DESIGN POINTS

FRAGRANT FOCAL POINT
A richly scented rose forms the centrepiece for this corner bed.

CRISP COLOURS
A restricted colour scheme in complementary shades of yellow and blue.

SPRING AND SUMMER
Hyacinths and tulips provide colour in spring before the perennials and shrubs take over for summer.

PLANTING PLAN

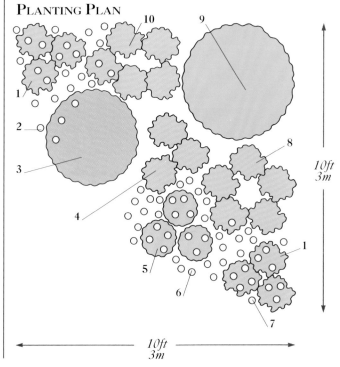

10ft
3m

10ft
3m

PLANT LIST
1 *Brunnera macrophylla* 'Hadspen Cream' x 6
2 *Hyacinthus orientalis* 'Delft Blue' and 'L'Innocence' (Hyacinths) x 25
3 *Phlomis fruticosa* (Jerusalem sage) x 1
4 *Hemerocallis* 'Marion Vaughn' (Daylily) x 3
5 *Ceratostigma willmottianum* x 3
6 *Tulipa* 'Candela' (Fosteriana tulip) x 25
7 *Tulipa* 'Bellona' (Single early tulip) x 25
8 *Campanula lactiflora* 'Prichard's Variety' x 5
9 *Rosa* 'Frühlingsgold' x 1
10 *Iris sibirica* x 5

SUMMERTIME BLUES

This border looks its best in early summer when the rose is in full bloom. It is complemented by Iris sibirica, *although you could use other blue irises instead. Additional blue comes from the forget-me-not flowers of* Brunnera macrophylla 'Hadspen Cream', *which has showy, variegated foliage.*

JERUSALEM SAGE

Both stems and leaves of the Jerusalem sage, *Phlomis fruticosa*, are covered in grey-green felt, enlivened in summer with whorls of yellow flowers.

MID-SPRING SCHEME

The blue and yellow theme starts in spring when the tulips take centre stage, sharing the limelight with blue and white hyacinths. The daylilies, more advanced, are showing spears of foliage about a foot high, matched by the bold, sword-like leaves of the irises.

HYACINTHS

Hyacinthus orientalis 'Delft Blue' is a rich, porcelain blue and early to come into flower. 'L'Innocence' has waxy, white flowers set loosely on each stem. Forced bulbs planted out after flowering indoors may take a season or two to recover, but will eventually give a good display.

TULIPS

The tulip 'Bellona' is a single early type, flowering usually in mid-spring with deep golden-yellow flowers. 'Candela' may flower a couple of weeks earlier. It is slightly taller and an equally good colour – clear, soft golden-yellow.

ROSE

Rosa 'Frühlingsgold' has only one season of flowering, but it is both early and beautifully scented.

IRIS

Although it grows best in damp soil and full sun, *Iris sibirica* is an adaptable plant and will flourish in a wide variety of situations.

CAMPANULA

Campanula lactiflora 'Prichard's Variety' makes a magnificent companion for most shrub roses. It may need staking in a windy site.

DAYLILY

Daylilies are as useful for their early spears of foliage as they are for their flowers, which in the vigorous *Hemerocallis* 'Marion Vaughn' are clear, lemon-yellow.

CERATOSTIGMA

Although it may be cut to the ground in winter, the new growths of *Ceratostigma willmottianum* give a plentiful display of searingly blue flowers by late summer.

BRUNNERA

Forget-me-not flowers are carried in abundance on stems held above the variegated leaves of *Brunnera macrophylla* 'Hadspen Cream', which grows best where there is moisture and some shade.

CARE AND CULTIVATION

SPRING
Plant phlomis and ceratostigmas. Dead-head tulips as they finish flowering but allow foliage to die down naturally. Top-dress irises with sifted compost. Mulch the rose. Cut out any brunnera foliage that reverts to plain green.

SUMMER
Spray the rose if necessary against mildew, aphids, and black spot. Phlomis does not need regular pruning, but cut back straggly branches after flowering. Cut out old, flowered stems of daylilies and brunneras. Allow foliage of irises to die down naturally.

AUTUMN
Plant campanulas, brunneras, and daylilies. Divide and replant established clumps if necessary. Plant irises, setting rhizomes no more than 2.5cm (1in) deep. Plant hyacinths and tulips. Cut down stems of campanulas when flowers have finished.

WINTER
Plant the rose, incorporating plenty of humus. In subsequent years, prune it lightly, taking out one or two old growths at the base.

COMPANION PLANTS *for a* SHRUB ROSE

Spring-flowering bulbs such as hyacinths and tulips are ideal for planting around a rose or other summer-flowering shrub. They provide another season of interest, before the perennials and shrubs have fully woken up and got into their stride, and you can alter the scheme with different varieties each year. Tulips do not always last well in the ground, so you may have to replace them every couple of years. This is not necessarily a disadvantage as it allows you to experiment with different kinds and colours. For example, a single early such as 'Bellona' can be preceded by an even earlier flush of a Fosteriana tulip such as 'Candela'. Take care to plant them deep so that when you are working among the plants, forking out weeds, you will not spear the bulbs accidentally on the end of your fork. There is no more mortifying experience.

If you want your tulips to flower reliably year after year, the best results come from lifting the bulbs at the end of each flowering season, drying them off, and storing them somewhere dry and mouse-proof until the following planting season. This is the counsel of perfection. It is easier to think of tulips as annuals instead.

Rosa 'Frühlingsgold' *Shrub rose with scented, clear yellow flowers in early summer. H 2.1m (7ft), S 1.5m (5ft).*

Hyacinthus orientalis 'L'Innocence' (Hyacinth) *Bulb with ivory-white flowers. H to 20cm (8in), S 10cm (4in).*

Phlomis fruticosa (Jerusalem sage) *Evergreen shrub forming a dome of woolly, grey leaves. H and S 75cm (2½ft).*

Hemerocallis 'Marion Vaughn' (Daylily) *Perennial with yellow flowers in mid-summer. H 1m (3ft), S 60cm (2ft).*

Tulipa 'Candela' (Fosteriana tulip) *Bulb with yellow flowers in mid-spring. H 40cm (15in), S 20cm (8in).*

Ceratostigma willmottianum *Deciduous shrub with a show of brilliant blue autumn flowers. H and S 1m (3ft).*

Iris sibirica *Rhizomatous perennial with purplish-blue flowers in late spring. H 1–1.2m (3–4ft), S indefinite.*

Hyacinthus orientalis 'Delft Blue' (Hyacinth) *Bulb with rich blue flowers in winter or spring. H to 20cm (8in), S 10cm (4in).*

Tulipa 'Bellona' (Single early tulip) *Early spring-flowering bulb with golden flowers. H 40cm (15in), S to 20cm (8in).*

Campanula lactiflora 'Prichard's Variety' *Perennial with bell-shaped flowers in summer. H 1.2m (4ft), S 60cm (2ft).*

Brunnera macrophylla 'Hadspen Cream' *Perennial with blue, forget-me-not flowers. H 45cm (18in), S 60cm (2ft).*

Altering *the* Planting Scheme

Where you have a corner site that is really hot, dry, and sheltered, too hot and dry for the rose, you can substitute this more tender collection of plants for some of those in the original scheme. All the plants used here are adapted to survive summer droughts, but not harsh winter frosts. Several have the grey foliage that is typical of drought-resistant plants.

Plants for a Dry, Sheltered Spot

Use the Cootamundra wattle for its finely cut foliage, more like bunches of glaucous blue feathers than leaves. It will grow larger than the rose, but its lightness and airiness stop it from ever becoming too dominant. The Russian sage – a native of Afghanistan and Tibet – is tougher, but it looks Mediterranean, with deeply cut leaves, greyish-white on their undersides.

The tall, stately flowers of the verbascum rise from astonishing rosettes of white, felted leaves. The eryngium is from a family that does not have a single duffer in it. Its sturdy, blue stems are topped with extravagant, thistle flowers, each surrounded by a complicated ruff of the same steely blue. They drift into death, fading to a pale buff, but are almost as handsome then as they are in life.

Verbascum olympicum (Mullein) *Biennial with large, grey, felt-like leaves and tall, downy stems that bear yellow flowers from mid- to late summer. H 2m (6ft), S to 1m (3ft).*

Acacia baileyana (Cootamundra wattle) *Graceful, evergreen tree with arching branches covered in blue-grey leaves and, in winter–spring, small, fluffy, golden flowers. H 6m (20ft), S 5m (15ft).*

Perovskia atriplicifolia 'Blue Spire' (Russian sage) *Deciduous sub-shrub that has ghostly grey-green stems and leaves and a mass of spires of violet-blue flowers in late summer to mid-autumn. H 1.2m (4ft), S 75cm (2½ft).*

Eryngium alpinum (Sea holly) *Upright perennial with deeply toothed, glossy foliage above which rise stems of conical flowerheads surrounded by soft spines during summer. H 1m (3ft), S 60cm (2ft).*

Argyranthemum frutescens, syn. *Chrysanthemum frutescens,* 'Jamaica Primrose' *Bushy, evergreen perennial with fern-like leaves, and soft yellow flowers in summer. H and S to 1m (3ft).*

VERTICAL SPACES

&.

*When you have used up all your horizontal
planting space, send plants up to the sky, trained
on trellis or wigwams, spread-eagled on a wall,
lolling against the arches of a pergola. It is vital
to consider the scale and style of vertical features
and how they will fit in with the rest of the garden.
A grand processional way through a lushly
planted pergola needs to lead somewhere more
exciting than the rubbish dump.*

PLANTS *for a* PERGOLA

F RESCOES AT POMPEII, the Roman town spectacularly swallowed up in an eruption of Vesuvius, show that even as early as AD79 pergolas were popular garden features. Covered in climbers, a pergola makes a living tunnel for you to walk through. Swathe it in clematis, roses, vines, and use it to enclose a path or to link two separate areas of the garden.

In Pompeii, pergolas would probably have been covered with vines to provide a crop of grapes and also shade in the garden. In hot countries, shade is still an important function of a pergola, the plants making a living roof of greenery.

SITING AND MATERIALS
Place your pergola with a purpose. It needs to lead somewhere, not look as though it has just dropped at random from the undercarriage of a passing helicopter. If you are building your own pergola, make it strong. There is a surprising amount of weight in a vine when it is in full leaf and an extraordinary strength in the twisting trunk of a wisteria. It may be slower than a boa constrictor, but it is no less crushing. Wood, brick, stone, and iron can all be used to construct

pergolas and the design will to a great extent depend on the materials you use. The most substantial are those with brick or stone pillars, connected by wooden beams across the top. Extremely pretty pergolas can be made from trellis work, which has an extra advantage for the plants: there are plenty of places for tendrils to get a hold and plenty of fixing points when you need to tie in stems. Use the sturdiest trellis you can find.

LEAFY COVERING
Clematis are popular plants for pergolas but can appear insubstantial if planted on their own. Think first of some handsome, leafy

GLORIOUS VINE
The leaves of Vitis coignetiae *can be as large as dinner plates. In autumn, they become richly coloured, earning the plant its common name, the crimson glory vine.*

PLANT LIST
1 *Wisteria sinensis* (Chinese wisteria) x 1
2 *Clematis viticella* 'Mme Julia Correvon' x 1
3 *Rosa* 'Félicité Perpétue' x 1
4 *Solanum jasminoides* 'Album' x 1
5 *Vitis coignetiae* (Crimson glory vine) x 1
6 *Clematis* 'The President' x 1
7 *Rosa* 'Rambling Rector' x 1
8 *Clematis macropetala* x 1
9 *Clematis* 'Elsa Spath' x 1
10 *Vitis vinifera* 'Purpurea' x 1
11 *Wisteria floribunda* 'Alba' x 1
12 *Clematis viticella* 'Etoile Violette' x 1

A CANOPY OF COLOUR
In late spring and early summer, the wisterias are heavy with tassels of flowers in lilac and white. Some of the clematis are in bloom, too, threading their colour through the backcloth of foliage.

PLANTING PLAN

10ft
3m

20ft
6m

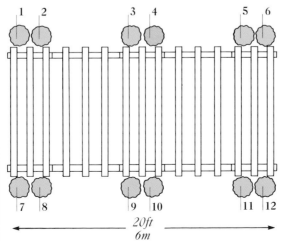

CHINESE WISTERIA
The purple flowers of *Wisteria sinensis*, Chinese wisteria, grow in racemes sprouting from stems that twine anti-clockwise. Hard pruning is necessary to encourage flowering.

CRIMSON CLEMATIS
Clematis viticella 'Mme Julia Correvon' is one of the large group of viticella cultivars flowering in late summer, all of which can be hard pruned in late winter.

DESIGN POINTS

HEAVEN SCENT
Roses and wisterias fill the air with fragrance, adding to the pleasure of sitting or walking beneath the pergola.

LUSH FOLIAGE
Plenty of leafy plants such as vines create a feeling of luxuriant abundance.

A BLOOMING SUMMER
Clematis, wisterias, and roses provide a glorious show of flowers throughout late spring and summer.

subjects to furnish the bare bones and add the clematis afterwards, like decorations on a cake. Vines are ideal. There are green- and purple-leaved versions; try *Vitis* 'Brant', *V. vinifera* 'Purpurea', or, for sweet grapes, *V.* 'Concord'.

Wisterias are also well suited to pergola life, their long racemes of blossom hanging like bunches of grapes from a vine. For the roses,

choose cluster-flowered climbers such as 'Rambling Rector'; some, particularly those developed from large-flowered types, have too stiff a growth habit to look comfortable.

On a long stretch of pergola, use the same plants more than once but in different combinations. This will help to give a sense of unity and cohesion to the planting.

VIOLET CLEMATIS
Clematis 'The President' flowers in early summer, bearing masses of single, purple blooms with silver undersides.

PALE PINK ROSE
The long, slender stems of *Rosa* 'Félicité Perpétue' are relatively easy to control on a pergola and the double flowers are sweetly scented.

SOLANUM
The white flowers of *Solanum jasminoides* 'Album' are carried over a long period from summer to autumn.

WHITE WISTERIA
The stems of *Wisteria floribunda* 'Alba' twine in a clockwise direction and need to be trained and well tied in as they grow.

CRIMSON GLORY VINE
This handsome species, *Vitis coignetiae*, is extremely vigorous with leaves that can be a foot across.

PURPLE CLEMATIS
The viticella forms of clematis such as this dark purple *Clematis viticella* 'Etoile Violette' are hardy and rarely subject to wilt.

CREAM ROSE
The individual flowers of *Rosa* 'Rambling Rector' are tiny but are borne in such large clusters that the overall effect is luxurious.

BLUE CLEMATIS
An early-flowering species with pale, ferny foliage, *Clematis macropetala* has fine double flowers of violet-blue.

LAVENDER CLEMATIS
Clematis 'Elsa Spath' often blooms twice in a season, the deep lavender-blue flowers studded with centres of reddish-purple anthers.

PURPLE VINE
Vitis vinifera 'Purpurea' is one of the best vines for a pergola with superb purple foliage that erupts in a blaze of crimson during autumn.

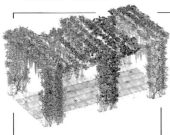

CLIMBERS *for a* PERGOLA

PATIENT TRAINING IS THE KEY to a well-furnished pergola. Little and often should be your motto, a job to be done on summer evenings while you are waiting for dinner to cook. Keep a pergola kit in a small basket – secateurs, soft brown twine, plastic ties – and take it with you on your evening stroll. As the clematis shoots grow, tweak each one in a different direction, so that when the plants come into flower, their blooms will cover the largest possible area. Be ruthless with the wisterias. Pruning twice a year is the only way to get them to flower profusely.

CARE AND CULTIVATION

SPRING

Mulch wisterias, vines, roses, and clematis. Tie in new growths of wisterias, vines, and roses. Plant the solanum and tie in firmly. In subsequent years, thin out weak growths and cut back any shoots damaged by frost. Plant clematis. 'Elsa Spath' and 'The President' may be lightly pruned by removing old, dead stems. *C. macropetala* needs no regular pruning.

SUMMER

Train and tie in stems of wisterias as they grow. Shorten shoots that are not needed for the main framework, cutting them back by half.

AUTUMN

Plant wisterias and vines, tying them in securely to their supports. Prune roses after flowering, untying and cutting out some of the old flowering stems and tying in new, whippy growth.

WINTER

Prune wisterias hard in late winter. Plant roses, cutting them hard back to produce strong, new growth. In late winter, prune *Clematis viticella* varieties to within 45cm (18in) of the ground.

Wisteria floribunda 'Alba' *Deciduous, twining climber with scented, white flowers in early summer. H to 9m (28ft).*

Rosa 'Rambling Rector' *Vigorous, rambling rose with clusters of fragrant, cream flowers in summer. H to 6m (20ft).*

Solanum jasminoides 'Album' *Semi-evergreen climber with star-shaped, white flowers in summer– autumn. H to 6m (20ft).*

Rosa 'Félicité Perpétue' *Climbing rose with clusters of blush-pink flowers in mid-summer. H 5m (15ft), S 4m (12ft).*

Clematis viticella 'Mme Julia Correvon' *Deciduous climber with red summer blooms. H 2.5–3.5 (8–11 ft), S 1m (3ft).*

Clematis macropetala *Deciduous climber with mauve-blue flowers in late spring and summer. H 3m (10ft), S 1.5m (5ft).*

Vitis vinifera 'Purpurea' *Deciduous, woody-stemmed, tendril climber with toothed, deeply lobed, purple leaves, and tiny purple grapes in late summer. H to 7m (22ft).*

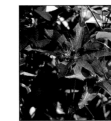

Clematis 'The President' *Deciduous climber with purple blooms in early summer. H 2–3m (6–10ft), S 1m (3ft).*

Vitis coignetiae (Crimson glory vine) *Deciduous climber with large, matt leaves that colour well in autumn. H to 15m (50ft).*

Clematis 'Elsa Spath' *Deciduous, large-flowered climber with mauve-blue blooms during summer. H 2–3m (6–10ft), S 1m (3ft).*

Wisteria sinensis (Chinese wisteria) *Deciduous climber bearing lilac flowers in early summer. H to 30m (100ft).*

Clematis viticella 'Etoile Violette' *Deciduous climber with violet flowers. H 3–4m (10–12ft), S 1.5m (5ft).*

ALTERING *the* PLANTING SCHEME

LUXURIANT FOLIAGE should always be the prime requirement in covering a pergola. But the vines and wisterias will take time to cover their allotted space. Gardeners in a hurry can use fast-growing climbers for quick results. If you want to spice up the soft colours of the scheme, include climbers such as eccremocarpus and campsis in cheerleader shades of orange and red.

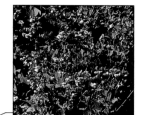

CLIMBERS FOR INSTANT RESULTS

Use fast-growing, tender climbers on the same supports as the vine to give instant cover. You will have to sacrifice the clematis, for their growths will become tangled, making it impossible to remove the tender climbers at the end of the season.

The cobaea and the lablab both grow vigorously. The convolvulus is more restrained and may be used instead of the solanum to twine its way through the rose. Its sky-blue flowers are vivid, but short-lived, opening in the morning and fading in the afternoon.

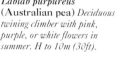

Lablab purpureus (**Australian pea**) *Deciduous, twining climber with pink, purple, or white flowers in summer. H to 10m (30ft).*

Convolvulus tricolor '**Heavenly Blue**' *Fast-growing, twining, annual climber that is covered in breathtaking, open blooms of purest blue from summer to early autumn. H to 3m (10ft).*

Cobaea scandens (**Cup-and-saucer vine**) *Tender climber, often grown as an annual, with flowers that change from yellow-green to purple as they age. H 4–5m (12–15ft).*

Tropaeolum speciosum (**Flame creeper**) *Deciduous climber with scarlet-red flowers followed by bright blue fruits. H to 3m (10ft).*

A FEAST OF FIERY COLOURS

These plants will set your pergola alight in summer and autumn, flames of tropaeolum licking up the supports among a mass of hand-shaped leaves. Use it to light up the vine and let the eccremocarpus flicker through the foliage of the wisteria. The campsis is only worth growing in mild areas as it needs a long, late summer to tease out a good performance. Used instead of one of the roses, it will change the atmosphere of the pergola, making it strange and tropical.

Campsis x tagliabuana '**Mme Galen**' (**Trumpet vine**) *Deciduous climber with vivid orange flowers in late summer–autumn. H to 10m (30ft).*

Eccremocarpus scaber (**Chilean glory flower**) *Climbing sub-shrub, often grown as an annual, with orange-red flowers in summer. H 2–3m (6–10ft).*

COLOUR *for* AUTUMN–WINTER

WALLS ARE OFTEN undressed of their clothes at the very time when they need them most, so this scheme suggests climbers and wall shrubs to keep a wall well covered throughout autumn and winter. Autumn colour comes from the fiery tones of a parthenocissus. Pyracantha adds brilliant winter fruit and jasmine defies the worst of winter weather with elegant sprays of bright yellow flowers.

LIVING GEMS
Thickly encrusting the stems like beads, the bright berries of Pyracantha *'Golden Charmer' are set off by evergreen leaves.*

CARE AND CULTIVATION

SPRING

Plant *Jasminum humile*, the garrya, and the clematis. Mulch all shrubs well. Prune out some old wood from *J. nudiflorum* and tie in new stems.

SUMMER

Train the pyracantha as necessary. Train clematis stems through the garrya.

AUTUMN

Plant the pyracantha, parthenocissus, and *J. nudiflorum*. Clip back parthenocissus as needed.

WINTER

Prune the pyracantha as necessary. In late winter, cut back clematis to within 45cm (18in) of the ground.

PLANTING PLAN

WARM COLOURS FOR A COOL WALL

You could use these plants on a house wall, for houses particularly look sad and naked when all their summer accessories are stripped away by the onset of frost. Do not waste a precious sheltered, sunny wall on shrubs such as pyracantha. In all but the most exposed and chilly locations, the combination would be ideal for a cool or partly shaded wall or fence. The cheering yellows, oranges, and reds of this scheme will provide at least an illusion of warmth in a semi-shaded spot.

Only the *Jasminum humile* and the garrya will grizzle and sicken in intensely exposed situations. The others are made of stouter stuff. If you want to reproduce the scheme in a cold area, substitute a chaenomeles, the

A LIVING WALL
A formally trained pyracantha contrasts well with the leafy abundance of the other shrubs and climbers. The glowing colours of flowers, foliage, and berries enliven even the gloomiest of walls.

PLANT LIST

1 *Parthenocissus tricuspidata* 'Lowii' x 1
2 *Pyracantha* 'Golden Charmer' x 1
3 *Clematis tangutica* x 1
4 *Garrya elliptica* x 1
5 *Jasminum humile* (Yellow jasmine) x 1
6 *Jasminum nudiflorum* (Winter jasmine) x 1

herringbone-branched *Cotoneaster horizontalis*, or a forsythia for the two less hardy shrubs.

Pyracanthas look most interesting when they are carefully trained. The branches are long and straight and fall very easily into parallel lines, squares, or diamonds. Although they are spiny, they are not vicious and the growths are easy to handle. Train one horizontally below a window, or bring the main stem up beside a window and tie in the growths to create a mirror image, a green and growing window squared off in panes.

PARTHENOCISSUS
The flaming leaves of *Parthenocissus tricuspidata* 'Lowii' have strikingly jagged edges.

PYRACANTHA
Pyracantha 'Golden Charmer' is a vigorous cultivar with relatively upright growth and bright autumn berries.

30ft
10m

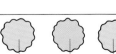
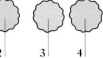

1   2   3   4   5   6

SUCCESSIONAL INTEREST

In autumn, the fiery berries of the pyracantha (yellow, orange, or red, depending on type) are complemented by the crimson leaves of the parthenocissus and the seedheads of the clematis. Garrya has extraordinary catkins of pale, greyish-green during late winter, but, exhausted by this bravura performance, it rests rather quietly for the rest of the year. Its foliage is evergreen, which is in its favour, but you can lend it jazzier summer clothes by allowing a clematis such as *Clematis tangutica* to thread through it. Choose your garrya with care. The catkins are less showy on female plants than they are on male. 'James Roof' is one of the best with extra long catkins, the calyces tinted with purple.

Spring is not without its attractions, too: the evergreen yellow jasmine, *Jasminum humile*, picking up the flowering baton from its cousin the winter jasmine. For greater contrast, you could try the more upright *Piptanthus nepalensis* instead. It is covered in bright yellow, pea-like blooms in spring and summer.

Parthenocissus tricuspidata 'Lowii'
Vigorous, deciduous climber with deeply cut, jagged leaves that turn brilliant crimson in autumn. H to 20m (70ft).

Clematis tangutica
Late-flowering, deciduous climber with yellow lantern flowers in summer–early autumn then fluffy, silvery seedheads. H to 6m (20ft), S 3m (10ft).

Jasminum humile (Yellow jasmine)
Evergreen shrub bearing bright yellow flowers on long, slender, green shoots from spring to autumn. H 2.5m (8ft), S 2.2m (7ft).

Pyracantha 'Golden Charmer' *Evergreen shrub with glossy leaves. Its white summer flowers are followed by orange berries in early autumn. H and S 3m (10ft).*

Garrya elliptica
Evergreen, bushy shrub with leathery leaves and, from mid-winter to early spring, long, grey-green catkins. H 4m (12ft), S 3m (10ft).

Jasminum nudiflorum (Winter jasmine)
Deciduous shrub with dark green leaves and, from winter to early spring, yellow flowers on bare stems. H and S 3m (10ft).

CLEMATIS
The silky seedheads of *Clematis tangutica* are as valuable an ornament as its nodding flowers.

GARRYA
As it is not reliably hardy, *Garrya elliptica* benefits greatly from the protection of a wall in winter.

YELLOW JASMINE
The bushy, evergreen *Jasminum humile* tends to sprawl, so looks better when trained against a support, as here.

WINTER JASMINE
One of the commonest winter-flowering shrubs, *Jasminum nudiflorum* is a cheering sight in the coldest months of the year.

PALE PERFECTION
The blooms of Rosa *‘Mme Alfred Carrière’, have a heady perfume and a fine creamy colour – flushed with the faintest blush of pink.*

DESIGN POINTS

DECORATIVE DIVISIONS
Screens covered in climbers may be used to divide a long, thin garden into more manageable, well-proportioned shapes.

PRECIOUS GOLD
Golden hops provide a glowing background for flowers of roses, honeysuckle, and clematis.

A SWATHE OF SCENT
Summer scent comes from old-fashioned climbing roses, white jasmine, and swags of apricot-coloured honeysuckle.

WOVEN COLOURS
Climbers mingle to provide a changing tapestry of yellow, white, and blue.

SCREENING *the* GARDEN

USING A SCREEN to divide one part of the garden from another creates the illusion that you are entering a different world, but because it is not solid, you do not feel that the one world is entirely divorced from the other. A screen will always introduce an element of surprise, too, for there is nothing more intriguing in a garden than not being able to see it all at once.

The screen is a useful device for dividing up a long, thin garden. It gives you spaces that are easier to work with and also creates separate areas that can be commandeered for different purposes, such as growing fruit or herbs. You could use a screen to mark a change of style in a garden, dividing a formally planted area from a wilder, more informal layout with fruit trees growing in long grass. It could also signal a change of colour schemes, perhaps marking a transition from cool to hot colours.

STYLE AND SUITABILITY
The style of the screen should be determined by the overall setting of the garden. For an informal effect, you can make a simple screen like a one-sided pergola, using larch poles for uprights and horizontals, and bracing the joints with diagonal poles in between. This type of screen is relatively inexpensive and easy to cover with plants, but in town gardens the faintly rustic aura may be inappropriate. Here, especially in paved gardens, something more architectural may be called for.

FLOWER POWER
In early summer, the clematis, roses, and honeysuckle are at their peak, filling the screen with colour and scent. The hops, with their handsome yellow leaves, provide a warm backdrop and contrast sharply with the dark-leaved jasmine.

DOUBLE SHOW CLEMATIS
In most seasons, the clematis ‘Lasurstern’ will give two shows of flower, one at each end of the summer.

COMMON JASMINE
Long cultivated in gardens, *Jasminum officinale* needs room to spread itself and some sun to ripen its wood if it is to flower freely.

GOLDEN HOP
The golden hop, *Humulus lupulus* ‘Aureus’, does not flower as freely as the plain green one, but the leaves are far superior in colour.

OLD ROSE
Delicately coloured and sweetly scented, *Rosa* ‘Gloire de Dijon’ is a beautiful old climbing rose.

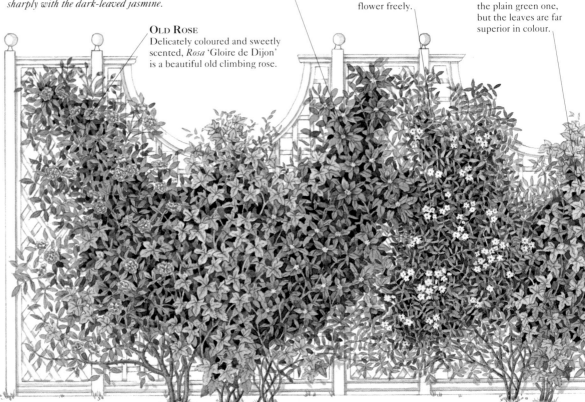

This scheme has been put together with a fairly elaborate trellis structure in mind, swooping through the garden in a series of elegant curves. Stains are more practical than paints for outside woodwork and either dark green or a greyish kind of blue would make a good background colour for the plants.

A formal, productive division could be made by planting cordon fruit trees, slanting in two directions to make a diamond pattern against taut wires and posts.

DRESSING THE SCREEN

The ratio of plants to structure needs to be considered carefully. Where you have an elaborate trellis screen, plants should be used only as set dressing. They should not completely swamp the underlying architecture. Where the screen itself is playing an entirely practical role, more vigorous plants will be needed as overall

cover. Here, the golden hop, *Humulus lupulus* 'Aureus', is used as an anchor plant along the four panels of a decorative trellis screen. Its warm yellow leaves set the tone for the rest of the plants: creamy roses such as 'Gloire de Dijon' and 'Mme Alfred Carrière', sweet-smelling honeysuckle, and clematis in varying shades of blue, yellow, and white.

PLANTING PLAN

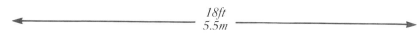

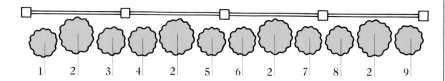

18ft
5.5m

PLANT LIST
1 *Rosa* 'Gloire de Dijon' x 1
2 *Humulus lupulus* 'Aureus' (Golden hop) x 4
3 *Clematis* 'Lasurstern' x 1
4 *Jasminum officinale* (Common jasmine) x 1
5 *Clematis orientalis* 'Bill Mackenzie' x 1
6 *Rosa* 'Mme Alfred Carrière' x 1
7 *Clematis* 'Perle d'Azur' x 1
8 *Lonicera* x *americana* (Honeysuckle) x 1
9 *Clematis* 'Henryi' x 1

YELLOW CLEMATIS
The vigorous *Clematis orientalis* 'Bill Mackenzie' has nodding flowers with thick, deep yellow petals.

LONG-LASTING ROSE
As well as being tolerant of shade, *Rosa* 'Mme Alfred Carrière' flowers almost continuously through the summer, with white blooms lightly tinged with pink.

BLUE CLEMATIS
A useful late-flowering clematis, 'Perle d'Azur' has china-blue flowers, the stamens tinged with green.

HONEYSUCKLE
The showy flowerheads of the honeysuckle, *Lonicera* x *americana*, have fortunately not sacrificed scent for the sake of size.

WHITE CLEMATIS
The most interesting clematis are usually those that, like *Clematis* 'Henryi', show a marked contrast between the colour of the stamens and the petals, here chocolate brown on white.

TRAINING *and* PRUNING PLANTS *on a* SCREEN

RELATIVELY FEW CLIMBERS are self-clinging and all those pictured here need to be fixed securely to supports as they grow. As with all climbing plants, you need to take care with the initial training.

The hop dies down in winter, and its stems should be cut back then. When it begins to grow again, it does so at speed and you need to fan out the growths and tie them in. The leaves make a good background to show off the clematis, which rarely have much to boast about by way of foliage.

Climbing roses often flower better if you bend the long growths down towards the horizontal position, making a low, gentle arch of the stem. The tension this creates along the top of the stem produces more flowering side shoots than would show if you left the stems vertical.

Apart from the architectural qualities of the screen itself, there will be no winter interest in this scheme, but in many ways this is an advantage for it leaves the trellis structure relatively clear each season for maintenance. You can re-stain the wood when necessary without first having to unpick a forest of greenery.

CARE AND CULTIVATION

SPRING
Mulch all plants liberally. Train hop stems over the trellis, fanning them out as they grow and tying them in securely. Thin out shoots of jasmine and tie in growth as necessary. Plant clematis before growth is too far advanced.

SUMMER
Cut out some of the old stems of the climbing roses and tie in new growths. Spray if necessary against black spot and mildew. Thin out the honeysuckle if necessary after flowering. Spray against aphids if these become troublesome. Tie in new clematis shoots.

AUTUMN
Plant hops, jasmine, and honeysuckle.

WINTER
Cut down stems of hops. Plant roses in ground that has been well prepared with added organic matter. Check that all ties are secure. Prune *Clematis orientalis* in late winter, cutting stems down to within 45cm (18in) of the ground. The other types of clematis need only light pruning to tidy up some of the brittle, old stems.

Clematis 'Lasurstern'
Vigorous, deciduous climber with large, single, blue flowers in summer. H 2–3m (6–10ft), S 1m (3ft).

Rosa 'Gloire de Dijon'
Climbing tea rose with fragrant, creamy-pink flowers in summer–autumn. H 4m (12ft), S 2.5m (8ft).

Humulus lupulus 'Aureus' (Golden hop)
Herbaceous, twining climber with rough, hairy stems and golden-yellow leaves. Greenish flower spikes are borne in hanging clusters in autumn. H to 6m (20ft).

Jasminum officinale (Common jasmine)
Semi-evergreen climber with fragrant, white flowers in summer. H to 12m (40ft).

Rosa 'Mme Alfred Carrière' *Climbing rose with fragrant, cream flowers in summer–autumn. H to 5.5m (18ft), S 3m (10ft).*

Clematis orientalis 'Bill Mackenzie' *Vigorous climber with yellow flowers in late summer. H 7m (22ft), S 3–4m (10–12ft).*

Clematis 'Perle d'Azur' *Twining climber with large, azure-blue flowers in late summer. H 3m (10ft), S 1m (3ft).*

Lonicera x americana (Honeysuckle) *Woody, deciduous climber with fragrant, yellow flowers in summer. H to 7m (22ft).*

Clematis 'Henryi'
Climber bearing large, white blooms with chocolate-brown anthers in summer. H 3m (10ft), S 1m (3ft).

ALTERING *the* PLANTING SCHEME

WHEN YOU ARE THINKING OF SUBSTITUTE PLANTS for a delicate trellis screen, avoid rampant climbers such as Russian vine or passion flower that will smother the entire structure.

Self-clinging plants such as the climbing hydrangea and ivies are best avoided here, too, as they are difficult to remove and may prise apart the wooden joinery.

SPLASH OUT FOR SUMMER

For a superabundant show, use the prolific rose 'Veilchenblau' in place of the hops on all four panels and replace the original roses with two leafy vines, either green or purple. The pretty parsley-leaved vine, *Vitis vinifera* 'Ciotat', would also work well here. Take out the yellow clematis and replace it with something redder such as 'Ville de Lyon' to tone with the new setting.

Vitis vinifera 'Purpurea' *Deciduous, woody-stemmed, climbing vine, with purple-bronze foliage. Tiny, pale green flowers appear in summer followed by green or purple berries. H to 7m (22ft).*

Clematis 'Ville de Lyon' *Deciduous climber covered in mid-summer with single, bright carmine-red flowers with yellow anthers and darker edged petals. H to 3m (10ft), S 1m (3ft).*

Rosa 'Veilchenblau' *Vigorous, summer-flowering rambling rose. The violet-pink rosettes are streaked with white and have a fruity scent. H 4m (12ft), S 2.2m (7ft).*

PALE COLOURS FOR A COOL EFFECT

By using another background plant to replace the hops, you can change the tone of the colour scheme, making it louder or softer. Vertically trained white-variegated euonymus, used with different sweet peas, either annual or perennial, will give a very soft, cool effect, with no yellow.

Euonymus fortunei 'Silver Queen' *Evergreen shrub with dark green leaves irregularly edged with a broad band of white. H 2.5m (8ft), S 1.5m (5ft).*

Lathyrus odoratus 'Lady Diana' (Sweet pea) *Annual climber with fragrant, pale violet flowers in summer – early autumn. H to 2m (6ft).*

Lathyrus odoratus 'Selana' (Sweet pea) *Vigorous, annual climber with large, scented flowers flushed with pink. H to 2m (6ft).*

A PLACE *in the* SUN

NEVER WASTE A SHELTERED, sunny wall on rock solid shrubs such as pyracantha or cotoneaster. You may as well feed caviare to a cart-horse. Use the warmest wall in your garden to gamble with plants that are on the borderline of hardiness. Disasters may strike in particularly cold seasons, but the euphoria of the roller-coaster ride in between will more than compensate for any accidents.

CLIMBERS OF FLAMING COLOURS

Hot places call for hot colours and this scheme is mostly composed of orange and yellow, with a soothing blue ceanothus to see you through late spring. This same ceanothus will later act as a prop for the scrambling yellow *Clematis tangutica*.

The display will be at its peak in late summer when the climbing trumpet vine, *Campsis* x *tagliabuana* 'Mme Galen', has started to perform. "Flower" is too tame a word for the event. Its blooms are orange-red trumpets, loud, but not discordant, which hold themselves clear of the well-cut foliage. The buds are held in clusters and open in succession over a long period. Frost eventually snuffs them out. The trumpet vine is self-clinging, but not in the sturdily tenacious way of ivy. Prudent gardeners should lash it to the wall at regular intervals, to nails or vine eyes, to prevent its being prised loose by wind in winter.

Flowering at the same time is the clear yellow clematis, which you can allow to ramble at will over the ceanothus. Cut all the stems of the clematis almost to ground level in late winter each year. This will keep it in good condition and also allow the ceanothus to have its space to itself for a while.

Setting fire to the winter-flowering mimosa in summer is another scrambling plant, *Eccremocarpus scaber*, the Chilean glory flower.

BLAZE OF COLOUR
In late summer, the star performer is the trumpet vine, its fiery colour echoed by the Chilean glory flower and contrasting with the yellow lanterns of the clematis.

PLANT LIST
1 *Acacia dealbata* (Mimosa) x 1
2 *Eccremocarpus scaber* (Chilean glory flower) x 1
3 *Ceanothus impressus* x 1
4 *Clematis tangutica* x 1
5 *Campsis* x *tagliabuana* 'Mme Galen' (Trumpet vine) x 1

MIMOSA
If the top-growth of *Acacia dealbata* is cut back during a harsh winter, it will often sprout with new growth from the base.

CHILEAN GLORY FLOWER
The usual type of *Eccremocarpus scaber* is orange, but there are also yellow and red forms, all having the same finely cut foliage.

PLANTING PLAN

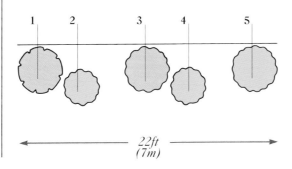

1 2 3 4 5

22ft
(7m)

TEXTURAL INTEREST
Both flowers and foliage of Acacia dealbata *have appealing textures – the leaves feathery and fern-like, the flowers in fluffy clusters of tiny balls.*

CARE AND CULTIVATION

SPRING
Plant the mimosa in late spring, and put in the eccremocarpus near the mimosa's base. Plant the campsis and cut it back to encourage basal growth.

SUMMER
Water the eccremocarpus in dry spells and remove seedheads as they appear. Tie in new growths of the ceanothus.

AUTUMN
Plant the ceanothus, training the growths flat against the wall. Plant the clematis, setting it at a little distance from the base of the ceanothus.

WINTER
In late winter, cut back the eccremocarpus and prune the clematis. Hard prune established campsis.

This often dies back in winter, sprouting afresh from the woody base in spring. If it does not die back naturally, cut it back before the mimosa begins to flower, for nothing should get in the way of that brilliant outburst.

TENDER PLANTS FOR A WARM SPOT

Some varieties of mimosa are hardier than others. Suggested here is the relatively hardy common florists' mimosa, *Acacia dealbata*, but you could equally well experiment with less hardy types such as the Cootamundra wattle, *A. baileyana*, or the Ovens wattle, *A. pravissima*. All have the same key attributes: flowers the colour of sunshine, a brave flowering season in late winter and early spring when little else is out, and finely divided, evergreen foliage that hovers on the greyish side of green.

If you have a conservatory rather than a sunny outside wall, you could grow these plants inside instead. The temptation then would be to experiment with even more tender subjects, substituting an ice-blue plumbago for the ceanothus and the tender golden trumpet, *Allemanda cathartica*, which has flowers of a glorious butter yellow, for the hardy clematis.

Acacia dealbata **(Mimosa)** *Fast-growing, evergreen tree with feathery leaves and fragrant, yellow flowers in winter–spring. H 8m (25ft), S 2m (6ft).*

Eccremocarpus scaber **(Chilean glory flower)** *Climbing sub-shrub, often grown as an annual, with orange flowers in summer. H 3m (10ft), S 2m (6ft).*

***Campsis* x *tagliabuana* 'Mme Galen' (Trumpet vine)** *Deciduous climber with orange flowers in late summer. H to 10m (30ft).*

Clematis tangutica *Climber with yellow flowers through summer and early autumn. H 5m (15ft), S 2.5m (8ft).*

Ceanothus impressus *Evergreen shrub with masses of blue flowers from mid-spring to early summer. H and S 3m (10ft).*

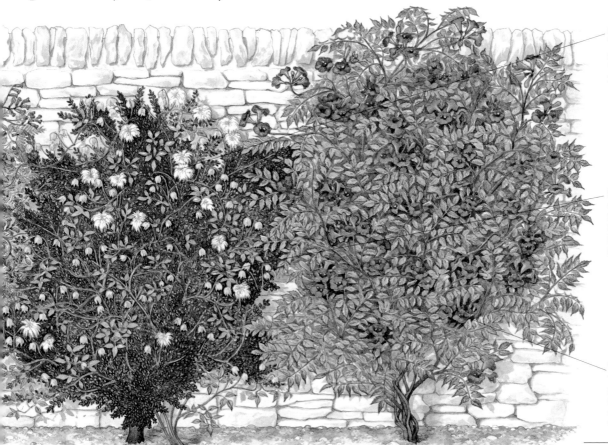

CLEMATIS
The silky seedheads of *Clematis tangutica* are as valuable as its nodding, yellow flowers.

CEANOTHUS
Ceanothus impressus is one of the hardiest of this family, with dark green foliage and flowers of a particularly rich blue.

TRUMPET VINE
The flowering shoots of *Campsis* x *tagliabuana* 'Mme Galen' hang from self-clinging growths. It needs the warmest wall you can give it.

CARE AND CULTIVATION

SPRING
Plant the thrift, erigerons, sempervivums, and the campanula. Shear over established erigerons in early spring to tidy them up before new growth starts.

SUMMER
Removed faded thrift and sedum flowerheads. Cut back trailing growths of the aubrieta by half. Tease out dying flowerheads and rosettes of sempervivums where necessary.

AUTUMN
Plant the aubrieta and sedum. Shear over clumps of campanula to clear away dead flowers.

WINTER
Birds sometimes dislodge plants such as sedum while searching for insects. Stretch cotton thread over plants if necessary to protect them.

A RETAINING WALL

ONLY MOUNTAINEERS CAN UNDERSTAND what it is like to hang spreadeagled on a vertical face of rock. Fortunately, there are more plants willing to adapt to this way of life than people. Aubrietas, thrifts, campanulas, sedums, drabas, lewisias, and arabis will all happily abandon the horizontal habit for the hanging. Ramondas will grow no other way.

Use a selection of these accommodating alpines to soften a retaining wall. You could also fit them in to a boundary wall, or where a low wall runs along by a drive. This scheme could be combined with *Border of Miniatures* (pp.52–55), where alpines are used in a raised bed.

The wall has to be made in such a way that you can squeeze the plants in between the stones or bricks from which it is made. If you are constructing it yourself, leave gaps for planting or, in a dry stone wall, position the plants as you go. In an existing wall, chip or scrape out mortar or soil to create a home for each plant. Choose small, young specimens for this type of planting. They will fit into smaller holes and will become established more easily than large, mature specimens. Trickle a little gritty compost around the roots as you plant.

NATURAL ALPINE PLANTING
Before you begin your planting, study the way nature arranges these things. Natural outcrops of limestone rock, even those as high as 3000m (8220ft), contain an astonishing range of wild alpine plants, trickling down vertical crevices, creeping along ledges. These habitats should be

PLANT LIST
1 *Erigeron karvinskianus* (Spanish daisy) x 5
2 *Sedum spathulifolium* 'Cape Blanco' x 1
3 *Aubrieta deltoidea* 'Argenteo-variegata' x 1
4 *Sempervivum arachnoideum* (Cobweb houseleek) x 3
5 *Armeria maritima* 'Vindictive' (Thrift) x 1
6 *Campanula cochleariifolia* (Fairy thimbles) x 1

AN UPRIGHT DISPLAY
This sort of planting is particularly worth trying in a small garden where horizontal space is in very short supply. It is also a good way of softening the look of an obtrusively new wall. The selection of plants used here would suit a sunny position.

your copybooks. Most of the plants suggested in this scheme will gradually spread to make large, natural-looking clumps. When you are placing the plants initially, try to avoid too mechanical an effect by varying the distances between the plants on the wall.

The Spanish daisy, *Erigeron karvinskianus*, flowers over a long period, unlike the alpines which tend to peak in spring. Its flowers gradually change colour as they age, starting off clear white, then flushing to ever-deeper shades of pink before dropping. If you are lucky, it will begin to seed into the wall, cramming itself in the narrowest of cracks where you could never hope to plant it.

SPANISH DAISY
Although an only slightly refined version of the common lawn daisy, *Erigeron karvinskianus* is a charming wall plant.

EVERGREENS FOR WINTER COLOUR

The sedum, sempervivum, aubrieta, and thrift are evergreen, so the wall will not look completely undressed in winter. They will all thrive on the excellent drainage provided by a vertical home. The thrift makes tight hummocks of needle-fine leaves, topped in summer with long-lasting, papery, pink flowers that are held out on fine stems.

Flowers are not such a blessing on the sempervivum for when a rosette flowers, it dies, bequeathing its space to the young baby sempervivums that cluster round the parent plant. The species suggested for this scheme, *Sempervivum arachnoideum*, has webs of fine hair round its leaves, as though it has been worked on by a hyperactive spider.

Aubrietas are one of the most common plants used in garden walls, and for good reason. They are adaptable and easy to grow. Colours range from pink through to a deep purple. The variety suggested for this scheme has variegated leaves and flowers of pinkish-lavender.

Erigeron karvinskianus (Spanish daisy)
Spreading perennial with lance-shaped leaves and white flowerheads that turn pink as they age. H 10–15cm (4–6in), S indefinite.

Sedum spathulifolium 'Cape Blanco'
Evergreen perennial with silvery-green, fleshy leaf rosettes and small clusters of tiny, yellow flowers in summer. H 5cm (2in), S indefinite.

Aubrieta deltoidea 'Argenteo-variegata'
Compact, evergreen perennial with trailing, variegated leaves, and pinkish-lavender flowers in spring. H 5cm (2in), S 15cm (6in).

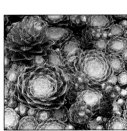

Sempervivum arachnoideum (Cobweb houseleek) *Evergreen, mat-forming perennial covered with white hairs. H 5–12cm (2–5in), S to 10cm (4in).*

Armeria maritima 'Vindictive' (Thrift) *Evergreen, clump-forming perennial with grass-like leaves, and pink flowers in summer. H 10–15cm (4–6in), S 20cm (8in).*

Campanula cochleariifolia (Fairy thimbles) *Spreading perennial bearing clusters of white, lavender, or pale blue flowers in summer. H 8cm (3in), S indefinite.*

SEDUM
The waxy foliage of *Sedum spathulifolium* 'Cape Blanco' is a year-round asset, spreading slowly to make a dense mat.

AUBRIETA
The leaves of *Aubrieta deltoidea* 'Argenteo-variegata' are thickly splashed with cream.

THRIFT
Full sun and good drainage are what this thrift, *Armeria maritima* 'Vindictive', needs to thrive.

FAIRY THIMBLES
Spreading by underground runners, *Campanula cochleariifolia* makes low mats of foliage topped by tiny, thimble-like flowers.

COBWEB HOUSELEEK
All the houseleeks make good wall plants, but *Sempervivum arachnoideum* is particularly intriguing with its web of fine filaments woven round the leaves.

CLIMBING FRAMES

A TRIPOD OR QUADRAPOD planted on its own, or incorporated into a bed or border, acts like a piece of sculpture in the garden. It provides a focal point. A vertical feature also breaks up the extent of a long, straight border in a useful way. Among the soft, humpy, rounded clumps of so many perennial plants, a well-planted tripod becomes a landmark, puncturing the hummocks like a lighthouse at sea.

This type of structure draws the eye, perhaps masking something beyond your boundary that you would rather not see. In a small space, it gives you extra room for planting. Horizontal spreads in a garden are quickly filled to bursting, but the vertical dimension is often under-used.

The style of the structure, as with pergolas and screens, will depend on the style of the garden. In a rustic setting, lash three or four stout hazel poles together and train plants up the poles. In a more formal scheme, use custom-designed structures, made from wrought iron or perhaps from trellis panels topped with decorative finials. Bamboo canes will not do; they look too temporary, too insubstantial.

CROCK OF GOLD
With fragrant, yellow blooms that fade to cream, Rosa 'Golden Showers' *flowers until late autumn and tolerates partial shade.*

CARE AND CULTIVATION

SPRING
Mulch all plants liberally. Tie in new growth of roses and honeysuckle. Plant clematis and fan out the shoots as they grow. Sow nasturtiums, raising seeds in pots and setting them out as plants, or sowing directly outside.

SUMMER
Dead-head roses and tie in new growth. Thin out wood on the honeysuckle after flowering. Spray against aphids if necessary.

AUTUMN
Plant the honeysuckle. Prune roses when flowering has finished, untying and cutting out some old, flowered stems and tying in new growth.

WINTER
Plant roses, cutting them hard back to produce new growth. In late winter, prune *Clematis* 'Ascotiensis' to within 45cm (18in) of the ground.

***Rosa* 'Golden Showers'**
Upright, climbing rose with fragrant, yellow blooms in summer–autumn. H 2m (6ft), S 2.2m (7ft).

CLIMBERS FOR A QUADRAPOD
In summer, warm colours are combined for a cheering effect. The soft, buttery-yellow of the rose is complemented by the bolder shades of the nasturtiums at its feet.

PLANT LIST
1 *Rosa* 'Golden Showers' x 1
2 *Clematis macropetala* 'Markham's Pink' x 1
3 *Tropaeolum majus*, single climbing mixed (Nasturtium) x 11

***Tropaeolum majus*, single climbing mixed (Nasturtium)** *Annual with trumpet flowers of red, yellow, or orange from early summer on. H 2m (6ft), S 1.2m (4ft).*

***Clematis macropetala* 'Markham's Pink'** *Early-flowering clematis with delicate, nodding, mauve-pink flowers in late spring–early summer. H 3m (10ft), S 1.5m (5ft).*

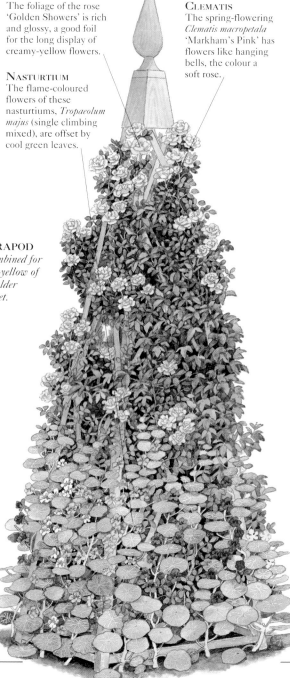

CLIMBING ROSE
The foliage of the rose 'Golden Showers' is rich and glossy, a good foil for the long display of creamy-yellow flowers.

EARLY-FLOWERING CLEMATIS
The spring-flowering *Clematis macropetala* 'Markham's Pink' has flowers like hanging bells, the colour a soft rose.

NASTURTIUM
The flame-coloured flowers of these nasturtiums, *Tropaeolum majus* (single climbing mixed), are offset by cool green leaves.

Wooden frames may be painted or, for a softer effect, stained so that the grain of the wood shows through. Frames are often painted black or white but this may look harsh; consider a gentler shade – grey, pale green, dark blue – instead.

LOFTY ASPIRATIONS

Use tripods and similar structures with restraint. Like exclamation marks and ultimatums, they quickly lose their effectiveness if over-exploited. Make sure they deserve their prominence. Choose positions and planting with care. In terms of colour, plants may either blend or contrast, but they must have the sort of habit that makes them look comfortable trained over a frame.

Old-fashioned rambling and climbing roses adapt well to tripod life. They have a yielding, relaxed habit of growth and many have abundant foliage, too. Steer clear of the stiffer large-flowered bush roses (Hybrid Teas) and avoid bullies, such as the Russian vine, and rampant climbing roses such as 'Kiftsgate', which would need a whole forest of tripods to contain it.

The planting for the quadrapod uses the climbing rose 'Golden Showers' with annual nasturtiums, which will continue to flower until the frosts. They are combined with the clematis 'Markham's Pink', an early-flowering variety that will provide spring interest. The tripod, planted in cooler colours, combines the semi-evergreen rose 'Albéric Barbier' with honeysuckle and the late-flowering clematis 'Ascotiensis'.

The fragrant climbing rose 'New Dawn' would make an equally good subject for a tripod, its pink flowers intertwined perhaps with a perennial sweet pea, or a later-flowering purple solanum. Clematis are naturals in this situation of course, but always better used in company with other plants than on their own.

PLANT LIST
1 *Rosa* 'Albéric Barbier' x 1
2 *Clematis* 'Ascotiensis' x 1
3 *Lonicera periclymenum* 'Belgica' (Honeysuckle) x 1

RAMBLING ROSE
Rosa 'Albéric Barbier', raised in France in 1900, is one of the best of the rambling roses with scrolled buds opening to small, creamy flowers.

HONEYSUCKLE
The scent of the early-flowering *Lonicera periclymenum* 'Belgica' is strongest in the evening, pulling in moths to pollinate the flowers.

LATE-FLOWERING CLEMATIS
The clear lavender-blue flowers of *Clematis* 'Ascotiensis' have a central boss of greenish stamens.

PLANTING UP A TRIPOD
The rich purple-blue flowers of the clematis make a sumptuous contrast with the creamy blooms of the rose. Fragrance comes from the rose and, in early summer, the honeysuckle. The rose's foliage is semi-evergreen and wonderfully glossy; it continues to provide bulk and textural interest long after its blowsy blooms have faded.

Rosa 'Albéric Barbier'
Vigorous, semi-evergreen rambler. Glossy leaves make a foil for soft yellow buds that open to creamy-white, scented blooms. H to 5m (15ft), S 3m (10ft).

Lonicera periclymenum 'Belgica' (Honeysuckle)
Deciduous, bushy climber with very fragrant flowers in early to mid-summer. H to 7m (22ft).

Clematis 'Ascotiensis'
Late, large-flowered clematis that bears flat, purple-blue flowers in summer. H 3–4m (10–12ft), S 1m (3ft).

COOL COLOUR
In a partially shaded position, pale flowers such as those of Clematis 'Mrs George Jackman' *gleam out from the gloom.*

CARE AND CULTIVATION

SPRING
Plant clematis. Dead-head hydrangeas and cut back growths that stray too far from their supports. Prune jasmines, taking out some of the old, flowered wood and tying in new stems that sprout from the base. Mulch all shrubs liberally.

SUMMER
Tie in growths of young hydrangeas. Train clematis through hydrangeas.

AUTUMN
Plant hydrangeas, jasmines, and the ivy.

WINTER
In late winter or early spring, take out any dry stems of clematis that show no signs of breaking into bud. On a house wall, keep the ivy well away from gutters and roof tiles.

WALLS *without* SUN

SHADY WALLS AND FENCES can be clothed as elegantly as sunny ones, provided that the shade is caused by lack of sun, rather than lack of light. You may not get as colourful a display as you could create on a sunny wall, but foliage will grow luxuriantly and plants such as ivy will be far happier here than they would be exposed to the full glare of the sun.

Some walls receive no direct sun at all, though in summer a few slanting beams may drop in at the beginning and the end of the day. At least you know where you are with this kind of wall. Others are far more treacherous. Those that get sun in a burst at the beginning of the day can be fatal to plants frosted overnight: the rapid thaw may rupture the walls of the plant cells.

SERENE PLANTS FOR SHADE
Your star plant on a shady wall or fence will be the climbing hydrangea. Once established, it sticks itself to a wall in the same way as ivy. The leaves are a brilliant fresh green when they first come out and, in some autumns, change to a fine clear yellow. It carries large, lacecap heads of creamy-white flowers in mid-summer.

PLANT LIST
1 *Jasminum nudiflorum* (Winter jasmine) x 2
2 *Hydrangea anomala* subsp. *petiolaris* x 2
3 *Clematis* 'Mrs George Jackman' x 1
4 *Hedera helix* 'Glacier' x 1
5 *Clematis* 'Nelly Moser' x 1

PLANTING PLAN

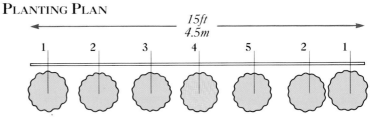

15ft
4.5m

SEASONAL CONTINUITY
At the start of summer, the clematis and hydrangeas will flower together but both clematis will continue to flower intermittently through the summer. Then you will have the hydrangeas' autumn display followed by the winter flowers of the jasmine.

JASMINE
An indispensible shrub in gardens, *Jasminum nudiflorum* has bright yellow flowers that are particularly welcome in winter.

HYDRANGEA
The climbing *Hydrangea anomala* subsp. *petiolaris* needs moist, cool soil to give of its best.

CREAM CLEMATIS
Flowering intermittently from early to late summer, *Clematis* 'Mrs George Jackman' has creamy flowers with dark brown stamens.

The plant sometimes seems slow to get going; this is because it does not want to risk too much growth until it feels safely attached to something. Secure growths tightly to their supports and if they still will not cling, strain them upwards with twine.

The winter-flowering jasmine, *Jasminum nudiflorum*, is common, but for a good reason. Little else chooses to start flowering at the onset of winter and, at that time of the year, its bright yellow flowers are particularly welcome. It cannot hold itself up without support, so is ideal growing in tandem with the hydrangea. This will be bare by the time the jasmine's display starts and you can tuck the thin green shoots in and around the hydrangea's stouter branches.

Some clematis do well on shady walls; some even prefer them. All appreciate the coolness at their roots. A cultivar such as 'Nelly Moser' keeps its colour better in shade than it does in sun. The pale tones of both types of clematis used here will show up far better in shade than would darker types.

IVY
Hedera helix 'Glacier' is a vigorous ivy handsomely variegated in grey-green and white.

PINK CLEMATIS
The early-flowering *Clematis* 'Nelly Moser' has a striking dark bar down the centre of each lilac-rose petal.

Jasminum nudiflorum **(Winter jasmine)** *Deciduous shrub that bears clear yellow flowers on leafless, whippy green shoots in winter and early spring. H and S to 3m (10ft).*

Hydrangea anomala subsp. ***petiolaris*** *Deciduous climber with frothy heads of white flowers in summer. H to 15m (50ft).*

***Clematis* 'Nelly Moser'** *Early, large-flowered clematis with rose-mauve flowers, each petal striped with dark pink. H to 3.5m (11ft), S 1m (3ft).*

***Hedera helix* 'Glacier'** **(Ivy)** *Variegated, evergreen climber covered in leaves patterned with grey-green and cream. H 3m (10ft), S 2m (6ft).*

***Clematis* 'Mrs George Jackman'** *Early, large-flowered clematis that bears creamy-white flowers in early summer. H 2–3m (6–10ft), S 1m (3ft).*

FORGOTTEN PLACES

꧂

These are the orphans of the garden scene: the area around the dustbins, the chilly little cliffs between stone steps, the tangle of drains and downpipes that you would like to disguise. Take heart. There are plenty of plants that actually prefer dark, dank corners to bright, sunny ones. And there are plants ample and generous enough to spread their foliage over the most unappetising patches of your garden.

A POTTED DISGUISE

DRAIN COVERS AND DOWN PIPES are not what you most want to see when you step out into your garden for a quick gulp of spiritual renewal. This exuberantly planted pot provides an excellent disguise for all kinds of necessary but ugly underpinnings of house and garden. Stand the pot on top of a drain cover or use it in a corner to camouflage plastic drain pipes and turn plumbing into paradise.

This sort of gesture has to look as though you mean it. You do not want the pot to seem as though it has accidentally fallen off somebody else's removal lorry. Use a big container, 60cm (2ft) across at least, but remember that this display must remain a moveable feast: if your plumbing plays up, you may have to investigate.

PLANTS FOR SPECTACLE AND SUBSTANCE

For maximum value, you need plants that give width as well as height so that they can mask problems that are both fat and tall. This is why the melianthus, the phormium, and the helichrysum will be your three best friends. Use a dark-leaved phormium, not one of the six-foot monsters, but something compact like 'Bronze Baby' or 'Tom Thumb'. The other

ingredients should be equally bold and leafy. *Begonia fuchsioides* is a winner with dark, glossy leaves and red bell-flowers just like those of a fuchsia. Weaving between these you could use a pelargonium, perhaps a variegated one as here, or one with scented, dark foliage, such as 'Chocolate Peppermint', or both. Include at least one free-flowering plant among all this leafy bulk: a daisy-flowered argyranthemum would be ideal.

All these plants are tender. If you have a sheltered porch, a greenhouse, or a conservatory, plant the pot up and keep it there until the danger of late frosts has passed. Harden off the plants gradually then, in early summer, you can stagger out with your pot already well furnished. In winter, you will have to put up with the sight of the drain covers, or design a different disguise.

UNFURLING FANS
The leaves of Melianthus major *unfold from tightly pleated fans into sprays of jagged-edged leaflets. It is the most sumptuous plant ever invented.*

CARE AND CULTIVATION

SPRING
In mid-spring, plant up the pot using fresh compost. Harden off plants before setting the pot outside.

SUMMER
Dead-head the argyranthemum. Remove any dead leaves and nip back plants such as the helichrysum, which may try and swamp the others. Feed and water regularly.

AUTUMN
Move the pot under cover before severe frosts set in. Overwinter mature plants or take cuttings each year and raise new ones. The phormium will last many years. The helichrysum, pelargonium, and argyranthemum are best raised afresh each spring.

WINTER
If retaining mature plants in the pot, keep them cool and make sure the compost is on the dry side.

Pelargonium crispum 'Variegatum' *Perennial with cream-variegated leaves. H 1m (3ft), S 45cm (18in).*

Melianthus major (Honeybush) *Evergreen shrub with large, glaucous leaves and brownish-red flowers. H and S to 2m (6ft).*

Helichrysum petiolare *Evergreen shrub with trailing, silver stems and grey, felted leaves. H 30cm (12in), S to 1.5m (5ft).*

Phormium tenax 'Bronze Baby' *Perennial with stiff, bronze, sword-like leaves. H and S to 60cm (2ft).*

Argyranthemum gracile 'Chelsea Girl' *Evergreen sub-shrub with grey-green foliage and daisy flowers. H and S to 75cm (2½ft).*

Begonia fuchsioides *Evergreen, shrub-like begonia with hanging, red flowers. H to 1.2m (4ft), S 30cm (12in).*

PLANT LIST

1 *Melianthus major* (Honeybush) x 1
2 *Argyranthemum gracile* 'Chelsea Girl' x 1
3 *Pelargonium crispum* 'Variegatum' x 1
4 *Helichrysum petiolare* x 1
5 *Phormium tenax* 'Bronze Baby' x 1
6 *Begonia fuchsioides* x 1

SMALL-SCALE PLANTING

A container scheme is like a bed in miniature, and the same design considerations of shape, colour, and texture apply.

BEGONIA
Although not as showy as the large-flowered members of its family, *Begonia fuchsioides* is an elegant plant with hanging, fuchsia-like flowers.

PHORMIUM
The stiffly vertical habit of *Phormium tenax* 'Bronze Baby' provides an excellent contrast to low-growing mounds of pelargonium.

HELICHRYSUM
One of the most widely used foliage plants in tubs and containers, *Helichrysum petiolare* spins a web of grey leaves around the other plants in the group.

PELARGONIUM
Pelargonium crispum 'Variegatum' is valued for its cream-marked leaves, which are more important than its small flowers.

HONEYBUSH
Grey-green, deeply serrated leaves are the chief attraction of *Melianthus major*. Nothing else has foliage that can match it.

ARGYRANTHEMUM
'Chelsea Girl' is a white-flowered cultivar of *Argyranthemum gracile* with particularly good foliage, silvery and finely cut.

**LONG-FLOWERING
WONDER**
*If dead-headed regularly,
heartsease, Viola tricolor,
will produce pansy-like
flowers from spring
right through summer
and autumn.*

CARE AND CULTIVATION

SPRING
Set all the plants in
pockets of good compost
mixed with some grit to
improve drainage.
Thymes and phloxes do
best in an open, sunny
position. The acaena will
tolerate partial shade as
will the violas and the
purple-leaved clover.

SUMMER
Shear off dead
flowerheads of thymes
to keep plants compact.
Leave some seedheads
on violas so that they
can seed themselves
randomly into cracks
in the paving.

AUTUMN
Clear away fallen leaves
that lodge among the
mats of foliage.

WINTER
No routine care
is required.

PATIO PLANTING

PATIO IS A TERM USED BY ESTATE AGENTS to describe any collection of paving stones vaguely adjacent to a house. Builders are keen on patios because they give an illusion of order to a new house. They shove all the muck that should never be left behind into a raft around the back door and then drop concrete slabs on top as they leave the site. A few low mats of plants growing in between the paving stones can go a long way towards softening the effect of a new and barren patio.

Growing plants in between paving is not everybody's idea of how such an area should be treated. Some people like to keep patios clear of all plants, so that they can be more easily swept and kept clean – and treated with weedkiller. If you are not one of those, read on. While you are reading, work out how you might fit the plants in between the slabs or stones. You will probably have to chip away a corner to make enough space. The builders may inadvertently have done this for you already. Treat it as a bonus rather than a black mark.

AROMATIC CREEPERS
The plants you choose should all have a low, spreading habit and should be able to survive the occasional shock of a foot crashing down on their heads. Choose colours that complement the background colour of the patio paving, whether this is stone, brick, or concrete.

Aromatic plants such as creeping thymes are very useful in this context. Far from sulking when trodden on, they give you the extra bonus

of scent. *Thymus serpyllum* is the most common form of creeping thyme, perfect for paving cracks. There is a particularly good variety called 'Pink Chintz', which has grey-green leaves spangled with tiny, pale pink flowers. You could, if you wished, create a whole scheme only using *T. serpyllum*, for there are ground-hugging varieties with white and deep red flowers as well as the pink. *Thymus caespititius* has a similar habit.

PLANT LIST
1 *Thymus serpyllum* 'Coccineus' x 1
2 *Trifolium repens* 'Purpurascens' (Purple-leaved clover) x 1
3 *Acaena microphylla* (New Zealand burr) x 1
4 *Viola tricolor* (Heartsease) x 4
5 *Phlox douglasii* 'Boothman's Variety' x 1
6 *Thymus serpyllum* 'Snowdrift' x 1

SITING PATIO PLANTS
Before you decide where to place your plants, consider access points to the patio and where you are likely to position garden furniture or plants in urns or tubs. If the patio is large enough, you could remove one or two entire slabs to provide more planting space.

CRIMSON THYME
The creeping stems of *Thymus serpyllum* 'Coccineus' are spangled with deep pinkish-red flowers.

Viola tricolor

COLOURFUL CARPET

The little New Zealand burr, *Acaena microphylla*, has no noticeable scent but like the thyme is evergreen and comes into its own in autumn and winter when decorative, tawny red burrs develop from the summer flowers. Creeping alpine phloxes adapt well to life between paving stones and, like the thymes, come in a wide variety of colours – pinks, mauves, and white. One of the lowest growing is *Phlox douglasii* 'Boothman's Variety', which has pale lavender flowers in early summer. Each flower has a prominent eye, marked round with blotches of a deeper violet-blue. For a fiercer splash of colour, try *P. d.* 'Crackerjack', which has magenta flowers.

Plants cannot grow in the plastic sacks, ancient newspapers, and solidified cement powder that often seem to make up the foundations of patio. Excavate this detritus and substitute decent compost. A good start will see the plants through a great deal of subsequent neglect.

Thymus serpyllum '**Coccineus**' *Creeping shrub with scented, green leaves and crimson flowers.* H 8cm (3in), S 20cm (8in).

Trifolium repens '**Purpurascens**' (**Purple-leaved clover**) *Ground-cover perennial.* H 8cm (3in), S 30cm (12in).

Acaena microphylla (**New Zealand burr**) *Mat-forming perennial with decorative autumn burrs.* H 5cm (2in), S 15cm (6in).

Viola tricolor (**Heartsease**) *Short-lived perennial or annual with flowers in combinations of white, yellow, and purple.* H and S 5–15cm (2–6in).

Phlox douglasii '**Boothman's Variety**' *Evergreen perennial with masses of pale lavender flowers.* H to 5cm (2in), S 20cm (8in).

Thymus serpyllum '**Snowdrift**' *Creeping shrub with small, faintly scented, bright green leaves and white flowers.* H 8cm (3in), S 20cm (8in).

PHLOX
The pretty flowers of *Phlox douglasii* 'Boothman's Variety' have prominent dark eyes.

PURPLE-LEAVED CLOVER
Each bronze clover leaf of *Trifolium repens* 'Purpurascens' is edged with brilliant green. Small, pea-like flowers are produced throughout summer.

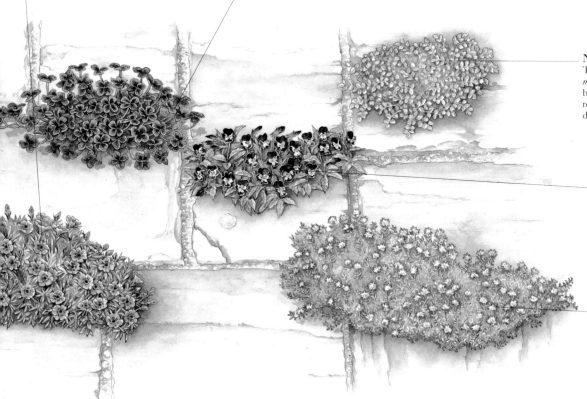

NEW ZEALAND BURR
The leaves of *Acaena microphylla* are tinged with bronze when young. It bears red summer bracts that develop into attractive burrs.

HEARTSEASE
Equally easy in sun or part shade, the charming pansy flowers of *Viola tricolor* are produced over a long season.

WHITE THYME
Dwarf and delightfully aromatic, *Thymus serpyllum* 'Snowdrift' is covered all summer with white flowers.

A NARROW STRIP

EVERY TEXTBOOK ON GARDEN DESIGN warns against the problems of the too narrow border. You lose the balance between a border's width and its length. You lose the opportunity to build up contrasting groups of plants. Flowers look as if they have been lined up for the school photograph. Sometimes, however, it is narrow or nothing. When you have little room for manoeuvre, make a virtue out of necessity and exploit the linear possibilities of a thin strip of ground.

WINTER WONDERS
The flower cups of winter aconites, Eranthis hyemalis, *form a golden carpet from late winter to early spring.*

CARE AND CULTIVATION

SPRING
Plant ferns, watering them in well. As new fronds unfurl, cut away old, tattered fronds. Plant crocosmias. In succeeding years, cut dead foliage down in early spring. Plant winter aconites "in the green" if available. Once the aconites have finished, plant pansies.

SUMMER
Clip box to shape in late summer. Keep soil around ferns moist. Dead-head pansies regularly; shear over in late summer to rejuvenate foliage.

AUTUMN
Plant box now or in spring, mixing plenty of bone meal into the soil. Plant cyclamen, barely covering the tubers with soil. Plant winter aconites if unavailable in spring.

WINTER
No routine care is required.

COMBINATIONS OF FORM

This scheme suggests a line of evergreen box, cut into alternating cones and balls, which can march single file along the whole length of the border. Setting out a bold single row like this gets round the problem of trying to shoehorn tiers of plants into insufficient space.

The way that you fill in the spaces between the box plants will depend on the amount of space you have to play with and whether the border is backed by a wall. This scheme would be ideal for a narrow strip of ground running between a path and a wall or fence. Shade will suit it even better than sun.

At the foot of a backing wall, try evergreen hart's tongue ferns, *Phyllitis scolopendrium*, perhaps planted alternately with crocosmia. The shiny, strap-shaped leaves of the ferns contrast well with the box's fussy foliage and the dramatic, sword leaves of the crocosmia, which have deeply incised veins running from leaf tip to base. Some hart's tongues explode into bizarre forms, the fronds endlessly subdividing until they look like bunches of parsley.

PLANTING PLAN

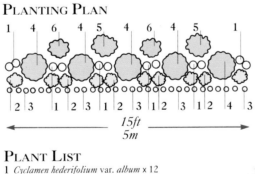

15ft
5m

PLANT LIST

1 *Cyclamen hederifolium* var. *album* x 12
2 *Viola* Clear Crystals Series (Pansy) x 10
3 *Eranthis hyemalis* (Winter aconite) x 30
4 *Buxus sempervirens* (Box) x 5
5 *Crocosmia* 'Lucifer' x 2
6 *Phyllitis scolopendrium*
   (Hart's tongue fern) x 2

Form in this border is more important than colour, but there will be a brilliant explosion of red from the arching flower stems of the crocosmia in summer. Choose a cultivar such as 'Lucifer' that is both vigorous and pleasingly violent in its tone. There is nothing worse in a garden than an apologetic red.

COLOUR WASHING

Use bulbs to provide washes of colour at different seasons in any spaces left between the box shapes. Start with aconites, as they are cheering in late winter and their clear, bright yellow flowers will contrast well with the sombre bulwarks of the box.

The plan here shows the aconites marching in a thin line in front of the box, but they could equally well be used in blocks between the box bushes. They die down completely by mid-spring so will not get in the way of later bulb

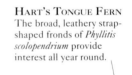

HART'S TONGUE FERN
The broad, leathery strap-shaped fronds of *Phyllitis scolopendrium* provide interest all year round.

WINTER ACONITE
In the wild, *Eranthis hyemalis* grows in woods, so is well adapted, if necessary, to shady positions in the garden.

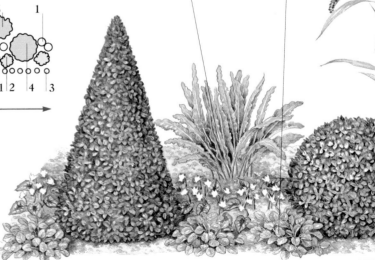

displays. Remember that aconites, if possible, should be planted "in the green", just after they have finished flowering. Dried bulbs, sold in late summer, do not establish so easily.

Snowdrops would be equally good for the first spring display, if you do not have them elsewhere. Like other white flowers, they look particularly cool and elegant with dark green foliage all around. Or you can wait for your white until early autumn and plant blocks of white *Cyclamen hederifolium* between the box bushes. The shuttlecock flowers are followed by intricately marbled leaves.

There remains only the choice of a flower to tide you over between the aconites and the cyclamen. Choose pansies or violas, but stick to a single shade. You are colour washing between the box bushes and need to keep the overall effect simple and clean.

FORMAL DISPLAY
A formal approach, with strongly patterned planting and a restricted colour scheme, creates an elegant, well-tailored effect in an awkwardly shaped piece of ground.

Buxus sempervirens **(Box)** *Dense, evergreen shrub with small, glossy, dark green leaves. H and S to 1.2m (4ft).*

***Crocosmia* 'Lucifer'** *Clump-forming corm with sword-shaped leaves and red flower spikes. H to 1.2m (4ft), S to 25cm (10in).*

Phyllitis scolopendrium **(Hart's tongue fern)** *Evergreen fern with tongue-like fronds. H 75cm (2½ft), S 45cm (18in).*

Eranthis hyemalis **(Winter aconite)** *Tuber bearing yellow flowers, each with a ruff-like bract. H and S to 10cm (4in).*

Cyclamen hederifolium var. ***album*** *Tuber with white flowers in autumn and marbled leaves. H to 10cm (4in), S 15cm (6in).*

***Viola* Clear Crystals Series (Pansy)** *Perennial, grown as an annual, with yellow flowers. H 15–20cm (6–8in), S 20cm (8in).*

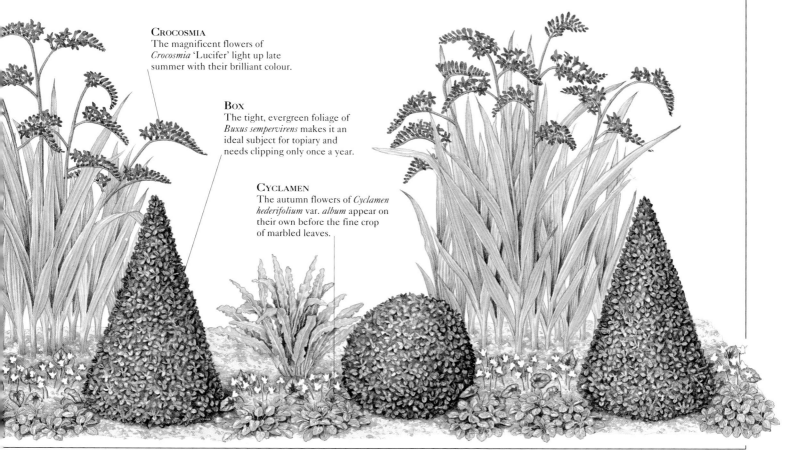

CROCOSMIA
The magnificent flowers of *Crocosmia* 'Lucifer' light up late summer with their brilliant colour.

BOX
The tight, evergreen foliage of *Buxus sempervirens* makes it an ideal subject for topiary and needs clipping only once a year.

CYCLAMEN
The autumn flowers of *Cyclamen hederifolium* var. *album* appear on their own before the fine crop of marbled leaves.

BETWEEN *the* STEPS

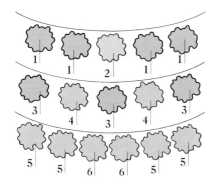

THE NEAT AND TIDY, no mess, no rough edges brigade will not want any plants to clutter up the carefully swept and weedkilled expanses of their steps and paths. Those with a more relaxed attitude to gardening may like to experiment with some of the plants suggested in this scheme for planting in the vertical spaces between the treads.

FLESHY FOLIAGE
The fleshy, spoon-shaped leaves of Sedum kamtschaticum *'Variegatum' have a subtle shine and are edged with a contrasting border of cream.*

CARE AND CULTIVATION

SPRING
Plant ferns in damp weather any time between mid-spring and early autumn, incorporating leaf mould in the planting mix.

SUMMER
Cut out the faded flowerheads of the euphorbia, saxifrages, and sedums.

AUTUMN
Plant the euphorbia, saxifrages, and sedums, incorporating grit if the soil is heavy and damp.

WINTER
Clear away any dead fern fronds in late winter before the new fronds emerge.

In some cases, of course, there are no spaces. Some steps are so firmly underpinned and anchored with cement and hardcore, you would need a pickaxe to plant even a pip. These are probably best left alone. Other steps are more accommodating. You may be able to ease out a few bricks from the risers. There may be cracks already there that you can utilize.

The easiest steps to plant between are those that are laid directly on earth, with the earth left uncovered between the different levels. These are the sort of steps you might have on an informal path winding its way up a bank between flower borders on either side.

SELECTING LEAFY PLANTS
Only certain sorts of plant will do in this situation. They must not grow too big, so that they trip you up, or obscure the path. They must not be so invasive that they make takeover bids for the territory on either side of the steps. And they must be plants that can take advantage of the cool root run underneath the steps.

PLANT LIST
1 *Asplenium trichomanes* (Maidenhair spleenwort) x 2
2 *Euphorbia cyparissias* x 1
3 *Ceterach officinarum* (Rusty-back fern) x 3
4 *Saxifraga moschata* 'Cloth of Gold' (Saxifrage) x 2
5 *Sedum kamtschaticum* 'Variegatum' x 2
6 *Sedum obtusatum* x 1

PLANTING PLAN

Planting must be simple. Two different plants is the most that you should use on each riser. If you use more, the effect will be messy and the steps will look too busy and cluttered. Choose plants for their leaves rather than their flowers. There is nothing better than foliage to soften the hard corners of over-aggressive masonry.

Small ferns are ideal and relish this kind of position where, even if they are in full sun, their roots are luxuriating in the cool, damp soil under the steps. The small rusty-back fern, *Ceterach officinarum*, would fit in well. So would the maidenhair spleenwort, *Asplenium trichomanes*, or, on acid soil, the parsley fern, *Cryptogramma crispa*.

SCULPTURAL STEPS
The hard, architectural lines of a flight of steps provide a sculptural setting for the lush fronds of ferns and the airy flower sprays of a euphorbia.

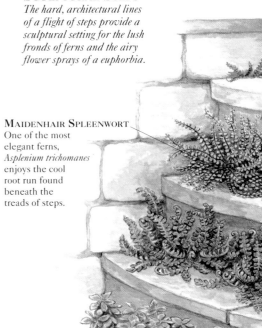

MAIDENHAIR SPLEENWORT
One of the most elegant ferns, *Asplenium trichomanes* enjoys the cool root run found beneath the treads of steps.

VARIEGATED SEDUM
The fleshy leaves of *Sedum kamtschaticum* 'Variegatum' are edged with cream.

SUN AND SHADE

If the steps lead from shade into sun, plant the ferns in the shade, which they will prefer. Try the rusty-back fern or a miniature polypody, such as *Polypodium polypodioides* or the taller but hardier *P. virginianum*, with one of the dwarf euphorbias, such as *Euphorbia cyparissias*. This euphorbia can be over-enthusiastic, but is very easy to pull out if you see it pushing its nose where it is not wanted. The feathery plumes of leaves are joined by brilliant lime-green flowers in late spring. Use the spleenwort alongside a soft, mossy saxifrage. *Saxifraga moschata* 'Cloth of Gold' has rosettes of fine, golden foliage and, like the ferns, prefers some shade.

If planting in a sunnier set of steps, use a couple of sedums, choosing between low, fleshy kinds, such as *Sedum kamtschaticum* 'Variegatum', or *S. spathulifolium* 'Cape Blanco', which has neat rosettes that are grey-green, sometimes suffused with purple. *S. obtusatum* has fat leaves that turn a lustrous bronze-red in summer. Sempervivums such as *Sempervivum arachnoideum*, which is covered in a cobweb of fine white hairs, would be equally suitable companions.

Asplenium trichomanes (Maidenhair spleenwort) *Semi-evergreen fern. H 15cm (6in), S to 30cm (12in).*

Euphorbia cyparissias *Leafy perennial with a mass of slender, grey-green leaves and lime-green flowers. H and S 30cm (12in).*

Ceterach officinarum (Rusty-back fern) *Semi-evergreen fern with lance-shaped, dark green fronds. H and S 15cm (6in).*

Saxifraga moschata 'Cloth of Gold' (Saxifrage) *Evergreen with white flowers. H 15cm (6in), S 30cm (12in).*

Sedum kamtschaticum 'Variegatum' *Semi-evergeen perennial with orange-yellow flowers. H to 8cm (3in), S 20cm (8in).*

Sedum obtusatum *Evergreen perennial with small, succulent leaves that turn bronze-red in summer. H 5cm (2in), S 15cm (6in).*

EUPHORBIA
The striking lime-green flowers of *Euphorbia cyparissias* are at their brightest in late spring.

SAXIFRAGE
Moist soil and some protection from the midday sun are what *Saxifraga moschata* 'Cloth of Gold' needs to prosper.

RUSTY-BACK FERN
The rusty-back fern, *Ceterach officinarum*, gets its name from the reddish-brown scales that cover the backs of the fronds.

BRONZE SEDUM
The fat, succulent leaves of *Sedum obtusatum* turn bronze-red in summer.

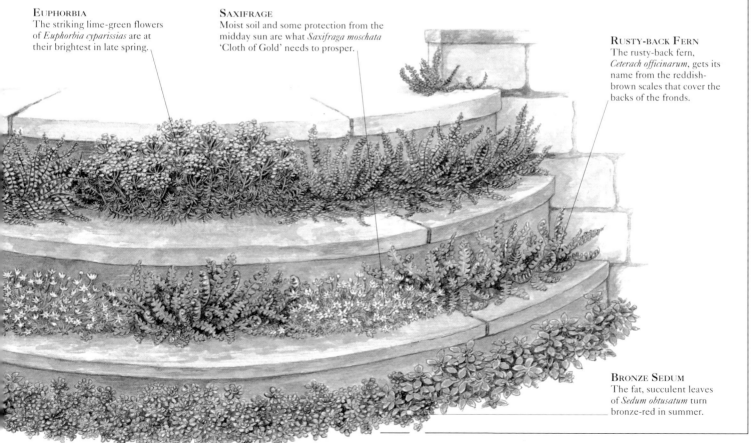

CARE AND CULTIVATION

SPRING
Plant the artemisia,
rosemary, and
ceratostigma. In
subsequent years, prune
out leggy or frosted
growths where necessary.
Sow chrysanthemum seed
in trays under cover and,
later, prick out seedlings.
Plant out seedlings as
soon as all danger of
frost has passed.

SUMMER
Dead-head plants
as necessary.

AUTUMN
Remove faded flower
stems from the artemisia
in early autumn. Plant
asphodels and
Welsh poppies.

WINTER
Cut back seedheads of
asphodels in late winter.

A STONY PATCH

THERE ARE TWO THINGS you can do with a dry, stony patch in your garden: set about removing all the stones by hand (the sort of job you usually find a good reason never to finish) or accept what fate has thrown at you and fill the area with plants that eat stone for breakfast. If you take the latter course, you will save yourself a great deal of back-breaking work and can also congratulate yourself on your ecological correctness.

There are plenty of plants that will positively enjoy this kind of well-drained billet, however unpromising it may look to you. They are the ones that you might find growing on the hillsides of the Mediterranean, or covering the slopes of the mountains of Eastern Turkey. Like these natural habitats, the site for this scheme needs to be open and sunny.

Soil that is packed with pebbles and stones will be very free draining. The most difficult period for the plants introduced here will be the initial one, immediately after planting. You will need to mulch and water assiduously until they are established and have sent their roots running deep underground in search of food and drink.

Do not try and make a formal edge to a patch such as this. The edges should be irregular and blend gently with the adjoining land. It should look like a small piece of mountainside, come to rest in your back yard. Enhance the effect by adding more gravel and pebbles, making a complete top-dressing of stone.

PLANT LIST
1 *Ceratostigma plumbaginoides* x 1
2 *Artemisia abrotanum* (Southernwood) x 1
3 *Chrysanthemum segetum* x 22
4 *Meconopsis cambrica* (Welsh poppy) x 22
5 *Rosmarinus officinalis* 'Severn Sea' (Rosemary) x 2
6 *Asphodeline lutea* (Yellow asphodel) x 5

A DISPLAY FOR DRY GROUND
A piece of dry, stony ground is transformed from an eyesore into an eye-catching display with hot-coloured flowers complemented by cool blues and grey.

WELSH POPPY
Though a determined self-seeder, *Meconopsis cambrica* bears welcome poppy flowers of sharp lemon or brilliant orange.

SPLASHES OF SUNNY YELLOWS
The bulk of this small scheme is provided by three plants: feathery artemisia, which makes an ever-grey mound of foliage, aromatic rosemary, studded with blue flowers, and the blue-flowered *Ceratostigma plumbaginoides*, which peaks at the end of summer. Lavender with its aromatic foliage and flowers would be equally suitable.

CERATOSTIGMA
The bushy *Ceratostigma plumbaginoides* has blue flowers and leaves that turn red in autumn.

Under this low canopy, you can spread carpets of yellow. Use the Welsh poppy, *Meconopsis cambrica*, for its long season of silky flowers. It seeds itself about with abandon, but in a rough site such as this, you will be glad of anything that is so willing to do its best.

Add height with spires of asphodel, which has grassy, blue-grey leaves and, in late spring, is covered with starry, yellow flowers. The seed spikes remain a feature long after the flowers have finished – leave them on the plants to add interest in winter.

To fill in at the end of the summer season, try a late-flowering annual, such as *Chrysanthemum segetum*, which will get into its stride as the poppies are finishing. This has small, bright yellow, daisy flowers on neat bushes, the flowers held on stout, stiff stems. There is little by way of foliage, but you will still have the poppy and the asphodel lending their leaves, as well as the foliage and flowers of the shrubs.

SOUTHERNWOOD
The stiff, erect stems of *Artemisia abrotanum* are clothed with lacy, aromatic foliage, which is unfortunately not evergreen.

Ceratostigma plumbaginoides Bushy perennial with blue flowers on reddish stems. H 30cm (12in), S 45cm (18in).

Artemisia abrotanum (Southernwood) Semi-evergreen shrub with yellow flowers and aromatic leaves. H and S 75cm (2½ft).

Chrysanthemum segetum Erect annual bearing daisy-like, yellow flowers. H 45cm (18in), S 30–45cm (12–18in).

Meconopsis cambrica (Welsh poppy) Perennial with yellow-orange blooms and fern-like foliage. H to 45cm (18in), S 30cm (12in).

Rosmarinus officinalis 'Severn Sea' (Rosemary) Evergreen shrub with blue flowers. H to 30cm (12in), S 1.2m (4ft).

Asphodeline lutea (Yellow asphodel) Neat perennial that bears star-shaped, yellow flowers. H to 1.2m (4ft), S to 1m (3ft).

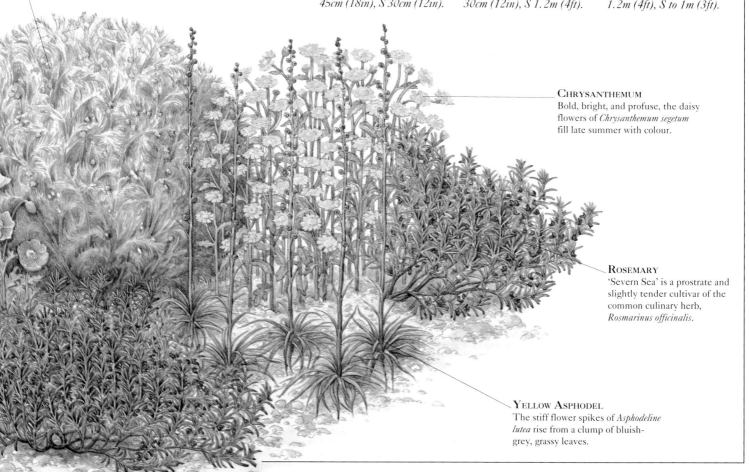

CHRYSANTHEMUM
Bold, bright, and profuse, the daisy flowers of *Chrysanthemum segetum* fill late summer with colour.

ROSEMARY
'Severn Sea' is a prostrate and slightly tender cultivar of the common culinary herb, *Rosmarinus officinalis*.

YELLOW ASPHODEL
The stiff flower spikes of *Asphodeline lutea* rise from a clump of bluish-grey, grassy leaves.

OCCASIONAL POTS

TARMAC AND CONCRETE have a disagreeable way of commandeering important places in a garden where we would much prefer to see flowers and foliage: beside the front door, directly outside the kitchen window, around a garden seat. In these situations, where there is little or no soil, pots and other containers packed with plants are your greatest allies.

In *A Potted Disguise* (pp.130–131) half a dozen plants are used all together in one large pot to conceal drain pipes and covers. Here, groups are built up by using plants in individual pots. You can mix and match the plants as you like to suit the time of year and the available space.

The advantage of growing plants in this way is that it is flexible and you can move particular ones out of the scheme when they are past their best. When the lilies' performance is over, for example, trundle them off to die down away from the limelight and move in another potted performer to take their place.

TAILOR-MADE PLANTING

Using collections of pots means that you can arrange them to fit any kind of space, whatever its shape. In a deep, narrow corner, you might use a potted evergreen to provide a backdrop to lilies and pelargoniums. By the front door, keep an ever-changing array of plants to reflect the seasons: camellias and early crocus giving way to scented-leaved pelargoniums, summer-flowering annuals, then neat winter evergreens.

Planting should always be adapted to suit a particular situation. Some plants such as the golden Japanese maple, *Acer japonicum* 'Aureum', scorch in full sun. Use this as the backdrop to pots of scented white regal lilies and lime *Alchemilla mollis* in a shady spot. White is always most effective when glowing from dark, shady corners.

This scheme uses brilliant flowers to sing out from a bare, concreted space, perhaps beside a front door. Hot colours suit hot spots and here there are bold orange lilies, rising behind pots of the dark-leaved pelargonium 'Mme Fournier'. This is a compact cultivar with clear red flowers, but any red pelargonium with dark foliage would be effective. If you want to use a pink type such as 'The Boar', which also has fine leaves, sharply zoned with a dark, central blotch, use different lilies: white or perhaps dark-flowered ones such as the crimson 'Empress of India'. Do not use

the tallest kinds, which would need staking in a pot. In a separate container, grow nasturtiums or pot marigolds, *Calendula officinalis*.

An evergreen gives substance to the group. This could be a clipped cone or sphere of box, or a shrub such as osmanthus, variegated euonymus, or pittosporum. If planted in the open ground these may become large shrubs. In pots, growth will be curtailed, and you can clip and snip to keep them in shape.

YELLOW LILY
Lilium 'Destiny' somtimes bears as many as ten flowers on a stem, each with petals curling back at the tip.

NASTURTIUM
Tropaeolum majus 'Alaska' is an unusual nasturtium, its leaves heavily marbled with white.

WELL CONTAINED
Spectacular in the border, lilies also make striking container plants. Lilium 'Enchantment' *will grow in sun or partial shade.*

CARE AND CULTIVATION

SPRING
Set out pelargoniums and the aeonium once all risk of frost has passed. Sow nasturtiums in the pot in which they will grow outside. Plant pittosporum; trim any straggly shoots as needed in late spring.

SUMMER
Dead-head pelargoniums. Keep lilies well fed and watered.

AUTUMN
Lift pelargoniums, cut them back, and overwinter in a frost-free greenhouse or shed. Or overwinter cuttings instead. Plant lilies as soon as available, setting them well down in the pots. Keep under cover until top-growth appears in spring.

WINTER
Overwinter the aeonium on a cool windowsill indoors. Do not overwater.

HARMONIOUS GROUP

When grouping containers, combine plants of contrasting form and habit to create a balanced display. Use upright plants for vertical emphasis and trailing plants for an informal, relaxed effect and to soften the hard lines of the pots.

PITTOSPORUM
The black stems of *Pittosporum tenuifolium* contrast well with the pale green, wavy leaves.

AEONIUM
Aeonium arboreum 'Schwarzkopf' is a lustrous dark succulent, but it is tender.

ORANGE LILY
The bright orange-red flowers of *Lilium* 'Enchantment' appear in mid-summer.

PELARGONIUM
Pelargonium 'Mme Fournier' is a zonal pelargonium with brilliant scarlet flowers offset by dark leaves.

PLANT LIST
1 *Lilium* 'Enchantment' (Lily) x 9
2 *Tropaeolum majus* 'Alaska' (Nasturtium) x 15
3 *Pittosporum tenuifolium* x 1
4 *Pelargonium* 'Mme Fournier' x 5
5 *Lilium* 'Destiny' (Lily) x 9
6 *Aeonium arboreum* 'Schwarzkopf' x 1

Lilium 'Enchantment' (Lily) *Early summer-flowering bulb that bears upward-facing, orange-red flowers with black-spotted throats. H 1m (3ft), S to 30cm (12in).*

Tropaeolum majus 'Alaska' (Nasturtium) *Annual with variegated leaves and trumpet-shaped, orange or yellow flowers in summer and early autumn. H and S 30cm (12in).*

Pittosporum tenuifolium *Evergreen shrub with wavy-edged, oval, glossy, mid-green leaves, bearing honey-scented, purple flowers in late spring. H and S 1.2m (4ft).*

Pelargonium 'Mme Fournier' *Tender perennial with almost black leaves and small, single, scarlet flowers. H 15–20cm (6–8in), S 10cm (4in).*

Lilium 'Destiny' (Lily) *Early summer-flowering bulb that bears upward-facing, cup-shaped, yellow flowers spotted with brown. H 1–1.2m (3–4ft), S to 30cm (12in).*

Aeonium arboreum 'Schwarzkopf' *Bushy, perennial succulent with stems each crowned by a rosette of long, spoon-shaped leaves of blackish-purple. H to 60cm (2ft), S 1m (3ft).*

SPLENDOUR *in the* GRASS

GRASS IN A GARDEN DOES NOT HAVE TO BE CUT every week. Once you grasp hold of this revolutionary notion, new possibilities open up on every side. Instead of toiling with a mower to shave grass off steep banks and awkward, tree-bound corners, allow the grass to grow tall. In orchards, or at the edge of a lawn where it meets countryside beyond, let the herbage grow under your feet. Mow wide paths through it. Contrast areas of mown and unmown turf.

Do not suppose, however, that you can persuade poppies and cornflowers to flutter beguilingly among the feathery grasses of your back yard meadow. Poppies and cornflowers will leap up brightly in the first year if sown on freshly prepared bare earth, but they are annuals, lasting only one year, and they favour newly disturbed ground. This is why they like cornfields, where after a neck and neck race with the corn, they seed themselves, ready to bob up after the next round of ploughing. Where grass is permanently established, as in an orchard, poppies die out.

PLANTS FOR A FLOWERY MEADOW
You can, however, tinker productively in unmown grass with a different range of plants: bulbs and perennials that grow like this in the wild and that can cope with the competition. Plant *Gladiolus byzantinus*, which will send up sheaves of sword leaves followed by searing spikes of magenta flowers. Plant camassia, whose tall spikes of white or blue stars can easily hold their own against the thin stems of

grasses. Both these will establish more easily if you put them in as growing plants rather than dry bulbs. Take out a square spadeful of turf and settle the plants in the bare earth so that they briefly have the space to themselves before their neighbours start jostling in.

Columbines can be used in the same way and look particularly pretty growing in grass. Transplant evening primroses into the wild grass areas in autumn, using plants grown from seed. All these are plants that peak in the first half of

FIELD OF BLOOMS
The colour scheme here is gloriously unrestrained in keeping with the wild look of the planting. Bright dabs of colour are seen through a feathery haze of grasses.

PLANT LIST
1 *Gladiolus byzantinus* x 3
2 *Geranium phaeum*
   (Mourning widow) x 2
3 *Aquilegia vulgaris* (Columbine) x 5
4 *Oenothera biennis*
   (Evening primrose) x 3
5 *Camassia leichtlinii* (Quamash) x 5

GLADIOLUS
In light soils, *Gladiolus byzantinus* will spread rapidly, throwing up sheaves of magenta flowers in early summer.

MOURNING WIDOW
Flourishing even in deep shade, *Geranium phaeum* has dark purple flowers that appear in late spring.

EVENING SCENT
The flowers of the evening primrose, Oenothera biennis, *have the heaviest perfume when they open in the evening. Each flower lasts only a day but there is a long succession of blooms.*

CARE AND CULTIVATION

SPRING
Plant gladioli and camassias as growing plants in holes cut into the turf. Add bone meal to the planting mix. Sow seed of evening primroses in late spring.

SUMMER
Towards the end of the summer, give the meadow grass its first cut. Transplant evening primrose seedlings in rows outside to grow on until autumn.

AUTUMN
Cut the grass several more times during autumn so that at the end of the growing season it has been reduced to a close-mown sward. Plant geraniums, columbines, and evening primroses in holes cut into the turf.

WINTER
No routine care is required in winter.

summer, for the meadow should be cut towards the end of the summer and if you have later-flowering plants you will behead them as you mow. After the first late summer cut, fit in perhaps three more cuts before late autumn. Then you will start off in spring with a close-mown sward against which plants such as primroses, fritillaries, and cowslips can display themselves to advantage.

Cranesbills, such as *Geranium pratense* 'Plenum Violaceum' and other reasonably tall-growing, herbaceous geraniums such as 'Kashmir Purple', 'Mrs Kendall Clarke', and *Geranium psilostemon* will be equally willing to supply splendour in the grass. Cut after the first crop of flowers. You may be lucky and get another, later show.

Any plant that includes the word "meadow" in its common name – meadow rue (*Thalictrum*), meadowsweet (*Filipendula*) – will be likely to have the right qualifications. Do not overdo the introductions or you will lose the meadow and find yourself with another herbaceous border.

QUAMASH
Long spikes of starry flowers, which range from white through to a rich, deep blue, rise from the bulbs of *Camassia leichtlinii* in early summer.

Geranium phaeum (Mourning widow) *Clump-forming perennial with maroon-purple flowers in late spring. H 75cm (2½ft), S 45cm (18in).*

Aquilegia vulgaris (Columbine) *Leafy perennial bearing pink, purple, or white flowers in early summer. H 1m (3ft), S 50cm (20in).*

Gladiolus byzantinus *Corm with upright spikes of deep pink flowers in summer. H 38–75cm (15–30in), S 6cm (2½in).*

Oenothera biennis (Evening primrose) *Erect biennial with pale yellow, fragant flowers in summer to autumn. H 1m (3ft), S 30cm (12in).*

Camassia leichtlinii (Quamash) *Bulb with erect leaves and star-shaped, bluish-violet or white flowers in summer. H 1–1.5m (3–5ft), S 30cm (12in).*

EVENING PRIMROSE
As its name suggests, *Oenothera biennis* is a biennial, the tall flowering spike arising from the basal rosette in the second season, giving a long succession of silky, yellow flowers.

COLUMBINE
The dumpy, short-spurred flowers of *Aquilegia vulgaris* are held above elegantly divided foliage.

PLANTER'S GUIDE

If you want to extend or adapt a planting scheme, use this planter's guide to help you. Plants featured in the book are grouped according to their suitability for particular sites or their characteristics, making it easy to find plants for any part of the garden. Use the lists to supplement any of the schemes: add plants to expand a design for a larger site, substitute plants to tailor a scheme to suit your taste or the growing conditions in your garden, or combine plants to create entirely new schemes.

PLANTS FOR SHADY SITES

Acer palmatum 'Dissectum'
Arum italicum 'Pictum'
Asplenium trichomanes
Astilbe x *arendsii*
Brunnera macrophylla
  'Hadspen Cream'
Camellia x *williamsii*
  'Brigadoon'
Carex elata 'Aurea'
Ceterach officinarum
Convallaria majalis
Cornus alba 'Elegantissima'
Crataegus laciniata
Cyclamen hederifolium
Decaisnea fargesii
Galanthus nivalis
Hamamelis x *intermedia*
  'Arnold Promise'

Helleborus orientalis

Helleborus
Hosta
Hydrangea
Ligularia przewalskii
Mentha x *gentilis* 'Variegata'
Pernettya mucronata
  'Mulberry Wine'
Phyllitis scolopendrium
Pieris 'Forest Flame'
Polygonatum x *hybridum*
Polygonum campanulatum
Polypodium
Polystichum setiferum
Rhododendron

Tellima grandiflora 'Purpurea'
Tiarella wherryi
Viburnum opulus
  'Compactum'
Viburnum plicatum 'Mariesii'

PLANTS THAT TOLERATE DRY SHADE

Ajuga reptans 'Atropurpurea'
Alchemilla mollis
Berberis thunbergii
  f. *atropurpurea*
Bergenia ciliata
Brunnera macrophylla
  'Hadspen Cream'
Buxus sempervirens
Cortaderia selloana
  'Sunningdale Silver'
Cotoneaster horizontalis
Epimedium perralderianum
Euonymus fortunei
  'Silver Queen'
Hedera helix
Iris foetidissima
Lamium maculatum
  'White Nancy'
Mahonia x *media* 'Charity'
Pittosporum tenuifolium
Pulmonaria saccharata
Salvia officinalis
  'Purpurascens'
Saxifraga x *urbium*
Vinca minor
  'Argenteovariegata'

PLANTS FOR LIGHT, SANDY SOILS

Acacia dealbata
Aeonium arboreum
  'Schwarzkopf'
Agave
Antirrhinum majus
Brachycome iberidifolia

Chrysanthemum segetum
Cistus x *corbariensis*
Cleome hassleriana
Crocus
Echeveria
Foeniculum vulgare
  'Purpureum'
Helianthemum 'Wisley Pink'
Iris (except *I. laevigata* and
  I. pseudacorus)
Juniperus
Lavandula
Linaria maroccana
  'Fairy Lights'
Nepeta 'Six Hills Giant'
Origanum vulgare 'Aureum'
Papaver orientale
Pelargonium
Pennisetum villosum
Pernettya mucronata
  'Mulberry Wine'
Rosmarinus
Scilla siberica 'Atrocoerulea'
Sedum
Sempervivum
Verbena
Vitis vinifera 'Purpurea'

Sempervivum tectorum

PLANTS FOR HEAVY, CLAY SOILS

Berberis thunbergii
  f. *atropurpurea*
Choisya ternata
Cornus alba 'Elegantissima'
Cotoneaster horizontalis
Crataegus laciniata
Eucalyptus gunnii
Eucalyptus niphophila
Filipendula

Hedera helix
Humulus lupulus 'Aureus'
Iris laevigata 'Variegata'

Lysichiton americanus

Lysichiton americanus
Malus
Matteuccia struthiopteris
Osmunda regalis
Philadelphus
Primula florindae
Primula japonica
Prunus 'Tai Haku'
Pyracantha
Pyrus communis
  'Marguerite Marillat'
Rosa filipes 'Kiftsgate'
Salix lanata
Sorbus
Viburnum
Vitis coignetiae

PLANTS THAT PREFER ACID SOIL

Abies koreana
Camellia x *williamsii*
  'Brigadoon'
Erica x *darleyensis*
  'Ghost Hills'
Gentiana sino-ornata
Hamamelis x *intermedia*
  'Arnold Promise'
Lithodora diffusa
  'Heavenly Blue'
Magnolia x *soulangeana*
Osmunda regalis
Pernettya mucronata
  'Mulberry Wine'
Pieris 'Forest Flame'
Pinus pumila 'Globe'
Rhododendron

PLANTS FOR BOGGY SITES

Astilbe x *arendsii*
Carex elata 'Aurea'
Cimicifuga simplex
Cornus alba 'Elegantissima'
Eupatorium ligustrinum
Eupatorium rugosum
Filipendula
Hemerocallis citrina
Iris laevigata 'Variegata'
Iris pseudacorus 'Variegata'
Iris sibirica
Ligularia przewalskii
Lobelia syphilitica
Lysichiton americanus
Matteuccia struthiopteris
Osmunda regalis
Polygonum campanulatum
Primula florindae
Primula japonica
Rodgersia
Zantedeschia aethiopica
　'Crowborough'

PLANTS FOR WINDY AND COASTAL SITES

✦=salt-tolerant plants
Antirrhinum majus
Arbutus unedo ✦
Bupleurum fruticosum
Calendula officinalis
Crinum x *powellii*
Eccremocarpus scaber
Erigeron karvinskianus ✦

Eryngium x oliverianum

Eryngium x *oliverianum*
Eschscholzia californica
Eucalyptus coccifera ✦
Eucalyptus gunnii ✦
Euonymus fortunei
　'Silver Queen' ✦
Euphorbia characias
　subsp. *wulfenii*

Felicia amelloides 'Santa Anita'
Galtonia candicans
Hyacinthus orientalis
Ilex aquifolium
　'Argentea Marginata' ✦

Kniphofia caulescens

Kniphofia caulescens
Kniphofia 'Percy's Pride'
Laurus nobilis
Lavandula angustifolia
　'Hidcote'
Matthiola
Narcissus
Nerine bowdenii
Phormium tenax ✦
Pulsatilla vulgaris
Pyracantha
Rosmarinus
Salvia argentea
Scilla siberica 'Atrocoerulea'
Sedum spathulifolium
　'Cape Blanco'
Sempervivum arachnoideum
Senecio maritima
　'Silver Dust' ✦
Senecio 'Sunshine' ✦
Viola cornuta
Wisteria sinensis

PLANTS FOR HEDGES AND WINDBREAKS

Arbutus unedo
Buxus sempervirens
Choisya ternata

Arbutus
unedo

Cortaderia selloana
　'Sunningdale Silver'
Crataegus laciniata
Ilex aquifolium
Laurus nobilis
Lavandula
Phormium tenax
Pittosporum tenuifolium
Pyracantha x *wateri*
Rosa 'Felicia'
Rosa 'Penelope'
Rosa rugosa
Rosmarinus officinalis

PLANTS FOR PAVING AND CREVICES

Acaena microphylla
Armeria maritima
Aubrieta deltoidea
Campanula carpatica
Campanula cochleariifolia
Erigeron karvinskianus
Helianthemum 'Wisley Pink'
Lithodora diffusa
　'Heavenly Blue'
Lobelia erinus
Phlox douglasii
Sedum spathulifolium
Sempervivum
Thymus praecox
Thymus serpyllum
Trifolium repens 'Purpurascens'
Viola tricolor

PLANTS WITH SCENTED FLOWERS

Acacia dealbata
Cheiranthus 'Bredon'
Choisya ternata
Daphne x *burkwoodii*
　'Somerset'
Daphne odora
　'Aureomarginata'
Dianthus
Galium odoratum

Hamamelis x *intermedia*
　'Arnold Promise'
Hyacinthoides hispanica
Hyacinthus
Iris graminea
Jasminum officinale
Lathyrus odoratus
Lavandula
Lilium
Lonicera
Mahonia x *media* 'Charity'
Malus floribunda
Narcissus
Nicotiana sylvestris
Oenothera biennis
Pelargonium (some)
Philadelphus
Pittosporum tenuifolium
Rhododendron luteum

Robinia pseudoacacia 'Frisia'

Robinia pseudoacacia
Rosa
Viburnum x *bodnantense*
　'Dawn'
Wisteria

PLANTS WITH AROMATIC FOLIAGE

Artemisia abrotanum
Calendula officinalis
Coriandrum sativum
Eucalyptus
Foeniculum vulgare
　'Purpureum'
Laurus nobilis
Mentha x *gentilis* 'Variegata'
Myrrhis odorata
Nepeta 'Six Hills Giant'
Origanum vulgare 'Aureum'
Pelargonium (some)
Rosmarinus
Salvia officinalis
　'Purpurascens'
Thymus

CARE AND CULTIVATION

PLANTS WILL MOSTLY TRY TO GROW, whatever you do to them. Sometimes they will also die, even if you are the world's acknowledged expert on their care. But there is a lot you can do to help, rather than hinder, their passage through life; this section is a practical guide that shows you how to keep your planting schemes looking their best.

The ideal way to learn about plants is by watching the way that they grow in your garden. The more time you spend with your plants, the more attuned you will become to their needs. Like people, some have quite specific requirements and it is foolish to ignore them. Work with the prevailing conditions in your garden, not against them.

PREPARING *the* SOIL *and* PLANTING

Soil is a mixture of organic matter, water, and small pieces of rock. The size of the rock particles and the amount of organic matter determine whether the soil is heavy or light, fertile or infertile. Adding manure, leaf mould, or compost helps improve soil structure. The extra humus closes up the spaces in sandy soil, making it capable of holding more water. In clay soils, humus opens up the spaces, so helps drainage. You can certainly improve your soil, but do not attempt to alter its basic type. You will be fighting a losing battle if you try to make an alkaline soil acid. If you want a garden filled with rhododrendrons and azaleas, move to an area with acid soil.

The perfect soil is loam, which is what good gardeners get when they go to heaven. Loam is neither too wet nor too dry, neither sticky nor sandy. It contains an ideal blend of clay, sand, and humus, with just the right amount of mineral seasoning. If you work hard at the humus, you may get your loam in the here and now rather than the hereafter.

SITE PREPARATION AND PLANTING
You cannot altogether avoid digging when preparing beds, but only a masochist will make this chore loom large in the gardening calendar. On heavy ground, digging exposes clods of earth that can then be broken up by frost. You also dig to get air into the soil and to bury weeds or other organic material. On light soils, you may not need to dig at all; forking over is often enough. A mulch of mushroom compost or other weed-free material may be spread thickly over the surface to prevent weed seeds germinating and will eventually be pulled down

PLANTING IN OPEN GROUND

1 *Dig a hole about twice the width of the plant's root ball. Mix the soil you have taken out with some compost or bone meal. Fork over the base of the hole. Place one hand over the compost in the pot and tip the pot over to ease out the plant. Gently tease out any tightly coiled roots. Settle the plant into the prepared hole.*

2 *Use a cane to check that the soil on top of the root ball is level with the ground around it. Adjust the depth if necessary by adding or removing soil underneath the plant. If planting a tree, drive in a supporting stake alongside, clear of the root ball (see p.148). Fill around the plant with the soil and compost mixture.*

3 *Firm the soil around the plant in stages to make sure there are no spaces between the roots, using your heel or knuckles. Water thoroughly and, for shrubs, trees, and moisture-loving perennials, spread a deep mulch of well-rotted compost or ground bark around the plant in a circle 30–45cm (12–18in) wide.*

4 *Your new plant may not need shaping or pruning at the outset. But if you can see diseased or damaged stems or wood, cut back to fresh, healthy growth. On a tree or shrub, prune out any stems growing towards the centre of the bush. Also remove any long, weak, or straggly stems that look as though they may spoil the balanced framework.*

by worms to enrich the earth. This is a lot easier than doing it yourself.

Where there are persistent weeds, use a non-residual weedkiller to clear the ground before using a mulch. Once the weeds have died down, you can plant direct into the ground without disturbing it any further. Tackle heavy clay soils at the beginning of winter, but leave light soils until late spring. The best time to plant trees, shrubs, and perennials is in spring or autumn. Most should be planted so that the surrounding soil is at the same level as the top of the root ball. Some perennials, such as irises, are best planted above the surface of the soil, however, while moisture-loving plants such as hostas, prefer to be slightly below ground level.

PLANTS IN CONTAINERS

You may want to create planting schemes using ornamental containers. Choose a container with drainage holes and add a layer of drainage material such as broken crocks in the base. Cover this with fibrous material such as coir fibre or upside-down turf. Set plants at the correct depth (see above) in a suitable compost, firming them in well, and water thoroughly.

If you are growing plants in a bed, that are too tender to overwinter outdoors, plunge them in the ground in pots. They can then be lifted easily when necessary and brought under cover until the following season.

PLANTING LEVELS

STANDARD PLANTING
(Aster)

SUNKEN PLANTING
(Hosta)

BULBS

Bulbs need to be planted as soon as you can get hold of them. Most are sold in a dried-off state but your success rate with the earliest flowering kinds, such as snowdrops and aconites, will improve significantly if you can plant them "in the green", that is lifted just after flowering, while still in full leaf. Plant these at the same depth as before, shown by the colour change near the base of the stem. Unless you are using them in bold blocks for formal bedding, all bulbs are best planted in random clumps or drifts, particularly if in a semi-wild setting, under trees or in grass. In general, light soils are kinder to bulbs than heavy ones. They warm up more quickly in spring and they are usually better drained.

PLANTING DEPTHS

The ideal planting depth depends on the size of the bulb. Use the length of the bulb as a rough guide and plant each bulb at two or three times its own depth.

PLANTING IN A WALL CREVICE

Before planting in a wall (or in the crevices of paving) chip out some mortar if necessary so you can add compost to support the plants. Choose plants such as sedums, saxifrages, and sempervivums that naturally grow in situations such as these.

1 *Ease the roots of the plant into a crevice, using a widger, teaspoon, or the tip of a small trowel. Firm the plants in place with your fingers, trickling in more compost if necessary.*

2 *When all the plants are in position, water them from the top of the wall, or mist them with a hand sprayer. Keep them moist until well established. Refirm any plants that become loose.*

WALL SHRUBS AND CLIMBERS

Before planting, secure any support such as vine eyes and wires or trellis (hinged so it can be lowered and the wall painted when necessary). The bottom of a wall is a dry place, so the most important thing when planting a wall shrub or climber is to set the plant at least 45cm (18in) away from the base of the wall. After that, regular training and tying in (see pp.150–51) are the keys to success. Keep climbers close to the wall, or they will crowd out other plants growing beneath.

TRELLIS SUPPORT

Fix trellis at top with hook and vine eye.

Fix hinge at base.

1 *Dig a hole larger than the plant's root ball. Loosen the soil in the hole. Soak the root ball, then settle the plant in the hole, leaning it at 45°. Spread out the roots away from the wall.*

2 *Fill in around the plant, firming in stages. Untie the plant from its cane and cut back any weak, damaged, or outward-growing stems. Spread out and tie in remaining shoots.*

CARING *for* PLANTS

In the wild, plants find their own billets and they choose what suits them best. In a garden, they have to make the best of what we give them. If you take the trouble to learn what requirements each plant has, you will be amply rewarded. The amount of care they need will depend on the plants you choose to grow.

FEEDING AND WATERING

Food and drink are as necessary to plants as they are to people. It is the gardener's duty to see that each plant has enough of both. Food means more than chemical fertilizers. These work fast, but they feed the plant rather than the soil and this upsets the soil's delicate balance. They do not supply as clever a balance of nutrients as the plant can supply for itself, if the soil is in good heart. Nitrates promote rapid growth, but plants fed only in this way have a high water content, which makes them sappy and more open to pest and disease attack.

Where plants are growing in unnatural circumstances, in the confined spaces of pots, hanging baskets, or window boxes, they are necessarily restricted to a diet of manufactured food. In the open ground, you can manage things differently, using fertilizers based on seaweed, bone meal, hoof and horn.

MULCHING AND WEEDING

Adding bulky organic matter to the soil will enhance its fertility and structure. The simplest way to do this is with a thick mulch. This also helps to retain moisture and control annual weeds. Different mulches provide different benefits. Gravel, for instance, will not do anything by way of feeding, but is excellent around alpines or Mediterranean herbs, which are used to thin rations. It prevents mud splashing on to low leaves or flowers and provides drainage around the necks of plants.

Weeds compete with your ornamental plants for food and water and may even smother their growth. Mulching helps to keep weeds in check but will not remove the need for weeding altogether. Take care to remove annual weeds while still young and certainly before they flower and set seed. Use a hoe, fork, or trowel to remove weeds or treat them with a weedkiller such as glyphosate that does not persist in the soil.

MULCHING
When mulching, spread the material around the plant to the same extent as its top-growth, keeping clear of the plant's stem. A mulch should be 5–10cm (2–4in) thick if it is to keep down annual weeds. No mulch will prevent the growth of perennial weeds.

STAKES AND TIES

The best answer to staking is to use plants that do not need it, for it is a difficult job to do well. The mechanics should not show, nor should the stake rule the plant, giving it the air of a patient in a neck brace. Some plants, such as delphiniums, you stake as a matter of course, for they have been bred far beyond the point where they can hold themselves up in a crisis. But to stake a foxglove is like caging a gazelle. You take away its soul. Any support you give a plant must be in keeping with its natural habit. Brushwood, either bent over and woven into an approximation of a lobster pot, or pushed in to make a stockade around a plant, provides the maximum support with the minimum interference. It is also attractive to look at before it is disguised by the plant's growth. That matters.

SINGLE CANE
Tie single-stemmed plants such as gladiolus to a bamboo cane before they are about 30cm (12in) tall. When flower buds begin to form, tie the stem to the cane just below the buds to provide support.

LINK STAKES
Use link stakes for clump-forming or multi-stemmed plants that need support. Push the stakes deep into the soil when the plant is still young, and raise them gradually as it grows.

ANGLED STAKE
A low, angled stake such as this allows a tree to move naturally in the wind. Drive it into the ground clear of the roots at a 45° angle so that it leans into the prevailing wind. Secure the tree to the stake with a buckle-and-spacer tie. Pull the tie taut, without damaging the bark, and adjust it as the tree grows.

CUTTING BACK AND DIVIDING

Many plants, including roses and some perennials, produce more flowers if the old, dying blooms are cut off (see right). Shrubs grown for their variegated foliage should have any plain leaves removed. A number of perennials and bulbs benefit from being divided and replanted if they are no longer flowering well and have become overcrowded (see p.152).

Herbaceous perennials may be cut down at the end of the season. As well as looking tidier, this helps prevent problems caused by diseased or decaying material.

PEST AND DISEASE CONTROL

If plants are growing well, as they will if you take care to give them what they need, they will be far less vulnerable to pests and diseases. The problem with using insecticides is that you wipe out the good guys along with the bad. There are plenty of good insects, but they seem slower on the uptake than the bad. Ladybirds, for instance, are good because they eat prodigious numbers of aphids. Encourage ichneumon flies, which prey on caterpillars, by planting golden rod and fennel. Centipedes and black ground beetles are both keen on slug breakfasts.

Weather conditions have a great influence on some diseases. There are good and bad years for mildew, rust, black spot, and blight. Fungicides help, but only if you doggedly apply them at the correct intervals. Help yourself by choosing varieties of plants that are resistant to disease.

DEAD-HEADING

The purpose of dead-heading, that is removing faded flowers, is to stimulate the earliest possible development of new, young shoots and further blooms throughout the flowering season. On a cluster-flowered bush rose such as this, cut out the central bloom of the truss first to stimulate the other buds into flower. When all the flowers have faded, remove the whole truss, cutting back to an emerging bud or a fully formed shoot.

REMOVING REVERTED SHOOTS

Many variegated shrubs are propagated from green-leaved plants that have produced mutated branches, known as sports. Sometimes branches of these variegated shrubs revert to the foliage of the parent. Since these branches have more chlorophyll and so are more vigorous, they may swamp the variegated growth. Cut them out as soon as you notice them.

PROTECTING PLANTS FROM FROST AND WIND

In general, you should garden with your climate, rather than against it, but all adventurous gardeners are constantly trying to extend the boundaries of what is possible in their patch. Plants that are on the borderline of hardiness in your area should be protected from the worst of winter, particularly while they are young and at their most vulnerable. Surround a tree or shrub with an insulating barrier of straw or bracken, for example, held in place with a cage of wire netting. Even if their top-growth has been cut to the ground by frost in winter, many shrubs will sprout again from the base once they have a well-established network of roots. Leafy plants such as palms and cordylines can be protected by having their leaves bound and wrapped in sacking. For small plants and seedlings, use glass or plastic cloches, low polytunnels, or a fleecy, floating mulch. Another solution is to pot up plants, then bring them under cover before the first frosts and overwinter them indoors.

DOUBLE NETTING
Protect vulnerable plants from wind with a barrier to diffuse the wind's strength. Most effective are permeable barriers such as this flexible netting which makes a temporary shelter for plants while they become established.

CLOCHE
Use a cloche to protect seedlings, tender herbaceous plants, or young shrubs. Cover the open ends with glass or plastic to stop wind blowing through. Water plants if necessary. Remove the cloches by day as the temperature warms up.

MOUNDING UP EARTH
In cold areas, protect tender bush roses or plants such as agapanthus from frost damage by mounding up earth around the crown to a depth of about 12cm (5in).

HESSIAN
To protect leafy plants against frost, tie in the leaves, then wrap them in hessian. Pack the base of the plant with straw.

PRUNING *and* TRAINING

Pruning is the gardener's way of enhancing the performance of a particular plant and encouraging it to produce better flowers, foliage, or fruit. It is something we do for our benefit rather than theirs. Shrubs do not die if they are left unpruned, as anyone who has taken over a neglected garden knows only too well. They just get bigger.

AIMS OF PRUNING
Good pruning is a matter of working with rather than against the natural habit and inclinations of a plant. If it flowers on new wood, as buddleia and perovskia do, then it is in your interests to persuade it to produce as much of this as possible by pruning hard each season. Shrubs such as dogwoods with decorative winter bark also benefit from hard pruning or coppicing (see opposite), as the bark colour is always brighter on new wood than old. Compensate for the extra work you are giving such shrubs by feeding them liberally.

Many trees, shrubs, roses, and climbers benefit from pruning to remove dead, unproductive, congested, or spindly growth. But do not look upon secateurs as offensive weapons to brandish round all plants in the garden. Abutilon, acer, camellia, cotoneaster, magnolia, and rhododendron do not need regular pruning. All you need to do with these is remove dead shoots and occasionally thin out overcrowded or crossing branches.

If you use shears on shrubs, you run the risk of reducing them all to the same barbered, bun-like shape. When pruning, do not cut back all branches by the same amount. Remove some stems entirely, cutting them back to the base or at the junction with another branch. In this way, you will be more certain of retaining the shrub's natural outline. If pruning stems partially, cut back to an outward-facing bud or shoot.

Before you make any cut, have its purpose clearly in mind. Some shrubs such as cotinus, forsythia, winter jasmine, spiraea, philadelphus, and weigela are best treated in a three-year

WHERE TO CUT
When pruning, cut back to just above a healthy bud or shoot or pair of buds or shoots.

Strong pair of buds

Make a straight cut on plants with opposite buds.

Angle the cut on plants with alternate buds.

Cut back to an outward-facing bud.

OLD WOOD
Periodically remove wood that is very old and no longer flowering well. Use secateurs or, for very thick stems, pruning loppers to remove a proportion of the oldest stems, cutting them back to within 5–8cm (2–3in) of the ground. On established suckering shrubs, cut back up to half the old wood to the base after flowering, and prune the remainder by half.

PRUNING ROSES
Prune roses when dormant, between autumn leaf fall and spring bud break. Large-flowered bush roses (Hybrid Teas) need the hardest pruning. Surprisingly, trials at the Royal National Rose Society's grounds in England showed that a quick haircut with a hedgetrimmer can yield better results than more traditional methods. Old shrub and species roses flower on old wood rather than new and so must be pruned more lightly. Most roses should be hard pruned after planting to stimulate vigorous growth.

REMOVING OLD STEMS
On mature roses, occasionally remove old, unproductive wood at the base to encourage the shrub to produce young, new growth.

SHORTENING SIDESHOOTS
Some shrub roses, such as the Gallicas, have an overabundance of twiggy sideshoots. Shorten these after flowering, cutting them back by about two-thirds.

DEAD WOOD
All shrubs at some stage in their lives have shoots or whole branches that die back, due to age, disease, or some kind of damage. This wood should be cut back to a healthy pair of buds, leaves, or shoots.

THIN STEMS
Prune back weak, twiggy, or straggly stems to just above soil level. Aim to create a balanced-looking shrub with an open centre. Prune very thin growth hard, but strong growth only lightly.

COPPICING

This is a useful technique for dogwoods and other plants grown for their winter bark as it stimulates the growth of new stems, which have a much brighter colour than the old. Cut down all the stems to the base in spring before new growth begins. After this hard pruning, mulch round the plants and feed well.

rotation. Each year after the shrub has flowered, you remove one-third of the oldest shoots to encourage fresh, young growth to sprout from the base. After three years of this treatment, you will have rejuvenated the entire bush.

Pinching out, or stopping, is a form of micro-pruning often used on argyranthemums and chrysanthemums to force plants to make more growth or flower buds. It is best done when plants are growing fast in spring.

WHEN TO PRUNE

In the most general terms, shrubs that flower in winter, spring, or early summer do so on growth made in the previous year. These can be pruned after flowering. Shrubs that flower in summer or autumn bear their flowers on the new wood they have made earlier in the growing season. These are best left until early spring the following year.

Pruning kicks a shrubs into top growing gear, causing it to pump energy into dormant growth buds to replace what it feels it has lost. If you prune a buddleia or caryopteris in late summer when it has just finished flowering, the resultant new growth will coincide fatally with the first frosts. For this reason these plants, as well as deciduous ceanothus, ceratostigma, lavatera, and perovskia, should be left until spring.

TRAINING

For wall shrubs and climbers, training and tying in is as important as pruning. Relatively few plants come complete with their own adhesive. The Virginia creepers and ivies have good self-sticking sucker pads. So does the climbing hydrangea, but most wall shrubs need careful attention in the early years while you build up a basic framework of branches and secure them strongly to their support. Once you have established this well tied-in framework, it is much clearer what can be pruned and what should be left alone.

Walls can provide shelter for relatively tender shrubs, such as ceanothus. If a shrub sticks its nose out too far from the shelter of its wall, it is far more likely to be damaged by wind and frost. Keep it spreadeagled flat for its own protection. If you tie in wall shrubs well, rather than letting them loll where they will, you create extra growing space under and around them. And by tying in branches, you stop them lashing around and smashing themselves in high winds. For a formal effect, train shrubs on parallel wires, strung through vine eyes fixed to the wall.

PRUNING CLEMATIS

Clematis can be divided into three separate pruning groups. The first group, mostly early-flowering species such as *Clematis alpina* and *C. macropetala*, need little or no pruning. The second group includes early, large-flowered cultivars such as 'Henryi' and 'Niobe' and needs only light pruning in early spring. The late-flowering types need the hardest pruning: those such as 'Perle d'Azur' and 'Jackmanii' should be cut hard back to within 45cm (18in) of the ground in late winter or early spring.

EARLY, LARGE-FLOWERED CLEMATIS
When pruning clematis in the second group, cut back old stems to a strong pair of buds to stimulate new, flowering wood.

LATE-FLOWERING CLEMATIS
In early spring, hard prune all stems just above the lowest pair of strong buds, about 15–45cm (6–18in) above the ground.

CLIMBERS ON PERGOLAS AND ARCHES

Little and often is the key to training plants on a pergola or arch. Stems should be tied in throughout the growing season. Spread them out to cover as much of the structure as possible. Train the stems of twining species around their supports, making sure that the shoots are going in the right direction. Some climbers grow clockwise, some anti-clockwise. When flowering is over, take out any dead or diseased shoots and prune the plants as necessary.

TYING IN
Tie in stray sideshoots to the support in their natural direction of growth. Encourage scramblers by wrapping wire netting round the posts to provide support.

CUTTING BACK
In late summer, cut back all the leading stems by one-third to promote lateral growth. Untie rambling roses, cut out old growth, and tie in new stems.

PROPAGATING PLANTS

Propagation is the catch-all phrase for the various means by which gardeners can increase their plant stock. Plants, being superbly profligate by nature, usually offer more than one means of doing this. Only annual plants, which complete their life cycle within a year, reproduce themselves solely by seed. Many other plants also set seed that can be germinated fairly easily, although many perennials and some bulbs may also be split and divided. Shrubs are usually propagated by vegetative methods such as taking cuttings or rooting layers.

GROWING PLANTS FROM CUTTINGS

Propagation can easily become an obsession. There is no more wildly parental feeling than watching your first successful cutting turn into a grown-up bush. If you are a beginner, start with pelargoniums. They are least likely to let you down, are always useful, and are expensive to buy. They are also difficult to overwinter unless you live in a frost-free area. Cuttings provide your insurance policy.

For your cuttings, look for bushy, new, bright green shoots without flowers. The reason for choosing shoots without flowers is that the cuttings can put all their effort into producing roots, without having to bother about what is happening on top. Take and prepare the cuttings (see above right) and push them into a compost that is easy for the roots to infiltrate. A mixture of peat and sand is traditional, but a mix of vermiculite and a fibrous medium such as coir compost is just as good.

Many cuttings root most easily in a moist, enclosed atmosphere and should be kept covered with a plastic bag or in a propagator. Pelargonium cuttings do not. Stand the pot in a light, airy place and keep the compost moist, but not sopping wet. The cuttings should root within ten days.

TAKING CUTTINGS
Take cuttings about 7–12cm (3–5in) long from the tips of strong, healthy shoots. Trim each just below a leaf joint and remove the lowest leaves. Push cuttings round the edge of a pot of compost and water in. Cover with a plastic bag, making sure it does not touch the cuttings. When the cuttings have rooted, set them in small pots.

You can take pelargonium cuttings at any time, but late summer is the best time to provide plants to set out the following late spring. This is also the best season to take cuttings of other tender perennials, such as osteospermums, argyranthemums, and penstemons. For a number of shrubs such as fuchsias, cuttings are best taken in spring.

Pelargoniums can also be propagated in early spring, but you need to overwinter the mother plants in a frost-free place. Force the overwintered plants into growth to provide plenty of juicy new cutting material by cutting them back and watering and feeding them generously in late winter.

DIVIDING PLANTS

Many perennials and some suckering shrubs that produce plenty of shoots from the base can be increased by division. This also allows you to discard old or unproductive parts and so helps rejuvenate the plant. The best time to divide plants is when they are dormant, between autumn and early spring, avoiding very cold, wet, or dry spells.

PROPAGATION BY DIVISION

1 *Perennials such as helianthus are most easily propagated by dividing mature clumps. The best and most vigorous pieces are usually at the edges of the clump. Lift the plant with a fork and chop off these sections with a spade.*

2 *Carefully pull these new, small segments away from the old clump, checking that each piece has several fresh, new shoots and good roots. Take care at all times to avoid any damage to the roots.*

3 *Cut back any long stems that remain on the new plants and replant them at the same depth as before in soil enriched with compost or bone meal. Firm them in and then water well. Keep them moist until well established.*

RAISING PLANTS FROM SEED

1 *There are various ways of ensuring that seed is sown thinly and evenly over the surface of the compost. You can scatter it from a folded piece of paper, as here, or sprinkle it with your finger and thumb. Cover with a fine layer of sieved compost or vermiculite.*

2 *Cover the pot with a pane of glass or with cling film to retain moisture. Check whether it needs to be kept in the dark or the light. An airing cupboard makes a good germination chamber for seed that needs darkness to germinate. An indoor windowsill is ideal for others.*

3 *Germination times vary widely, so check the pots frequently and uncover them as soon as the seedlings emerge. When they have developed their first true leaves, prick them out into a larger container – either a seed tray or individual pots.*

4 *Plants need to grow on without check, so regular watering is essential. Gradually harden off the plants, putting the trays or pots out on warm days and bringing them in at night. When this hardening off is complete, you can set out your plants.*

SOWING SEED

To the uninitiated, seed sowing is the impenetrable rite of passage that separates the novice from the seasoned gardener. But it is not as difficult as experts would have you believe, nor do you need batteries of equipment. A heated propagator speeds up the germination process, but is not vital. At some stage seedlings have to face real life. The tougher they are raised, the better they will cope.

If you are a beginner, avoid sowing seeds that have complicated germination mechanisms. Some seeds need frost, or alternating periods of cold and heat before they germinate. These conditions usually mirror the circumstances that occur in their natural habitats. Most just need warmth and moisture.

Not all need light. Nemesia, pansy, and verbena, for example, germinate best in total darkness. Ageratum, alyssum, snapdragon, lobelia, mimulus, impatiens, nicotiana, and petunia, on the other hand, all need light.

The basic routine for seed sowing is simple. Use a clean plastic pot or seed tray for the initial sowing. Fill it with compost and firm it down gently. Scatter the seed over the surface of the compost, then cover it with a thin layer of compost or vermiculite. The latter drains quickly and you do not have to worry about the exact depth of the covering, as you must if you are using compost. Water the pot thoroughly before covering it with a sheet of glass or plastic or piece of cling film. Remove the cover once the seedlings are visible.

OVERCROWDED BULBS

If bulbs are happy, they will increase, each bulb gradually building up into a large clump. This is a joy of course, but if they get too congested, you may get fewer flowers. Then you need to split them up and replant them, discarding any that have dried up.

1 *When the bulbs are dormant and the foliage has died down, lift the entire clump from the ground and sort through the bulbs, discarding any that seem unsound.*

2 *Gently pull the bulbs apart. Early-flowering bulbs such as snowdrops and aconites are best split "in the green" just as they have finished flowering.*

DIVIDING RHIZOMATOUS PERENNIALS

Rhizomatous plants such as bearded iris can also be propagated by splitting congested clumps. The best pieces are usually on the edges of the clump. Replant the rhizomes, each with plump roots, level or just above the soil surface.

1 *Lift a clump of iris and split it into pieces, each with a single fan of leaves. Discard any unproductive rhizomes with old, dark roots and no leaves.*

2 *Trim the rhizomes with a sharp knife, cutting back any very long roots. Shorten the foliage and replant the rhizomes about 12cm (5in) apart.*

INDEX

Page numbers for plant entries that appear in **bold** refer to a plant featured in a main scheme or supplementary planting. Page numbers given in normal type direct you to text on a plant or topic, while those in *italic* indicate that there is a picture and caption.

A

Abies (Fir)
    A. koreana (Korean fir) **82–5**, 144
Abutilon 28, 150
Acacia (Mimosa)
    A. baileyana (Cootamundra wattle) **107**, 121
    A. dealbata **120–21**, 144, 145
    A. pravissima (Ovens wattle) 121
Acaena 14
    A. microphylla (New Zealand burr) **132–3**, 145
Acanthus (Bear's breeches) 14
Acer (Maple) 150
    A. japonicum 'Aureum' (Golden-leaved Japanese maple) 140
    A. japonicum 'Dissectum' (Japanese maple) **82–5**
    A. palmatum 'Dissectum' 144
Adiantum
    A. pedatum (Northern maidenhair fern) 18
    A. venustum 20
Aeonium 10
    A. arboreum 'Atropurpureum' *11*
    A. arboreum 'Schwarzkopf' **32–5**, **62–5**, **140–41**, 144
Aeroplane propeller, see *Crassula falcata*
Agapanthus 16
    A. Headbourne Hybrids 31
Agave 10, 144
    A. americana 'Variegata' **62–5**
    A. parryi **62–5**
Ageratum 153
Ajuga reptans 'Atropurpurea' (Bugle) **24–7**, 144
Albizia julibrissin (Silk tree) **65**
Alchemilla (Lady's mantle) *14*, 16, 20
    A. mollis *21*, **58–61**, **88–91**, **92–5**, 140, 144
Allemanda cathartica (Golden trumpet) 121
Allium
    A. christophii **74–7**
    A. giganteum **28–31**
    A. schoenoprasum (Chives) **74–7**
Alpine snow gum, see *Eucalyptus niphophila*
Alpine strawberry, see *Fragaria vesca*
Alpines 148; see also Border of Miniatures 52–5, A Retaining Wall 122–3
Alyssum 153
Amelanchier 70
Anaphalis triplinervis **58–61**

Anemone
    A. blanda 55
    A. coronaria De Caen Group **81**
    A. x hybrida 'Honorine Jobert' (Japanese anemone) *16*, **47**
    A. x japonica, see *A. x hybrida*
Anethum graveolens (Dill) *15*
Angelica archangelica **39**
Angel's fishing rod, see *Dierama pulcherrimum*
Angels' trumpets, see *Datura x candida*
Annuals 80, 99
    in containers, see Occasional Pots 140–41
    perennials and sub-shrubs used as, see Instant Flowers 66–9
    propagating 152, 153, *153*
Anthriscus cerefolium (Chervil) 74
Antirrhinum majus (Snapdragon) 144, 145
    A. majus, rust resistant yellow **66–9**, 153
Aquilegia (Columbine)
    A. vulgaris (Granny's bonnets) **44–7**, **142–3**
Arabis 122
Aralia elata 'Variegata' *18*, **35**
Arbutus unedo (Strawberry tree) **82–5**, 145
Arches *17*; see also Pergolas
Argyranthemum *19*, 151, 152
    A. frutescens 'Jamaica Primrose' **32–5**, **107**
    A. gracile 'Chelsea Girl' *15*, **66–9**, **130–31**
Armeria maritima (Thrift) 145
    A. maritima 'Vindictive' **122–3**
Artemisia 20
    A. abrotanum (Southernwood) **138–9**, 145
Arum italicum 'Pictum' **24–7**, 144
Arum lily, see *Zantedeschia aethiopica* 'Crowborough'
Asphodeline lutea (Yellow asphodel) **138–9**
Asplenium trichomanes (Maidenhair spleenwort) **136–7**, 144
Aster (Michaelmas daisy) 20, *147*
    A. x frikartii 'Mönch' **28–31**
Astilbe x arendsii **36–9**, 144, 145
Astrantia (Masterwort)
    A. major 'Shaggy' **28–31**
    A. major 'Sunningdale Variegated' **95**
Aubrieta deltoidea 145
    A. deltoidea 'Argenteo-variegata' **122–3**
Australian pea, see *Lablab purpureus*
Autumn schemes *12*, *71*, *101*; see also Bright Berries for Autumn 40–43, An Autumn–Winter Display 48–51, A Low-maintenance Scheme 82–5, Colour for Autumn–Winter 114–15
Azalea, see *Rhododendron*
    Karume azalea, see *R.* 'Hatsugiri', *R.* 'Hinodegiri'

B

Baby's breath, see *Gypsophila paniculata*
Banana palm, see *Ensete ventricosum*
Banks, schemes for, see A Low-maintenance Scheme 82–5, Splendour in the Grass 142–3
Barberry, see *Berberis*

Bay tree, see *Laurus nobilis*
Bear's breeches, see *Acanthus*
Begonia
    B. fuchsioides **65**, **130–31**
    B. rex 'Helen Lewis' **62–5**
Bellflower, see *Campanula*
Bellis (Daisy) 20
    B. perennis 'Pomponette' (Double daisy) **44–7**
Berberis (Barberry) 31
    B. thunbergii f. *atropurpurea* **92–5**, 144
Bergenia 20, 153
    B. ciliata **70–73**, 144
Berries, schemes for, see Bright Berries for Autumn 40–43, Colour for Autumn–Winter 114–15
Biennials 99
Black false hellebore, see *Veratrum nigrum*
Bluebell, see *Hyacinthoides*
    Spanish bluebell, see *H. hispanica*
Boggy ground
    plants for *10*, 145
    scheme for, see A Lush Poolside 36–9
Borago officinalis (Borage) *15*
Borders, schemes for 22–55; see also A Narrow Strip 134–5
Boundaries, schemes for, see Bright Berries for Autumn 40–43, A Retaining Wall 122–3, Walls without Sun 126–7
Bowles' golden sedge, see *Carex elata* 'Aurea'
Box, see *Buxus*
Brachycome iberidifolia (Swan River daisy) 69, 144
Bronze fennel, see *Foeniculum vulgare* 'Purpureum'
Broom, see *Cytisus*
Brunnera macrophylla 'Hadspen Cream' **104–107**, 144
Buddleia 150, 151
Bugbane, see *Cimicifuga*
Bugle, see *Ajuga reptans* 'Atropurpurea'
Bulbs 13, 51, 78, 106
    for colour 134–5
    dwarf bulbs 55, 95
    in meadows 142
    planting *147*, *147*
    propagating by division 153, *153*
    for scent 96
    for spring colour 52, 61, 81
Bupleurum fruticosum (Shrubby hare's ear) **103**, 145
Busy lizzie, see *Impatiens*
Buxus (Box) 14, *15*, 76, 140
    B. sempervirens **134–5**, 144, 145

C

Calendula officinalis (Pot marigold) 140, 145
Californian poppy, see *Eschscholzia californica*
Callicarpa bodinieri **40–43**
Camassia leichtlinii (Quamash) **44–7**, **142–3**
Camellia 27, 91, 140, 150
    C. x williamsii 'Brigadoon' **85**, 144
Campanula (Bellflower)
    C. carpatica (Dwarf bellflower) **52–5**, 145

Campanula (cont.)
    C. cochleariifolia (Fairy thimbles) **122–3**, 145
    C. lactiflora 'Prichard's Variety' **44–7**, **104–107**
    C. medium (Canterbury bells) 28
Campsis x tagliabuana 'Mme Galen' (Trumpet vine) **113**, **120–21**
Canna indica **32–5**
Canterbury bells, see *Campanula medium*
Carex elata 'Aurea' (Bowles' golden sedge) **24–7**, **36–9**, 144, 145
Caryopteris 151
Castor oil plant, see *Ricinus communis*
Ceanothus 151
    C. impressus **120–21**
Centaurea
    C. cyanus (Cornflower) 142
    C. moschata (Sweet sultan) 99
Ceratostigma 151
    C. plumbaginoides **138–9**
    C. willmottianum **104–107**
Ceterach officinarum (Rusty-back fern) **136–7**, 144
Chaenomeles 114
Chain fern, see *Woodwardia unigemmata*
Chamaerops humilis (European fan palm) *11*
Cheddar pink, see *Dianthus gratianopolitanus*
Cheiranthus (Wallflower)
    C. 'Bredon' 99, 145
Cherry, see *Prunus*
    Great white cherry, see *P.* 'Tai Haku'
Chervil, see *Anthriscus cerefolium*
Chilean glory flower, see *Eccremocarpus scaber*
Chimonanthus 48
Chinese wisteria, see *Wisteria sinensis*
Chionodoxa 55, 95
Chives, see *Allium schoenoprasum*
Chlorophytum comosum 'Vittatum' (Spider plant) 69
Choisya 91
    C. ternata (Mexican orange blossom) **70–73**, 144, 145
Chrysanthemum 151
    C. frutescens, see *Argyranthemum frutescens*
    C. segetum **138–9**, 144
Cimicifuga (Bugbane)
    C. simplex **39**, 144
Cistus x corbariensis (Rock rose) **100–103**, 144
Clematis 95, 151, *151*
    C. alpina 151
    C. alpina 'Frances Rivis' **31**
    C. 'Ascotiensis' **125**
    C. 'Comtesse de Bouchaud' **51**
    C. 'Elsa Spath' **110–13**
    C. 'Henryi' **116–19**, 151
    C. 'Jackmanii' 151
    C. 'Jackmanii Superba' **74–7**
    C. macropetala **43**, **110–13**, 151
    C. macropetala 'Markham's Pink' **124–5**
    C. 'Mrs George Jackman' **126–7**
    C. 'Nelly Moser' **126–7**
    C. 'Niobe' 151
    C. orientalis 'Bill Mackenzie' **116–19**
    C. 'Perle d'Azur' **47**, **116–19**, 151

(entry cont.)

Clematis (cont.)
  C. 'The President' **110–13**
  C. tangutica **114–15, 120–21**
  C. 'Ville de Lyon' **119**
  C. viticella 'Etoile Violette' **110–13**
  C. viticella 'Mme Julia Correvon'
    110–13
  C. viticella 'Purpurea Plena Elegans' **73**
  large-flowered cultivars 151, *151*
Cleome hassleriana (Spider flower) 144
  C. hassleriana 'Colour Fountain' **32–5,
    78–81**
Climbing hydrangea, see *Hydrangea
  anomala* subsp. *petiolaris*
Climbing plants, see Vertical Spaces
    108–27
  for autumn interest 113, 114–15
  fast-growing 113, 119
  planting 147, *147*
  pruning and training 150–51, *151*
  for summer interest 119, 120; see also
    Plants for a Pergola 110–13,
    Screening the Garden 116–19,
    Climbing Frames 124–5, Walls
    without Sun 126–7
  supports for 74, 110, 114, 116–17,
    124–7
  training 151, *151*
  for winter display 114–15; see also
    Walls without Sun 126–7
Coastal gardens
  plants for 145
  scheme for, see Planting by the Sea
    100–103
Cobaea scandens (Cup-and-saucer vine)
    113
Cobweb houseleek, see
  Sempervivum arachnoideum
Colchicum 13
  C. agrippinum **55**
Colour schemes
  cool 16, 39, 65, 89, 119, 125; see also
    Cool Colours for Damp Shade 24–7
  fiery *12*, 32, 113, 120, 140
  garden design and 16, *16*, *17*
  grey *14*, 16, 92
  pastel 16, 58; see also Pretty Pastels
    28–31
  pink 51, 61, 85, 102
  purple *16*, 61, 92
  rich 31, 33, 47, 61, 114
  white 16, 17, 25, 33, 40, 85, 102
  yellow 16, 92, 93, 138–9
Columbine, see *Aquilegia*
Coneflower, see *Rudbeckia*
Conifers, dwarf 52–3, 70
Conservatories
  plants for 130
  schemes for, see A Bold Desert Bed
    62–5, A Place in the Sun 120–21,
    A Potted Disguise 130–31,
    Occasional Pots 140–41
Container gardening, schemes for *10*,
    14, *15*, *128–9*; see also A Potted
    Disguise 130–31, Occasional Pots
    140–41
Convallaria (Lily-of-the-valley) 17
  C. majalis **27**, 144
Convolvulus
  C. cneorum **52–5**
  C. sabatius **77**
  C. tricolor 'Heavenly Blue' **113**

Cootamundra wattle, see *Acacia
  baileyana*
Coppicing 151
Cordyline 149
  C. australis 'Atropurpurea' **35**
Coriander, see *Coriandrum sativum*
Coriandrum sativum (Coriander) **77**, 145
Corner sites, schemes for 86–107
Cornflower, see *Centaurea cyanus*
Cornus (Dogwood) 150, *151*
  C. alba 'Elegantissima' **39**, 70–73, 95,
    144, 145
Cortaderia selloana 'Sunningdale Silver'
    (Pampas grass) **35**, 144, 145
Corylopsis 48
Cosmos 'Sensation' **32–5**
Cotinus 16, 150
  C. coggygria 'Notcutt's Variety' (Smoke
    tree) **31**
Cotoneaster 120, 150
  C. horizontalis 114, 144
  C. horizontalis 'Variegatus' **24–7**
Cottage gardens, schemes for, see
    Pretty Pastels 28–31, Cottage-garden
    Border 44–7, A Formal Herb Design
    74–7, A Scheme for Scent 96–9,
    Between the Steps 136–7, A Stony
    Patch 138–9
Courtyards, schemes for *10*, *19*, 20; see
    also A Tropical Summer Border 32–5,
    A Bold Desert Bed 62–5, A Potted
    Disguise 130–31, Patio Planting
    132–3, Occasional Pots 140–41
Cowslip, see *Primula veris*
Crab apple, see *Malus*
Crambe 18
  C. cordifolia **78–81**
Cranesbill, see *Geranium*
Crassula falcata (Aeroplane propeller)
    62–5
Crataegus (Hawthorn) 70
  C. laciniata **100–103**, 144, 145
Creeping plants, see Ground cover,
  plants for
Crimson glory vine, see *Vitis coignetiae*
Crinum x *powellii* **100–103**, 145
Crocosmia 16
  C. 'Lucifer' *13*, **134–5**
Crocus 52, 55, 61, 144
  C. 'E.A. Bowles' **95**
  C. 'Snow Bunting' **81**
  C. tommasinianus **55**, 81
  dwarf crocus 95
  early crocus 81, 140
Cryptogramma crispa (Parsley fern) 136
Cup-and-saucer vine, see *Cobaea
  scandens*
Cupressus (Cypress)
  C. macrocarpa (Monterey cypress) 100
Cuttings, propagating plants by 152, *152*
Cyclamen
  C. coum subsp. *coum* **48–51**, 55
  C. hederifolium **48–51, 70–73,
    91**, 144
  C. hederifolium var. *album* **134–5**
  C. neapolitanum 72
  C. persicum 49
Cypress, see *Cupressus*
  Monterey cypress, see *C. macrocarpa*
Cytisus (Broom)
  C. x *praecox* (Warminster broom)
    28–31

D

Daffodil, see *Narcissus*
Dahlia 12
  D. 'Bishop of Llandaff' *13*, **35**
Daisy, see *Bellis*
  Daisy bush, see *Olearia*
  Double daisy, see *Bellis perennis*
    'Pomponette'
Daphne 48
  D. bholua 44
  D. x *burkwoodii* 44
  D. x *burkwoodii* 'Somerset' **44–7**, 145
  D. odora 'Aureomarginata' **96–9**, 145
Daylily, see *Hemerocallis*
Dead nettle, see *Lamium*
Dead-heading 149, *149*
Decaisnea fargesii **24–7**, 144
Delphinium 19, 144
Dianthus (Pink) 47, 54, 145
  D. barbatus (Sweet william) 47, 99
  D. 'Charles Musgrave' **58–61**
  *D. gratianopolitanu*s (Cheddar pink)
    52–5
  D. 'Prudence' **96–9**
Diascia rigescens **66–9**
Dierama pulcherrimum (Angel's fishing
  rod) **88–91**
Digitalis (Foxglove) 14, 148
  D. purpurea 'Suttons Apricot' **78–81**
Dill, see *Anethum graveolens*
Diseases, protecting plants from 149
Division, propagating plants by 152,
    152, 153, *153*
Dog's-tooth violet, see *Erythronium
  dens-canis*
Dogwood, see *Cornus*
Draba 122
Driveways, schemes for, see Bright
    Berries for Autumn 40–43, Border of
    Miniatures 52–5, A Retaining Wall
    122–3, A Narrow Strip 134–5
Dryopteris affinis (Shield fern) 20
Dwarf pine, see *Pinus mugo* 'Humpy'

E

Eccremocarpus scaber (Chilean glory
  flower) **113, 120–21**, 145
Echeveria 144
  E. elegans **65**
  E. gibbiflora var. *metallica* **62–5**
Echium 16
Ensete ventricosum (Banana palm)
    32–5
Epimedium
  E. perralderianum **24–7**, 144
  E. pubigerum **70–73**
Eranthis hyemalis (Winter aconite)
    134–5, 147, 153
Erica (Heather)
  E. x *darleyensis* 'Ghost Hills' **43**, 144
Erigeron karvinskianus (Spanish daisy)
    122–3, 145
Eryngium (Sea holly) 28
  E. alpinum **107**
  E. giganteum *18*
  E. x *oliverianum* **28–31**, 145

Erythronium dens-canis (Dog's-tooth
  violet) **48–51**
Escallonia 'Iveyi' **100–103**
Eschscholzia californica (Californian
  poppy) **74–7**, 145
Eucalyptus (Gum tree) 145
  E. coccifera (Tasmanian snow gum)
    103, 145
  E. gunnii 144, 145
  E. niphophila (Alpine snow gum)
    62–5, 144
Eucryphia glutinosa **85**
Euonymus 20, 140
  E. europaeus 'Red Cascade' (Spindle
    tree) **40–43**
  E. fortunei 'Silver Queen' **119**, 144,
    145
Eupatorium
  E. ligustrinum **28–31**, 145
  E. micranthum 30
  E. rugosum **36–9**, 145
Euphorbia (Spurge) 15, *19*
  E. characias subsp. *wulfenii* *12*, *14*,
    70–73, 92–5, 145
  E. cyparissias **73, 136–7**
  E. seguieriana **88–91**
European fan palm, see *Chamaerops
  humilis*
Evening primrose, see *Oenothera biennis*
Evergreens
  as foil for grey-leaved plants 91
  formal gardens and 14
  planting schemes for 82, 140; see also
    An Autumn–Winter Display 48–51,
    A Year-round Display 70–73,
    A Narrow Strip 134–5
Exotic gardens, scheme for, see
    A Tropical Summer Border 32–5

F

Fairy thimbles, see *Campanula
  cochleariifolia*
False acacia, see *Robinia pseudoacacia*
    'Frisia'
Fatsia 91
Feather top, see *Pennisetum villosum*
Feeding plants 148
Felicia amelloides 'Santa Anita' **32–5**, 145
Fences, schemes for, see Colour for
    Autumn–Winter 114–15, A Place in
    the Sun 120–21, Walls without Sun
    126–7, A Narrow Strip 134–5
Fennel, see *Foeniculum vulgare*
  Bronze fennel, see *F. vulgare*
    'Purpureum'
Ferns *12*, *20*, 49, 51, 136, *136*
  Chain fern, see *Woodwardia
    unigemmata*
  Hart's tongue fern, see *Phyllitis
    scolopendrium*
  Ostrich feather fern, see *Matteuccia
    struthiopteris*
  Parsley fern, see *Cryptogramma crispa*
  Royal fern, see *Osmunda regalis*
  Shield fern, see *Dryopteris affinis*
Ficus carica (Fig) 19
Fig, see *Ficus carica*
Filipendula (Meadowsweet) 143, 144, 145
Fir, see *Abies*
  Korean fir, see *A. koreana*

Flame creeper, see *Tropaeolum speciosum*
Foamflower, see *Tiarella*
Foeniculum vulgare (Fennel) *21*, 149
  F. vulgare 'Purpureum' (Bronze fennel) **77**, 144, 145
Foliage interest 20, *20*, *21*
  plants for *13*, *16*, 48, 110, 145
  schemes for, see Pretty Pastels 28–31, A Tropical Summer Border 32–5, A Lush Poolside 36–9, A Bold Desert Bed 62–5, A Formal Herb Design 74–7, Waterside Textures 88–91, Coloured Foliage 92–5, A Narrow Strip 134–5, Between the Steps 136–7
  structural plants and 12
  variegated 20, *20*, 95, 149
Formal gardens
  plants for 14, *14*, *19*
  schemes for 14, 99, 116–17; see also A Tropical Summer Border 32–5, A Bed of Roses 58–61, Instant Flowers 66–9, A Formal Herb Design 74–7, Climbing Frames 124–5, A Narrow Strip 134–5
Forsythia 114, 150
Fragaria vesca (Alpine strawberry) **78–81**
French lavender, see *Lavandula stoechas*
Fritillaria (Fritillary) 52, 143
Frosts, protecting plants from 149, *149*
Fuchsia 152
  F. 'Thalia' **62–5**
  F. magellanica 'Versicolor' **100–103**

G

Galanthus (Snowdrop) 147
  G. nivalis **40–43**, **48–51**, 135, 144, 153
Galium odoratum (Sweet woodruff) **74–7**, 145
Galtonia candicans (Summer hyacinth) **81**, 145
Garrya elliptica **114–15**
  G. 'James Roof' 115
Gazania 10
  G. uniflora **62–5**
Gentiana (Gentian)
  G. sino-ornata **82–5**, 144
Geranium (Cranesbill) 28
  G. cinereum 'Ballerina' **92–5**
  G. endressii **58–61**
  G. himalayense 95
  G. 'Johnson's Blue' **78–81**
  G. phaeum (Mourning widow) **142–3**
  G. pratense 'Flore-pleno' **44–7**
  G. pratense 'Kashmir Purple' 143
  G. pratense 'Mrs Kendall Clarke' 143
  G. pratense 'Plenum Violaceum' 143
  G. psilostemon **58–61**, **78–81**, 143
Geranium, see *Pelargonium*
  Peppermint-scented geranium, see *P. tomentosum*
Giant cowslip, see *Primula florindae*
Ginger, see *Zingiber officinale*
Ginger mint, see *Mentha* x *gentilis* 'Variegata'
Gladiolus 148
  G. byzantinus **142–3**
  G. 'Robin' **35**

Golden feverfew, see *Tanacetum parthenium* 'Aureum'
Golden hop, see *Humulus lupulus* 'Aureus'
Golden marjoram, see *Origanum vulgare* 'Aureum'
Golden rod, see *Solidago*
Golden trumpet, see *Allemanda cathartica*
Golden-leaved Japanese maple, see *Acer japonicum* 'Aureum'
Granny's bonnets, see *Aquilegia vulgaris*
Grassy areas, scheme for, see Splendour in the Grass 142–3
Greenhouses, see Conservatories
Griselinia 100
Ground cover
  plants for 24, 43, 51
  schemes for 13, 27, 49, 50; see also Patio Planting 132–3
Gum tree, see *Eucalyptus*
  Alpine snow gum, see *E. niphophila*
  Tasmanian snow gum, see *E. coccifera*
Gunnera 18, 36
Gypsophila paniculata 'Bristol Fairy' (Baby's breath) **44–7**

H

Hamamelis (Witch hazel) 48
  H. x *intermedia* 'Arnold Promise' **43**, 144, 145
Hart's tongue fern, see *Phyllitis scolopendrium*
Hawthorn, see *Crataegus*
Heartsease, see *Viola tricolor*
Heather, see *Erica*
Hebe
  H. albicans **88–91**
  H. 'La Séduisante' *20*, 31
  H. pinguifolia 'Pagei' **52–5**
Hedera (Ivy) 92, 119, 151
  H. helix 144
  H. helix 'Adam' **48–51**
  H. helix 'Glacier' **126–7**
Hedges 14, 145
Helianthemum 'Wisley Pink' **78–81**, 144, 145
Helianthus 152
Helichrysum 15
  H. petiolare **130–31**
  H. petiolare 'Limelight' **28–31**
  H. petiolatum 30
Heliotropium (Heliotrope) 74, 99
Hellebore, see *Helleborus*
  Black false hellebore, see *Veratrum nigrum*
  Stinking hellebore, see *H. foetidus*
Helleborus (Hellebore, Lenten rose) 144
  H. foetidus (Stinking hellebore) **40–43**, **73**
  H. lividus subsp. *corsicus* **48–51**
  H. orientalis *12*, **48–51**
Hemerocallis (Daylily)
  H. 'Cartwheels' 104
  H. citrina **96–9**, 145
  H. 'Hyperion' 104
  H. 'Marion Vaughn' **104–107**
Herbs *17*, 148; see also A Formal Herb Design 74–7, A Scheme for Scent 96–9

Holly, see *Ilex*
Honesty, see *Lunaria*
Honeybush, see *Melianthus major*
Honeysuckle, see *Lonicera*
  Early Dutch honeysuckle, see *L. periclymenum* 'Belgica'
Hop, see *Humulus*
  Golden hop, see *H. lupulus* 'Aureus'
Horned violet, see *Viola cornuta*
Hosta 18, 144, *147*
  H. fortunei 'Albopicta' **58–61**
  H. 'Gold Standard' **27**
  H. plantaginea **66–9**
  H. 'Royal Standard' **82–5**
  H. sieboldiana var. *elegans* **88–91**
Houseleek, see *Sempervivum*
  Cobweb houseleek, see *S. arachnoideum*
Humulus (Hop)
  H. lupulus 'Aureus' (Golden hop) **74–7**, **116–19**, 144
Hyacinthoides (Bluebell) 14
  H. hispanica (Spanish bluebell) **48–51**, 145
Hyacinthus (Hyacinth) 145
  H. orientalis 145
  H. orientalis 'Delft Blue' **61**, **104–107**
  H. orientalis 'L'Innocence' **104–107**
  Summer hyacinth, see *Galtonia candicans*
Hydrangea 144, 151
  H. anomala subsp. *petiolaris* (Climbing hydrangea) 119, **126–7**
  H. aspera subsp. *aspera* **24–7**
  H. quercifolia (Oak-leaf hydrangea) **24–7**
  H. villosa 24

I

Ice plant, see *Sedum spectabile*
Ilex (Holly) 91
  I. aquifolium 145
  I. aquifolium 'Argentea Marginata' *21*, **40–43**, 145
Impatiens (Busy lizzie) 153
  I. 'Accent Pink' **65**
Informal gardens
  plants for *14*, *15*, *19*
  schemes for, see Pretty Pastels 28–31, Cottage-garden Border 44–7, A Low-maintenance Scheme 82–5, Screening the Garden 116–117, Climbing Frames 124–5, Patio Planting 132–3, Between the Steps 136–7, A Stony Patch 138–9, Splendour in the Grass 142–3
Instant gardens, scheme for, see Instant Flowers 66–9
Iris 144, 147, 153
  I. colchica 96
  I. ensata 'Alba' (Japanese flag) **88–91**
  I. foetidissima (Stinking iris) **40–43**, 144
  I. germanica **58–61**
  I. graminea **96–9**, 145
  I. laevigata 'Variegata' **39**, 144, 145
  I. pseudacorus 'Variegata' **36–9**, 145
  I. reticulata 'Cantab' **55**
  I. sibirica 10, *18*, **104–107**, 145
Ivy, see *Hedera*

J K

Japanese anemone, see *Anemone* x *hybrida*
Japanese cartwheel tree, see *Trochodendron araloides*
Japanese flag, see *Iris ensata* 'Alba'
Japanese maple, see *Acer japonicum* 'Dissectum'
Jasminum (Jasmine)
  J. humile (Yellow jasmine) **114–15**
  J. nudiflorum (Winter jasmine) **114–15**, **126–7**, 150
  J. officinale (Common jasmine) 17, **116–19**, 145
Jerusalem sage, see *Phlomis fruticosa*
Jonquil, see *Narcissus jonquilla*
Juniperus (Juniper) 144
  J. communis 'Compressa' (Dwarf juniper) **52–5**
  J. horizontalis 'Turquoise Spreader' **91**
  J. squamata 'Blue Star' **73**
Karume azalea, see *Rhododendron* 'Hatsugiri', *R.* 'Hinodegri'
Kniphofia (Red hot poker) 14, *16*
  K. caulescens **62–5**, 145
  K. 'Percy's Pride' **65**, 145
Korean fir, see *Abies koreana*
Korean mountain ash, see *Sorbus alnifolia*

L

Lablab purpureus (Australian pea) **113**
Lady's mantle, see *Alchemilla*
Lamb's tongue, see *Stachys byzantina*
Lamium (Dead nettle)
  L. maculatum 'White Nancy' **73**, 144
Large gardens
  adapting plans for 47
  planting styles in 14
  plants for 100
Lathyrus
  L. latifolius (Perennial sweet pea) 125
  L. odoratus (Sweet pea) *17*, 99, 145
  L. odoratus 'Lady Diana' **119**
  L. odoratus 'Selana' **119**
Laurus nobilis (Bay tree) **74–7**, 145
Lavandula (Lavender) 28, 138, 144, 145
  L. angustifolia 'Hidcote' **96–9**, 145
  L. stoechas (French lavender) 98
Lavatera 151
Lavender, see *Lavandula*
  French lavender, see *L. stoechas*
Lenten rose, see *Helleborus*
Lesser periwinkle, see *Vinca minor* 'Argenteovariegata'
Lewisia 122
Ligularia przewalskii **36–9**, 144, 145
Lily, see *Lilium*
  Arum lily, see *Zantedeschia aethiopica* 'Crowborough'
  Daylily, see *Hemerocallis*
  Madonna lily, see *Lilium candidum*
  Regal lily, see *L. regale*
Lilium (Lily) 18, 145
  L. 'Black Beauty' **70–73**
  L. candidum (Madonna lily) 17, **96–9**
  L. 'Destiny' **140–41**

(entry cont.)

Lilium (cont.)
  L. 'Empress of India' 140
  L. 'Enchantment' **140–41**
  L. regale (Regal lily) **28–31**, 140
Lily-of-the-valley, see *Convallaria*
Linaria (Toadflax)
  L. maroccana 'Fairy Lights' **66–9**, 144
Liriodendron tulipifera (Tulip tree) 66
Lithodora diffusa 'Heavenly Blue' **52–5**, 144, 145
Lobelia 153
  L. erinus 145
  L. erinus 'Crystal Palace' **69**
  L. syphilitica **36–9**, 145
London pride, see *Saxifraga* x *urbium*
Lonicera (Honeysuckle) 17, 47, 145
  L. x *americana* **116–19**
  L. periclymenum 'Belgica' (Early Dutch honeysuckle) **47**, 125
Low-maintenance gardens
  plants for 50
  schemes for, see Bright Berries for Autumn 40–43, A Low-maintenance Scheme 82–5, Coloured Foliage 92–5
Lunaria (Honesty)
  L. annua 'Variegata' **40–43**
Lungwort, see *Pulmonaria*
Lupinus arboreus (Tree lupin) **103**
Lychnis coronaria **44–7**
Lysichiton americanus (Skunk cabbage) **39**, 144, 145

M

Madonna lily, see *Lilium candidum*
Magnolia 150
  M. x *soulangeana* **66–9**, 144
Mahonia 18
  M. x *media* 'Charity' **48–51**, 144, 145
Maidenhair spleenwort, see *Asplenium trichomanes*
Malus (Crab apple) 14, 70, 144
  M. floribunda 40, 145
  M. 'Golden Hornet' 40
  M. 'John Downie' **40–43**
  M. 'Red Sentinel' 40
Maple, see *Acer*
  Golden-leaved Japanese maple, see *A. japonicum* 'Aureum'
  Japanese maple, see *A. japonicum* 'Dissectum'
Marjoram, see *Origanum majorana*
  Golden marjoram, see *O. vulgare* 'Aureum'
Masterwort, see *Astrantia*
Matteuccia struthiopteris (Ostrich-feather fern) 19, 51, 144, 145
Matthiola (Stock) 47, 99, 145
Meadow rue, see *Thalictrum*
Meadows, flowers in, see Splendour in the Grass 142–3
Meadowsweet, see *Filipendula*
Meconopsis
  M. cambrica (Welsh poppy) **138–9**
  M. regia 20
Melianthus 15
  M. major (Honeybush) 20, **28–31**, **130–31**
Mentha (Mint)
  M. x *gentilis* 'Variegata' (Ginger mint) **24–7**, 144, 145

Mexican orange blossom, see *Choisya ternata*
Michaelmas daisy, see *Aster*
Mimulus 153
Mint, see *Mentha*
  Ginger mint, see *M.* x *gentilis* 'Variegata'
Mock orange, see *Philadelphus*
Monterey cypress, see *Cupressus macrocarpa*
Monterey pine, see *Pinus radiata*
Morus (Mulberry) 66
Mossy saxifrage, see *Saxifraga* 'Sanguinea Superba'
Mountain ash, see *Sorbus*
  Korean mountain ash, see *S. alnifolia*
Mourning widow, see *Geranium phaeum*
Mulberry, see *Morus*
Mulching plants **146**, 147, 148, *148*
Mullein, see *Verbascum*
Myrrhis odorata (Sweet cicely) **74–7**, 145

N

Narcissus (Daffodil) 14, 55, 61, 81, 145
  N. 'Hawera' **55**
  N. jonquilla (Jonquil) **96–9**
  N. 'Pheasant's Eye' **81**
  N. 'Thalia' **40–43**
Narrow gardens, schemes for, see Screening the Garden 116–19, Climbing Frames 124–5, A Narrow Strip 134–5
Nasturtium, see *Tropaeolum*
Nemesia 153
Nemophila 16
Nepeta 'Six Hills Giant' (Catmint) **58–61**, **92–5**, 144, 145
Nerine bowdenii **31**, **81**, 145
New Zealand burr, see *Acaena microphylla*
New Zealand flax, see *Phormium*
Nicotiana (Tobacco plant) 153
  N. langsdorfii **100–103**
  N. sylvestris **32–5**, 99, 145
Northern maidenhair fern, see *Adiantum pedatum*

O

Oak-leaf hydrangea, see *Hydrangea quercifolia*
Oenothera biennis (Evening primrose) 17, **142–3**, 145
Old-fashioned gardens 22
  schemes for, see Cottage-garden Border 44–7, A Bed of Roses 58–61, Formal Herb Design 74–7, A Scheme for Scent 96–9
Olearia (Daisy bush)
  O. x *haastii* **103**
Omphalodes cappadocica **27**
Onopordum 19
Opium poppy, *see Papaver somniferum*
Oriental poppy, see *Papaver orientale*
Origanum
  O. majorana (Marjoram) 74
  O. vulgare 'Aureum' (Golden marjoram) **92–5**, 144, 145

Osmanthus 48, 140
Osmunda regalis (Royal fern) **36–9**, 144, 145
Osteospermum 152
  O. 'Whirlygig' **69**
Ostrich-feather fern, see *Matteuccia struthiopteris*

P Q

Paeonia (Peony)
  P. 'Sarah Bernhardt' **44–7**
Pampas grass, see *Cortaderia selloana* 'Sunningdale Silver'
Pansy, see *Viola* Clear Crystals Series
Papaver (Poppy) 14, 142
  P. orientale (Oriental poppy) **31**, 144
  P. rhoeas 47
  P. somniferum (Opium poppy) *13, 15*
Parsley, see *Petroselinum crispum*
Parsley fern, see *Cryptogramma crispa*
Parthenocissus
  P. quinquefolia (Virginia creeper) 151
  P. tricuspidata 'Lowii' **114–15**
Pasque flower, see *Pulsatilla vulgaris*
Passiflora (Passion flower) 119
Paths
  garden design and 18
  plants for 145
  schemes for, see Patio Planting 132–3, Between the Steps 136–7
Patios
  planting in crevices 147, *147*
  plants for 145
  schemes for, see A Bold Desert Bed 62–5, A Potted Disguise 130–31, Patio Planting 132–3, Occasional Pots 140–41
Pear, see *Pyrus*
Pelargonium (Geranium) 144, 145, 152
  P. 'The Boar' 140
  P. 'Chocolate Peppermint' 130
  P. crispum 'Variegatum' **130–31**
  P. 'Mabel Grey' **96–9**
  P. 'Mme Fournier' **140–41**
  P. 'Royal Oak' **32–5**
  P. 'Sweet Mimosa' *17*
  P. tomentosum (Peppermint-scented geranium) **77**
Pennisetum villosum (Feather top) **70–73**, 144
Penstemon 20, 28, 152
Peony, see *Paeonia*
Peppermint-scented geranium, see *Pelargonium tomentosum*
Perennials 149
  herbaceous 149, 153
  propagating 152–3, *152, 153*
  rhizomatous 153, *153*
Pergolas 116
  scheme for, see Plants for a Pergola 110–113
  training plants on 151, *151*
Periwinkle, see *Vinca*
  Lesser periwinkle, see *V. minor* 'Argenteovariegata'
Pernettya mucronata 'Mulberry Wine' **43**, 144
Perovskia 150, 151
  P. atriplicifolia 'Blue Spire' (Russian sage) **107**

Pests, protecting plants from 149
Petroselinum crispum (Parsley) **74–7**
Petunia 153
Philadelphus (Mock orange) 17, 47, 144, 145, 150
  P. 'Belle Etoile' **47**
  P. coronarius 'Aureus' **92–5**
Phlomis
  P. fruticosa (Jerusalem sage) **92–5**, **104–107**
  P. russeliana **100–103**
Phlox 16
  P. douglasii 145
  P. douglasii 'Boothman's Variety' **132–3**
  P. douglasii 'Crackerjack' **133**
Phormium (New Zealand flax) 20, 33
  P. tenax 145
  P. tenax 'Bronze Baby' **130–31**
  P. tenax 'Dazzler' **100–103**
  P. tenax 'Maori Sunrise' **100–103**
  P. tenax 'Purpureum' **62–5**
  P. tenax 'Tom Thumb' **130**
Phuopsis 16
Phyllitis
  P. scolopendrium (Hart's tongue fern) *20*, **48–51**, **134–5**, 144
  P. scolopendrium 'Crispum' **91**
  P. scolopendrium 'Marginatum' **51**
Pieris 10
  P. 'Forest Flame' **27**, 144
Pinching out plants 151
Pine, see *Pinus*
  Dwarf pine, see *P. mugo* 'Humpy'
  Monterey pine, see *P. radiata*
Pink, see *Dianthus*
  Cheddar pink, see *D. gratianopolitanus*
Pinus (Pine)
  P. leucodermis 'Schmidtii' 53
  P. mugo 'Humpy' (Dwarf pine) **52–5**, **103**
  P. pumila 'Globe' 53, 144
  P. radiata (Monterey pine) 100
Piptanthus nepalensis 115
Pittosporum tenuifolium **140–41**, 144, 145
Plant forms, see Shapes of plants
Planting
  considerations when 10–21
  in containers 147
  in open ground 146, *146*
  styles 14, *14, 15*; see also Cottage gardens, Exotic gardens, Formal gardens, Informal gardens, Old-fashioned gardens, Traditional gardens, Tropical gardens, Wild gardens, Wooded gardens
  against walls 147, *147*
Plumbago 121
Polygonatum (Solomon's seal)
  P. x *hybridum* **24–7**, 144
Polygonum
  P. baldschuanicum (Russian vine) 119, 125
  P. campanulatum **100–103**, 144, 145
Polypodium (Polypody) 144
  P. polypodioides 137
  P. virginianum 137
  P. vulgare **82–5**
Polypody, see *Polypodium*

Polystichum
  P. setiferum (Soft shield fern) **70–73**, 144
  P. setiferum 'Densum' **70–73**
Poppy, see *Papaver*
  Californian poppy, see *Eschscholzia californica*
  Opium poppy, *see Papaver somniferum*
  Oriental poppy, see *Papaver orientale*
  Welsh poppy, see *Meconopsis cambrica*
Pot marigold, see *Calendula officinalis*
Primula (Primrose) 143
  P. florindae (Giant cowslip) **36–9**, 144, 145
  P. japonica (Japanese primrose) **36–9**, 144, 145
  P. pulverulenta 10
  P. veris (Cowslip) 143
  P. vulgaris 'Gigha White' 47
Propagating plants 152–3, *152*, *153*
Pruning plants *146*, 150–51, *150*, *151*
Prunus (Cherry) 70
  P. 'Tai Haku' (Great white cherry) **70–73**, 144
Pulmonaria (Lungwort)
  P. saccharata **78–81**, 144
Pulsatilla vulgaris (Pasque flower) **52–5**, 145
Purple sage, see *Salvia officinalis* 'Purpurascens'
Purple-leaved clover, see *Trifolium repens* 'Purpurascens'
Purple-leaved violet, see *Viola labradorica* 'Purpurea'
Puschkinia 55, 95
Pyracantha 92, 120, 144, 145
  P. 'Golden Charmer' **114–15**
  P. x *wateri* 73, 145
Pyrus communis 'Marguerite Marillat' (Pear) **78–81**, 144
Quamash, see *Camassia leichtlinii*

R

Ramonda 122
Red hot poker, see *Kniphofia*
Regal lily, see *Lilium regale*
Rejuvenation of plants 149, *149*, 150–51, *150*, *151*
Reverted plant shoots, removal of 149, *149*
Rhododendron 10, 14, 144, 150
  R. 'Frome' (Azalea) **82–5**
  R. 'Hatsugiri' (Karume azalea) 85
  R. 'Hinodegiri' (Karume azalea) 85
  R. hippophaeoides **82–5**
  R. luteum (Azalea) **82–5**, 145
  R. 'Narcissiflorum' (Azalea) **82–5**
  R. 'Palestrina' (Azalea) **82–5**
  R. 'Snow' 27
  R. 'Strawberry Ice' (Azalea) 85
  R. yakushimanum 85
Rhus typhina (Stag's-horn sumach) *20*
Ricinus communis (Castor oil plant) **32–5**
  R. communis 'Carmencita' **32–5**
Robinia pseudoacacia (False acacia) 145
  R. pseudoacacia 'Frisia' **92–5**
Rock rose, see *Cistus* x *corbariensis*
Rodgersia 11, 18, 145
  R. aesculifolia **36–9**
  R. podophylla 10, **36–9**

Rosa (Rose) *17*, 104, 145, 149, 150, *150*; see also A Bed of Roses 58–61
  R. 'Albéric Barbier' **125**
  R. 'The Fairy' 99
  R. 'Felicia' **58–61**, 145
  R. 'Félicité Perpétue' **58–61**, **110–13**
  R. filipes 'Kiftsgate' 58, 125, 144
  R. 'Frühlingsgold' **104–107**
  R. 'The Garland' 59
  R. 'Gloire de Dijon' **116–19**
  R. 'Golden Showers' **124–5**
  R. 'Mme Alfred Carrière' **116–19**
  R. moyesii 'Geranium' **40–43**
  R. 'New Dawn' 125
  R. 'Penelope' **58–61**, 145
  R. 'Rambling Rector' **110–13**
  R. 'Regensberg' 99
  R. rugosa 145
  R. rugosa 'Alba' **103**
  R. rugosa 'Blanc Double de Coubert' 103
  R. rugosa 'Frau Dagmar Hartopp' **43**, **61**, **100–103**
  R. rugosa 'Roseraie de l'Haÿ' **61**, **100–103**
  R. 'Veilchenblau' 61, **119**
  R. virginiana 43, *43*
  Alba roses *17*
  climbing roses 58–9, 116, 118, 124–5
  cluster-flowered bush roses *149*
  Gallica roses 150
  Hybrid Musk roses, see A Bed of Roses 58–61
  large-flowered bush roses (Hybrid Teas) 58, 104, 125, 150
  patio roses 99
  pruning and training 150, *150*
  rambling roses 125, *125*
  Rugosa roses 43, 61, 100, 103
  shrub roses 43, 58, 104, 106, 150
  species roses 41, 150
  standard roses 75, 99
Rose, see *Rosa*
Rosemary, see *Rosmarinus*
Rosmarinus (Rosemary) 144, 145
  R. officinalis 145
  R. officinalis 'Miss Jessop's Upright' **96–9**
  R. officinalis 'Severn Sea' **138–9**
Rowan, see *Sorbus*
Royal fern, see *Osmunda regalis*
Rudbeckia (Coneflower) *14*
  R. hirta 'Marmalade' 69
Russian sage, see *Perovskia atriplicifolia* 'Blue Spire'
Russian vine, see *Polygonum baldschuanicum*
Rustic gardens, see Informal gardens
Rusty-back fern, see *Ceterach officinarum*

S

Sage, see *Salvia*
  Jerusalem sage, see *Phlomis fruticosa*
  Purple sage, see *Salvia officinalis* 'Purpurascens'
  Russian sage, see *Perovskia atriplicifolia* 'Blue Spire'
  Vatican sage, see *Salvia sclarea* var. *turkestanica*

Salix (Willow) 36
  S. lanata (Woolly willow) **88–91**, 144
Salvia (Sage)
  S. argentea **88–91**, 145
  S. farinacea 'Victoria' **66–9**
  S. officinalis 'Purpurascens' (Purple sage) **74–7**, 144, 145
  S. sclarea var. *turkestanica* (Vatican sage) **44–7**
Saxifraga (Saxifrage) 147
  S. moschata 'Cloth of Gold' **136–7**
  S. 'Sanguinea Superba' (Mossy saxifrage) **52–5**
  S. 'Southside Seedling' **52–5**
  S. x *urbium* (London pride) **78–81**, 144
Saxifrage, see *Saxifraga*
Scent
  flowers for 17, *17*, 33, 47, 110, 116, *125*, 145
  foliage for 17, 145; see also A Formal Herb Design 74–7, A Scheme for Scent 96–9
  schemes for 17, 48, 132; see also A Scheme for Scent 96–9
Scilla 52, 55
  S. siberica 'Atrocoerulea' **24–7**, 95, 144, 145
Screens, scheme for, see Screening the Garden 116–19
Sea holly, see *Eryngium*
Seaside gardens
  plants for 145
  scheme for, see Planting by the Sea 100–103
Sedum 144, 147
  S. kamtschaticum 'Variegatum' **136–7**
  S. obtusatum **136–7**
  S. spathulifolium 145
  S. spathulifolium 'Cape Blanco' **122–3**, 137, 145
  S. spectabile 'Brilliant' (Ice plant) **78–81**, 92–5
Seed, raising plants from 153, *153*
Sempervivum (Houseleek) 144, 145, 147
  S. arachnoideum (Cobweb houseleek) **122–3**, 137, 145
  S. tectorum **52–5**
Senecio
  S. maritima 'Silver Dust' (Silver fern) **66–9**, 145
  S. 'Sunshine' **78–81**, **92–5**, 145
Shade
  plants for *20*, 137, 144
  schemes for, see Cool Colours for Damp Shade 24–7, An Autumn–Winter Display 48–51, A Low-maintenance Scheme 82–5, Colour for Autumn–Winter 114–15, Walls without Sun 126–7
Shapes of plants, importance when selecting 12, 18, *19*, 20
Sheltered areas
  plants for 100
  schemes for, see Sunny Yellows and Blues 104–107, Colour for Autumn–Winter 114–15, A Place in the Sun 120–21
Shield fern, see *Dryopteris affinis*
Shrubby hare's ear, see *Bupleurum fruticosum*

Shrubs *146*
  acid-loving 10, 27, 43, 144; see also A Low-maintenance Scheme 82–5
  for autumn display 48; see also Bright Berries for Autumn 40–43
  importance in gardens 12
  planting against walls 147, *147*; see also Colour for Autumn–Winter 114–15
  propagating 152
  pruning and training 149, *149*, 150–51, *150*, *151*
  for winter display 48, 51; see also Colour for Autumn–Winter 114
Silk tree, see *Albizia julibrissin*
Silver fern, see *Senecio maritima* 'Silver Dust'
Sisyrinchium graminoides **52–5**
Sizes of plants, importance when selecting 19
Skunk cabbage, see *Lysichiton americanus*
Small gardens
  importance of plant shapes and sizes in 18, 19
  planting styles in 14
  plants for 85
  schemes for, see Border of Miniatures 52–5, A Formal Herb Design 74–7, Vertical Spaces 108–27, A Potted Disguise 130–31, Patio Planting 132–3, A Narrow Strip 134–5, Occasional Pots 140–41
Smoke tree, see *Cotinus coggygria* 'Notcutt's Variety'
Snapdragon, see *Antirrhinum*
Snowdrop, see *Galanthus*
Soft shield fern, see *Polystichum setiferum*
Soil
  preparation 146–7
  schemes for different types of
    acid soil 27, 43, 144; see also A Low-maintenance Scheme 82–5
    dry or well-drained soil *11*, 98, 107, 144; see also Pretty Pastels 28–31, A Bold Desert Bed 62–5, A Stony Patch 138–9
    heavy soil 47, 144
    moist soil *10*, 20, 47, 145; see also Cool Colours for Damp Shade 24–7, A Lush Poolside 36–9
    poor soil 94; see also A Stony Patch 138–9
    sandy soil 144
Solanum 125
  S. jasminoides 'Album' **110–13**
Solidago (Golden rod) 149
Solomon's seal, see *Polygonatum*
Sorbus (Mountain ash, rowan) 144
  S. alnifolia (Korean mountain ash) 40
  S. 'Joseph Rock' *12*, **40–43**
Southernwood, see *Artemisia abrotanum*
Spanish bluebell, see *Hyacinthoides hispanica*
Spanish daisy, see *Erigeron karvinskianus*
Spider flower, see *Cleome hassleriana*
Spider plant, see *Chlorophytum comosum* 'Vittatum'
Spindle tree, see *Euonymus europaeus* 'Red Cascade'
Spiraea 150

Spring schemes 27, 39, 61, 75, 91; see also Bright Berries for Autumn 40–43, Cottage-garden Border 44–7, Border of Miniatures 52–5, A Year-round Display 70–73, A Low-maintenance Scheme 82–5, Sunny Yellows and Blues 104–107, A Retaining Wall 122–3
 early spring schemes *12*, 81
 late spring schemes *12, 25, 37, 41, 45, 49, 52, 79, 82, 110*
 mid-spring schemes *29, 97, 105*
Spurge, see *Euphorbia*
Stachys
 S. byzantina (Lamb's tongue) 20, **28–31**, 60, **88–91**
 S. lanata, see *S. byzantina*
 S. macrantha **58–61**
Stag's-horn sumach, see *Rhus typhina*
Stakes for plants, types of 148, *148*
Steps, scheme for, see Between the Steps 136–7
Stinking hellebore, see *Helleborus foetidus*
Stinking iris, see *Iris foetidissima*
Stock, see *Matthiola*
Stopping plants 151
Strawberry tree, see *Arbutus unedo*
Summer hyacinth, see *Galtonia candicans*
Summer schemes *12*, 17; see also A Tropical Summer Border 32–5, Cottage-garden Border 44–7, A Bed of Roses 58–61, Instant Flowers 66–9, A Scheme for Scent 96–9, Sunny Yellows and Blues 104–107, Plants for a Pergola 110–13, Screening the Garden 116–19
 early summer schemes *89, 105, 116, 125*
 late summer schemes *13, 15, 24, 28, 31, 53, 58, 80, 120, 120*; see also Waterside Textures 88–91
 mid-summer schemes *15, 36, 59, 93, 101*; see also A Formal Herb Design 74–7
Sun
 plants for *11*, 85, 98, 137
 schemes for 107; see also Pretty Pastels 28–31, A Tropical Summer Border 32–5, A Bold Desert Bed 62–5, Coloured Foliage 92–5, A Place in the Sun 120–21, A Stony Patch 138–9
Swan River daisy, see *Brachycome iberidifolia*
Sweet cicely, see *Myrrhis odorata*
Sweet pea, see *Lathyrus odoratus*
 Perennial sweet pea, see *Lathyrus latifolius*
Sweet sultan, see *Centaurea moschata*
Sweet william, see *Dianthus barbatus*
Sweet woodruff, see *Galium odoratum*

T

Tamarix (Tamarisk) 100
Tanacetum parthenium 'Aureum' (Golden feverfew) **74–7**
Tasmanian snow gum, see *Eucalyptus coccifera*
Taxus baccata (Yew) 14

Tellima grandiflora 'Purpurea' **70–73**, 144
Tetrapanax 33
Textures of plants, importance when selecting 20, *20, 21*
Thalictrum (Meadow rue) 143
 T. delavayi 44–7
Thrift, see *Armeria maritima*
Thymus (Thyme) 74, 145
 T. caespititius 132
 T. x citriodorus 'Silver Queen' (Lemon thyme) **96–9**
 T. praecox 145
 T. serpyllum (Wild thyme) **96–9**, 145
 T. serpyllum 'Coccineus' **132–3**
 T. serpyllum 'Pink Chintz' 132
 T. serpyllum 'Snowdrift' **132–3**
Tiarella (Foamflower)
 T. wherryi 27, 144
Ties for plants, types of 148, *148*
Toadflax, see *Linaria*
Tobacco plant, see *Nicotiana*
Town gardens
 formal gardens and 14
 schemes for, see An Autumn–Winter Display 48–51, Border of Miniatures 52–5, Walls without Sun 126–7, A Potted Disguise 130–31, Patio Planting 132–3, A Narrow Strip 134–5, Between the Steps 136–7
 screens in 116–17
Traditional gardens, schemes for, see Cottage-garden Border 44–7, A Bed of Roses 58–61, Instant Flowers 66–9, A Formal Herb Design 74–7
Training plants 151, *151*
Tree lupin, see *Lupinus arboreus*
Trees 146, 148
 for autumn display 40, 42
 fruit 14, 78–9, *79*, 117
 pruning and training 149, 150–51
Trellis screens
 scheme for, see Screening the Garden 116–19
 support for 147, *147*
Trifolium (Clover)
 T. repens 'Purpurascens' (Purple-leaved clover) **132–3**, 145
Trillium (Trinity flower, Wood flower) *20*
Trinity flower, see *Trillium*
Trochodendron araloides (Japanese cartwheel tree) 33
Tropaeolum (Nasturtium) *12*, 74, 77
 T. majus 'Alaska' **140–41**
 T. majus, single climbing mixed **124–5**
 T. speciosum (Flame creeper) **113**
Tropical gardens, schemes for, see A Tropical Summer Border 32–5, A Bold Desert Bed 62–5, A Place in the Sun 120–21
Trumpet vine, see *Campsis x tagliabuana* 'Mme Galen'
Tulip, see *Tulipa*
Tulip tree, see *Liriodendron tulipifera*
Tulipa (Tulip) 52, 55, 74, 75
 T. 'Angélique' **28–31**
 T. 'Bellona' (Single early tulip) **104–107**
 T. 'Candela' (Fosteriana tulip) **104–107**
 T. 'Estella Rijnveld' (Parrot tulip) 61
 T. linifolia (Species tulip) **55**

Tulipa (cont.)
 T. 'Orange Favourite' (Parrot tulip) **74–7**
 T. 'Purissima' (Fosteriana tulip) 61
 T. 'Queen of the Night' 75
 T. saxatilis (Species tulip) **91**
 T. tarda (Species tulip) **91**
 T. turkestanica (Species tulip) **91**
 T. 'White Triumphator' **28–31**
 Fosteriana tulips, see *T.* 'Candela', *T.* 'Purissima'
 Parrot tulips 28; see also *T.* 'Estella Rijnveld', *T.* 'Orange Favourite'
 Single early tulip, see *T.* 'Bellona'
 Species tulips, see *T. linifolia*, *T. saxatilis*, *T. tarda*, *T. turkestanica*

V

Vatican sage, see *Salvia sclarea* var. *turkestanica*
Veratrum nigrum (Black false hellebore) **88–91**
Verbascum olympicum (Mullein) **107**
Verbena 99, 144, 153
 V. bonariensis 19
 V. patagonica **35**
 V. 'Sissinghurst' **66–9**
Viburnum 48, 51, 144
 V. x bodnantense 'Dawn' 51, 145
 V. opulus 'Compactum' **40–43**, 144
 V. plicatum 'Mariesii' **24–7**, 144
Vinca (Periwinkle)
 V. minor 'Argenteovariegata' (Lesser periwinkle) 51, 144
Vine, see *Vitis*
 Crimson glory vine, see *Vitis coignetiae*
 Cup-and-saucer vine, see *Cobaea scandens*
 Trumpet vine, see *Campsis x tagliabuana* 'Mme Galen'
Viola (Violet)
 V. Clear Crystals Series (Pansy) **134–5**, 153
 V. cornuta (Horned violet) **28–31**, 145
 V. labradorica 'Purpurea' (Purple-leaved violet) **44–7**
 V. 'Moonlight' **78–81**
 V. 'Nellie Britton' **78–81**
 V. tricolor (Heartsease) **132–3**, 145
Violet, see *Viola*
 Horned violet, see *V. cornuta*
 Purple-leaved violet, see *V. labradorica* 'Purpurea'
Virginia creeper, see *Parthenocissus quinquefolia*
Vitis (Vine)
 V. 'Brant' 111
 V. coignetiae (Crimson glory vine) **110–13**, 144
 V. 'Concord' 111
 V. vinifera 'Ciotat' 119
 V. vinifera 'Purpurea' **110–13**, 119, 144

W

Wallflower, see *Cheiranthus*
Walls
 large gardens and 14

Walls *(cont.)*
 planting in crevices 147, *147*
 plants for 145
 schemes for, see Sunny Yellows and Blues 104–107, Colour for Autumn–Winter 114–15, A Place in the Sun 120–21, A Retaining Wall 122–3, Walls without Sun 126–7, A Narrow Strip 134–5
Warm areas, plants for, see A Tropical Summer Border 32–5, A Bold Desert Bed 62–5, A Place in the Sun 120–21
Warminster broom, see *Cytisus x praecox*
Watering plants 148
Waterside schemes *10*; see also A Lush Poolside 36–9, Waterside Textures 88–91
Weeds, tackling
 annual 148
 perennial 147, 148
Weigela 150
Welsh poppy, see *Meconopsis cambrica*
Wild gardens
 plants for 14, *15*
 schemes for, see A Low-maintenance Scheme 82–5, Splendour in the Grass 142–3
Willow, see *Salix*
 Woolly willow, see *S. lanata*
Wind
 plants tolerant of 145
 plants suitable as windbreaks 145
 protecting plants from 149, *149*
Winter aconite, see *Eranthis hyemalis*
Winter schemes 39, 91; see also An Autumn–Winter Display 48–51, Colour for Autumn–Winter 114–15, A Narrow Strip 134–5
 plant colour in 40
 late winter schemes *49*
Wisteria 66, 145
 W. floribunda 'Alba' **110–13**
 W. sinensis (Chinese wisteria) **110–13**, 145
Witch hazel, see *Hamamelis*
Wood flower, see *Trillium*
Wooded gardens, schemes for *19*; see also Cool Colours for Damp Shade 24–7, A Low-maintenance Scheme 82–5
Woodwardia unigemmata (Chain fern) *20*
Woolly willow, see *Salix lanata*

YZ

Year-round interest
 plants for 12, 100
 schemes for 31; see also A Year-round Display 70–73, A Narrow Strip 134–5
Yellow asphodel, see *Asphodeline lutea*
Yew, see *Taxus baccata*
Yucca 19, 20, 32
 Y. filamentosa 'Variegata' *11*
 Y. whipplei **62–5**
Zantedeschia aethiopica 'Crowborough' (Arum lily) **39**, 145
Zingiber officinale (Ginger) 10

ACKNOWLEDGMENTS

AUTHOR'S ACKNOWLEDGMENTS

Most of the schemes in this book have no direct provenance, arising, often, out of experiments in my own garden. Some however, do and I would like to thank Mr and Mrs Paice of Bourton House, whose garden was the inspiration for the large planted pot on pp.130–31, and the superb gardeners at Kingston Maurward, Dorset's college of agriculture, where I first saw the border that was adapted for the tropical scheme on pp.32–5.

A book such as this is made by a large team – writing is only the first step – and I am grateful to Dorling Kindersley for providing such superb support. I would particularly like to thank Claire Calman, Jill Andrews, and Melanie Tham for their tenacity, good humour, and exemplary attention to detail.

Dorling Kindersley would like to thank: Jackie Bennett, Marion Boddy-Evans, Diana Craig, Kate Swainson for editorial assistance; Joanna Chisholm for the index; Karen Ward, Karen Mackley, Suzanne Stevenson for design and DTP assistance; Sarah Fuller and Hilary Stephens for production; Cooling Brown for typesetting.

ILLUSTRATORS

Sharon Beeden pp.24–5, pp.28–9, pp.32–3, pp.36–7, pp.44–5, pp.48–9, pp.52–3, pp.58–9, pp.66–7, pp.78–9
Martine Collings pp.40–41, pp.62–3, pp.70–71, pp.74–5, pp.82–3, pp.88–9, pp.92–3, pp.96–7, pp.100–101, pp.104–105
Catharine Slade pp.110–11, pp.114–15, pp.116–17, pp.126–7
Vanessa Luff pp.120–21, pp.132–3, pp.134–5, pp.138–9
Ann Winterbottom pp.122–3, pp.124–5
Gill Tomblin pp.136–7, pp.140–41, pp.142–3
David Ashby pp.130–31
Karen Cochrane all planting plans
Additional illustrators Sally Hynard, Will Giles, Liz Pepperell, Sandra Pond, Michael Shoebridge, Ross Watton

PHOTOGRAPHY CREDITS

tl=top left; tr=top right; tcl=top centre left; tc=top centre; tcr=top centre right; ul=upper left; ur=upper right; ucl=upper centre left; ucr=upper centre right; lcl=lower centre left; lc=lower centre; lcr=lower centre right; bl=bottom left; br=bottom right; bc=bottom centre; bcl=bottom centre left; bcr=bottom centre right.

CREATIVE PLANTING
p.10 Eric Crichton: bl; Steven Wooster: cr.
p.11 Will Giles: br.
p.12 Stephen Robson: tl; Steven Wooster: tr; Will Giles: bc.
p.13 Steven Wooster: tr, bl.
p.14 Eric Crichton: bl; Steven Wooster: tc.
p.15 Steven Wooster: tl; Eric Crichton: br.
p.16 Stephen Robson: bl; Steven Wooster: tr.
p.17 Steven Wooster: bl; Stephen Robson: tr, br.
p.18 Steven Wooster: uc; Will Giles: bc.
p.19 Steven Wooster: main pic.
p.20 Steven Wooster: tr, br.
p.21 Steven Wooster: bl; Stephen Robson: tr.

MIXED BORDERS
Cool Colours for Damp Shade
p.26 Harry Smith: cr; Will Giles: bcr, br.
p.27 Eric Crichton: ucl; Will Giles: ucr; Gillian Andrews: br.
Pretty Pastels
p.30 A–Z Botanical Collection: tcl, br; Andrew Lawson: tr.
p.31 Guernsey Clematis Nursery Ltd: bl.
A Tropical Summer Border
p.34 Harry Smith: cl, tr.
p.35 The Garden Picture Library: bcr.
A Lush Poolside
p.38 Neil Holmes: ucl; Harry Smith: tl, tcr.

Bright Berries for Autumn
p.42 Harry Smith: ucl; Will Giles: tr.
p.43 Harry Smith: tl.
Cottage-garden Border
p.46 Harry Smith: bl; Pat Brindley: lcl; Will Giles: tr; Harry Smith: br.
p.47 Pat Brindley: bcl.
An Autumn–Winter Display
p.51 Harry Smith: br, bl; The Garden Picture Library: tl.
Border of Miniatures
p.54 Harry Smith: ul; Gillian Beckett: bcl; Will Giles: ur; Gillian Beckett: bcr; Eric Crichton: tr.

ISLAND BEDS
A Bed of Roses
p.61 Pat Brindley: br, bl; Eric Crichton: bc.
A Bold Desert Bed
p.64 Gillian Beckett: br; Harry Smith: ucl.
p.65 Will Giles: bcl; Harry Smith: tl.
Instant Flowers
p.68 Will Giles: ucr; Harry Smith: br; Pat Brindley: tr.
p.69 Derek Gould: bc.
A Formal Herb Design
p.76 Harry Smith: bl.
Flowers and Fruits
p.80 Will Giles: ucl; A–Z Botanical Collection: lcl; Harry Smith: bcr; Brogdale Slide Library: lc.
A Low-maintenance Scheme
p.84 Harry Smith: tl.
p.85 Christopher Brickell: br.

CORNER SITES
Waterside Textures
p.90 Diana Grenfell: tcr.
p.91 Harry Smith: bl.

Coloured Foliage
p.95 Harry Smith: tr.
A Scheme for Scent
p.98 Harry Smith: cr.
p.99 Photos Horticultural: bl; Harry Smith: br.
Planting by the Sea
p.102 Eric Crichton: bcr; Will Giles: bcl.
p.103 Hazel le Rougetel/Biofotos: cl; Will Giles: bl.
Sunny Yellows and Blues
p.106 Harry Smith: lcl, tl, lcr, bl; Pat Brindley: tr.
p.107 Harry Smith: lcl, bl.

VERTICAL SPACES
Planting up a Pergola
p.112 Hazel le Rougetel/Biofotos: ul; Harry Smith: lc.
p.113 Harry Smith: bl; Pat Brindley: ucr.
Screening the Garden
p.118 Harry Smith: bl.
p.119 Harry Smith: bl, br, ur.
A Place in the Sun
p.121 Harry Smith: tl, tc, tr.
Climbing Frames
p.124 Suttons Seeds: bl.
Walls without Sun
p.127 Pat Brindley: br.

FORGOTTEN PLACES
A Potted Disguise
p.130 Will Giles: tr, bl.
A Stony Patch
p.139 Harry Smith: tl, bc.
Occasional Pots
p.141 Harry Smith: bl.
Splendour in the Grass
p.143 Harry Smith: tl.